IMAGES
of America

MAHOPAC

I0807090

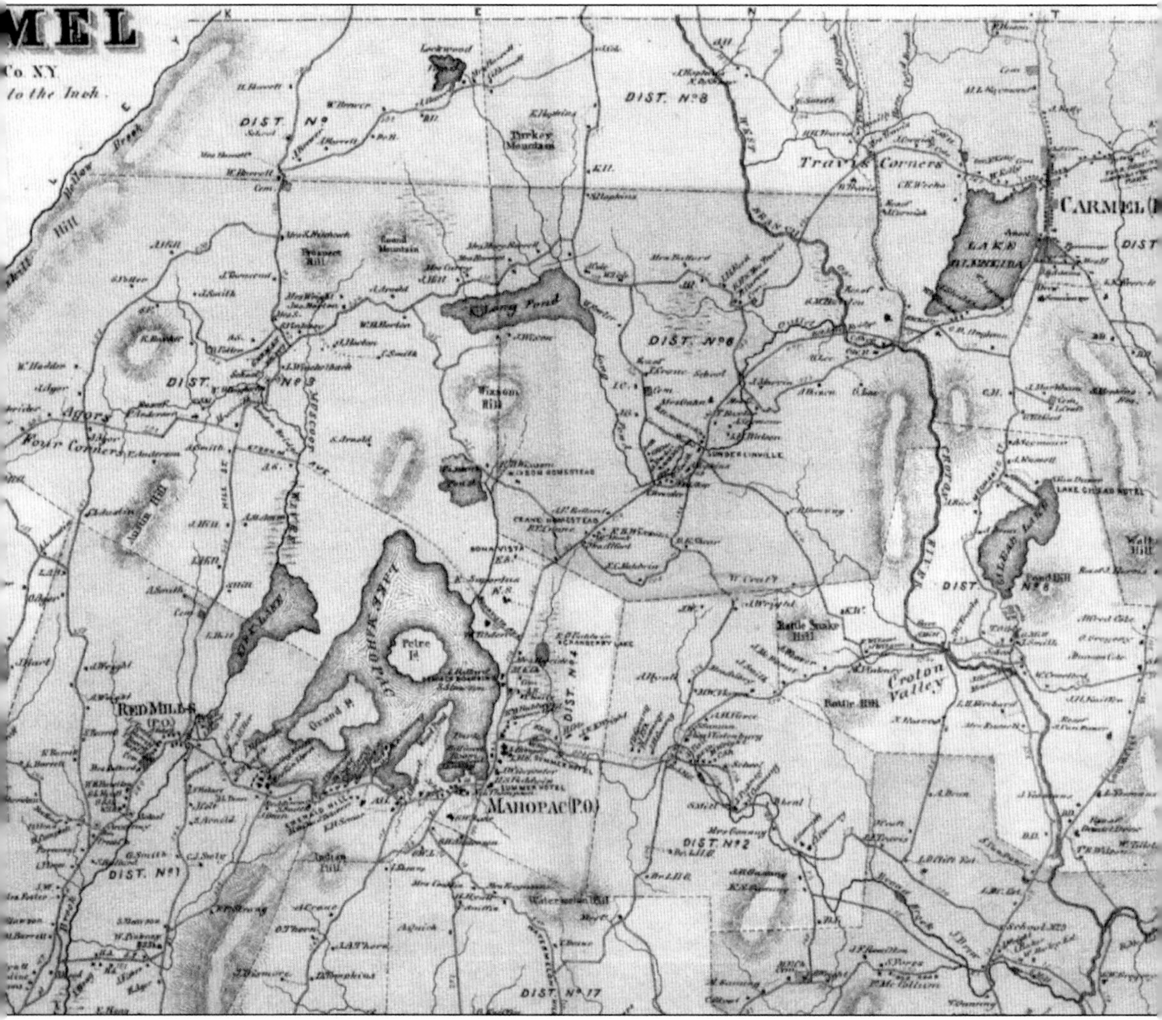

The 1867 Beers Atlas Map of the Town of Carmel shows Lake Mahopac and the surrounding area. Many modern roads are recognizable on the map, but others such as Route 6 did not exist. Residence locations are shown on the map as dots along with the names of those who resided there. (Eugene J. Boesch.)

ON THE COVER: The *Dew Drop*, a double-deck steamboat took passengers around Lake Mahopac during the late 19th century. The craft sometimes hosted a band to entertain passengers as it plied the lake. This 1885 photograph shows a time of Victorian Romanticism, when Mahopac was a bustling resort destination with vacationers taking the railroad to Croton Falls and then to the hamlet via carriage to enjoy the beauty of the lake. (The Town of Carmel Historical Society.)

IMAGES
of America

MAHOPAC

Eugene J. Boesch, Gregory J. Amato,
and Barbara Lacina Bosch

ARCADIA
PUBLISHING

ISBN 978-0-7385-7689-3

Published by Arcadia Publishing
Charleston, South Carolina

Printed in the United States of America

Library of Congress Control Number: 2011937114

For all general information, please contact Arcadia Publishing:
Telephone 843-853-2070
Fax 843-853-0044
E-mail sales@arcadiapublishing.com
For customer service and orders:
Toll-Free 1-888-313-2665

Visit us on the Internet at www.arcadiapublishing.com

Contents

ACKNOWLEDGMENTS

We are grateful to those who offered their photographic collections and gave their time to provide historical information, anecdotes, and their encouragement for this project.

A special thank you goes to Brian Vangor, Carmel town historian. He provided much information and served as the technical wizard behind formatting the photographs. Brian is a multitalented individual with limited free time, which was generously shared with us. As much as any of us, he deserves the title coauthor.

The Putnam County Historian's Office, particularly Sallie Sypher and Reggie White, and Lillian Eberhardt, president of the Carmel Historical Society, are specially noted for the knowledge and information they provided. We also thank the following for providing us historic photographs, maps, and other information: Joy Alter, John Agor, Stewart Agor, Laura Amato, American Legion Post 1080, Lee and Ann Archer, George and Olive Bennett, Loretta Billington, Clara Boesch, Amy Boesch, Charlotte Boesch, Jack Casey, Karen Czysz, Edward and Ann Dazi, Ted Dwyer, Karen Faulkner, Debra Feiman, Ann Garris, district clerk of the Mahopac Central School District Dorothy Gilroy, Frido Goerlich, Rabbi Eytan Hammerman, Muriel Hill, Aaron Kass, Patricia Kaufman, Jeffrey Kellogg, Terry Komendowski, Darleen Lampe, Karen and Jerry Levitis, Mahopac and Mahopac Falls Fire Departments, Susan Mauldin, Rev. Willett Porter, Kevin and Barbara Neary, Ellen Lupinacci, Rev. Ken Mast, Richard Smith, William Spain Jr., Bob and Claudia Stevens, "Chipper" Swarm, Carol and Randy Tompkins, Jo Wegel, Lottie Weschler, and Rev. Claudia Wilson.

Our objective for the book was to share part of the collected memory of Mahopac's past with future generations. To lead those unfamiliar with Mahopac's past to a new place. Hopefully not a day will pass where readers will not view a landscape or building in Mahopac, or anywhere, and not think of what was occurring there a century or more ago. There are hundreds of other photographs that could have been used but we hope we have made a start in bringing Mahopac's past to all. As with any book, there may be some inaccuracies contained here, slight or otherwise, for which we apologize in advance. We hope all who read this enjoy it and learn as much as we did.

INTRODUCTION

The hamlet of Mahopac is within the town of Carmel, Putnam County, New York. Its population is approximately 8,700 people. The community is about 6.4 square miles in size with about 1.1 miles being lake surface. Mahopac sits within the eastern margin of the Hudson Highlands, part of a mountain range that extends from Pennsylvania to Connecticut. Its predominant landmark is Lake Mahopac, a picturesque 587-acre lake, which gives the hamlet its name. Other large and small lakes also dot the land. Much of the hamlet, especially its commercial corridor, is centered on Route 6 with its intersection with Route 6N being the commercial heart of the community. The first settlers entered Mahopac during the early 18th century as tenant farmers on the Philipse patent. It is likely, however, that hunters, trappers, adventurers, and squatters entered the Mahopac wilderness even earlier. Such immigrants were not the first people to inhabit the area as Native Americans were living here for millennia before the arrival of the first colonists. Their heritage is seen in the Algonquian term *Mahopac* (likely pronounced Ma-HOE-pac) for the lake that defines the community. Various translations are recorded for the term, including "Big Pond," "Lake of the Great Serpent," and "Snake Lake," but its exact meaning is uncertain.

Mahopac's prehistory includes the PaleoIndian, Archaic, Transitional, and Woodland periods. PaleoIndian (10,000–8,000 BC) represents the earliest occupation of the region. Archaic (8,000 1,700 BC) refers to a time prior to the introduction of horticulture and pottery manufacture. Transitional (1,700–1,000 BC) witnessed a gradual change in archaic lifestyles with the development of Woodland traits. Woodland (1,000 BC–1,600 AD) is characterized by the use of pottery and reliance on horticulture.

The Contact period (AD 1600–c. 1700) represents the initial contacts between Native Americans and European colonists. By the end of the Woodland period, Native American cultures began to resemble those of groups that were encountered by early colonists. At that time, Native Americans of the lower Hudson Valley, including Mahopac, were part of the Algonquian cultural and linguistic stock. Specifically, they were a group of Munsee speakers who migrated into southeastern New York and southwestern Connecticut during late Woodland times. East of the Hudson River, their descendants were known as the Wappinger and numbered about 13,200 people at the beginning of European contact.

In political terms, the Wappinger were divided into a number of groups. However, the political, linguistic, and social relationships among them will never be understood. The Natives had no fixed boundaries and ownership of particular areas may have overlapped with use rights shared. Colonists also misunderstood Native American associations with particular areas. Finally, early pressure on Native groups by colonial expansion resulted in shifts of villages and territories. Such confusion over relationships was particularly true for bands inhabiting relatively unexplored interior areas, such as Mahopac.

The Wappinger group traditionally associated with Putnam County was the Nochpeem. Little information concerning them is recorded. They were located east of the Hudson River in the wild mountain region of Putnam County. Their territory appears to have extended from Anthony's Nose on the south to Fishkill Creek on the north and eastward to Connecticut. A Nochpeem village was located in Canopus Hollow with another settlement in what is now Putnam Valley. The Nochpeem, however, may have been restricted to the region around the Hudson River with the eastern portion of the Hudson Highlands, including Mahopac, being part of the traditional lands of the Tankiteke, another main division of the Wappinger. It is possible that portions of Putnam County were a boundary zone between the Nochpeem and Tankiteke. If so, traditional Native American rights to the area may have been vague, duel, or shifting, and probably misunderstood by the Europeans.

Problems and conflicts during the 17th century between lower Hudson Valley Natives and the Dutch and English resulted in countless Indian deaths. The introduction of European diseases further devastated local Native populations. The populations of the Nochpeem and Tankiteke are estimated at approximately 600 individuals each around 1600. A century later, the number of remaining Wappinger was reduced to approximately 1,000 individuals.

Putnam County, named for Revolutionary War general Israel Putnam and reflecting the area's social and economic ties to New England, came into being on June 12, 1812. Before that date, the region was part of Dutchess County. Although references by travelers through Dutchess County during the mid to late 17th century are known, it was not until the 1680s that Euro-Americans began to enter the region and reside in its forests and mountains. These first arrivals were transients and squatters who possessed no deeds to the land they settled. By 1697, however, Adolph Philipse, a New York City merchant, had acquired legal rights to almost 200,000 acres in the area.

During the late 17th to mid-18th century, most of Dutchess County, including Mahopac, was sparsely inhabited. Only 445 people resided there in 1714. Most were tenant farmers. In Mahopac, early occupation did not occur, most likely due to the area's rough terrain. The earliest recorded settler in Mahopac was Eleazar Hamblin, who arrived in 1739 from Cape Cod. His homestead was located along the West Branch of the Croton River. The first known settler at Lake Mahopac was George Hughson, who settled near its north end about 1740. By 1762, eighty-eight families resided in Mahopac.

The hamlet was of strategic importance during the Revolutionary War because of its position in a line of American military outposts established between West Point and Connecticut. The rugged nature of the terrain ensured safety for American forces from British attacks.

No engagement occurred in Mahopac during the Revolutionary War. American encampments, however, were located there and troops were a common site given the proximity of the American lines at the Croton River and the important logistical depot at Red Mills in Mahopac. An outpost was located near Lake Mahopac during the latter years of the war with another encampment situated near Baldwin Place and Myrtle Avenue.

Growth occurred throughout Mahopac after the Revolutionary War. The hamlet's main occupation was farming with grain, apples, sheep, pork, and beef produced. Goods were transported by wagon to Peekskill and shipped by boat down the Hudson River to New York City. The coming of the railroad to Croton Falls in 1849 enabled items to be shipped quickly to markets in New York City.

Lake Mahopac became a tourist resort when Stephen Monk opened the first hotel there around 1835. It soon became a successful destination with tourists traveling up the Hudson River to Peekskill and from there via stages to Lake Mahopac. Other hotels and boardinghouses quickly opened and the tourist trade on the lake boomed. This was particularly true after the railroad reached Croton Falls. Travel by stage from there to Lake Mahopac over Croton Falls Road was quicker and easier than over the road from Peekskill. Travelers from New York City could reach Lake Mahopac within a few hours, making it an easily reached vacation destination. The opening of the Mahopac Branch Railroad to Mahopac in 1871 further supported tourism at the lakeside resorts. Land speculation also occurred with companies formed to purchase land and build residences for use as boardinghouses or hotels.

One

EARLY DAYS

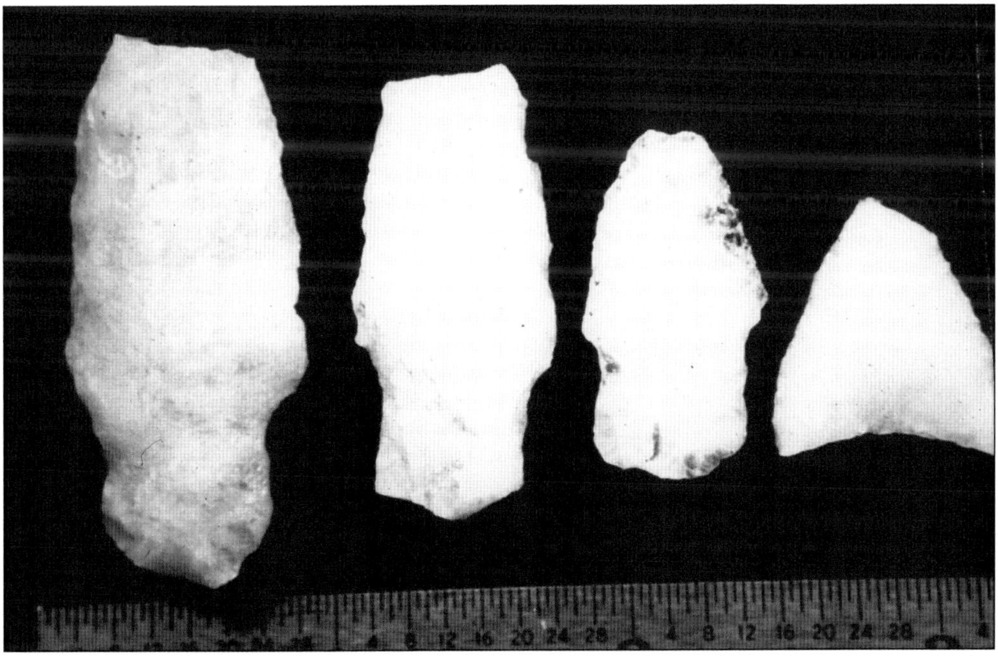

Native American artifacts recovered from Mahopac Falls indicate that Indians frequented the area for at least the last 5,000 years. The three artifacts on the left are spear points and a knife dating to the Late Archaic (3,000–1,500 BC). The artifact on the right is an arrow point dating to between AD 900–1200. The broken tips are impact fractures suggesting that the artifacts struck something. The artifacts were used for hunting and butchering game in the Mahopac Falls area. All of the items are made from quartz. (Eugene J. Boesch.)

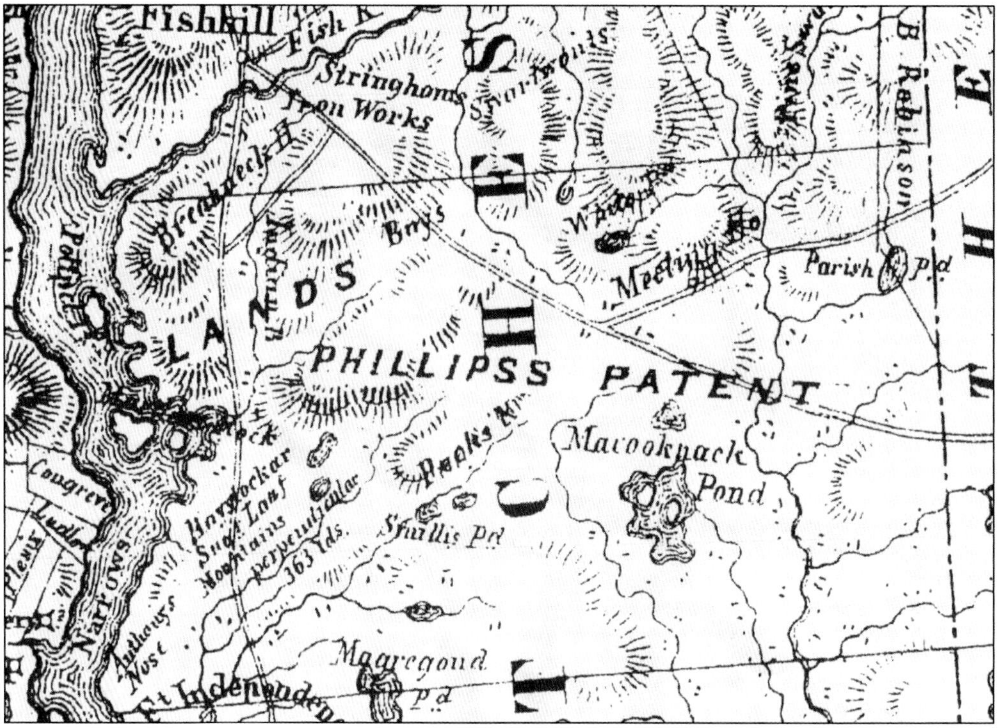

The 1779 map was prepared by Claude Joseph Sauthier, a mapmaker for the British Army during the Revolutionary War. Sauthier's map depicts Lake Mahopac, referring to it as Macookpack Pond, reflecting its Algonquian name. The outlet shown east of the lake is probably Turtle Creek. Dots indicate dwelling locations. Areas away from the lake are unsettled although such locales could have been used for cultivation. (Eugene J. Boesch.)

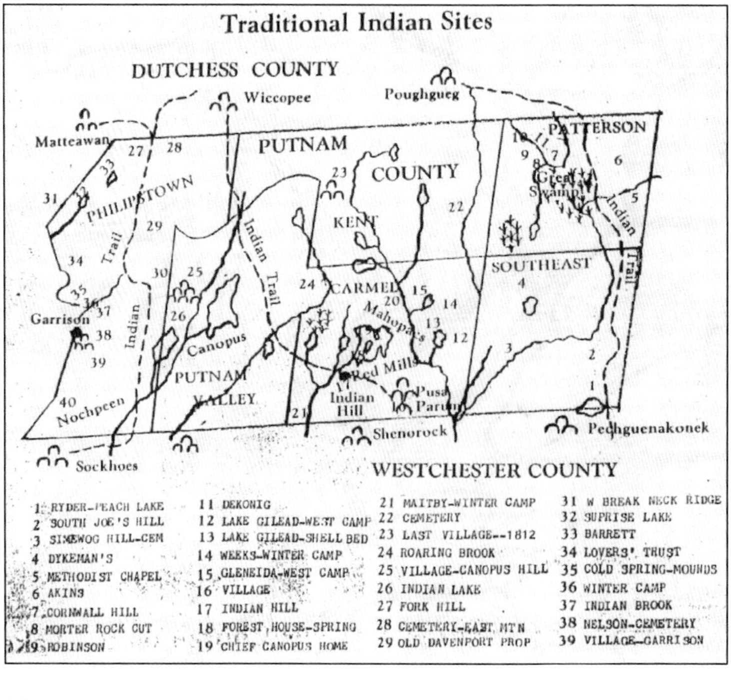

This map shows traditional locations of Native American sites in Putnam County. Six sites are in Mahopac, including No. 17 at Red Mills and No. 18 Forest House Spring, where the Nochpeem leader Canopus was killed by colonists. Native American sites are located on high, well-drained ground near a fresh water source, a pattern similar to that seen for colonial occupation on the Sauthier map. (Putnam County Historian's Office.)

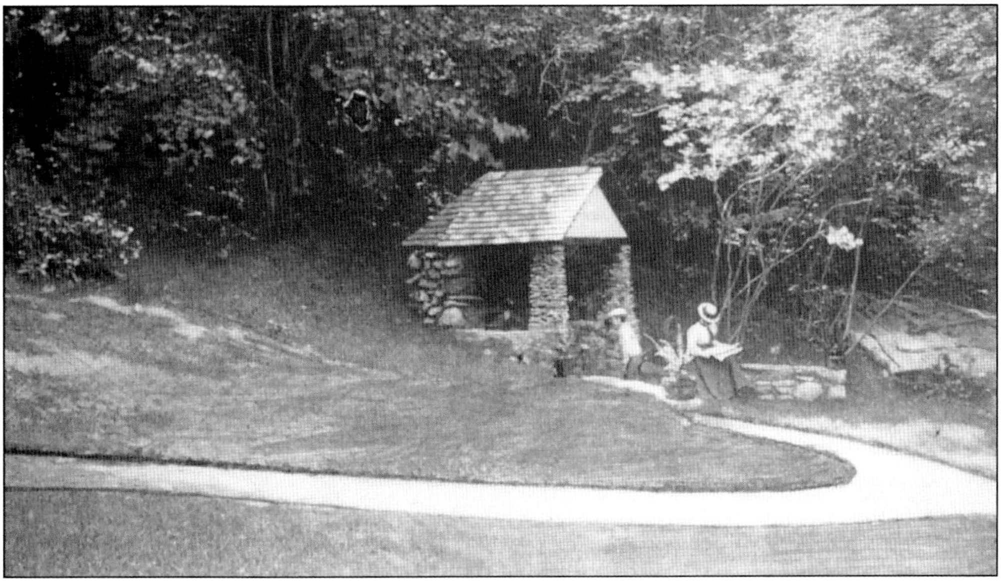

This 1897 image shows the stone springhouse covering the natural rock spring, traditionally referred to by its Algonquian name Minomah, located near the Forest House hotel on North Lake Boulevard. Visitors were able to stroll to the spring to partake its waters to improve health. The spring is the traditional site where Canopus was killed during a skirmish with colonists. The fight reportedly was the last conflict between colonists and Indians in Putnam County. The spring was located along what is now Tennis Court Road near West Lake Boulevard. (Susan Brady Mauldin.)

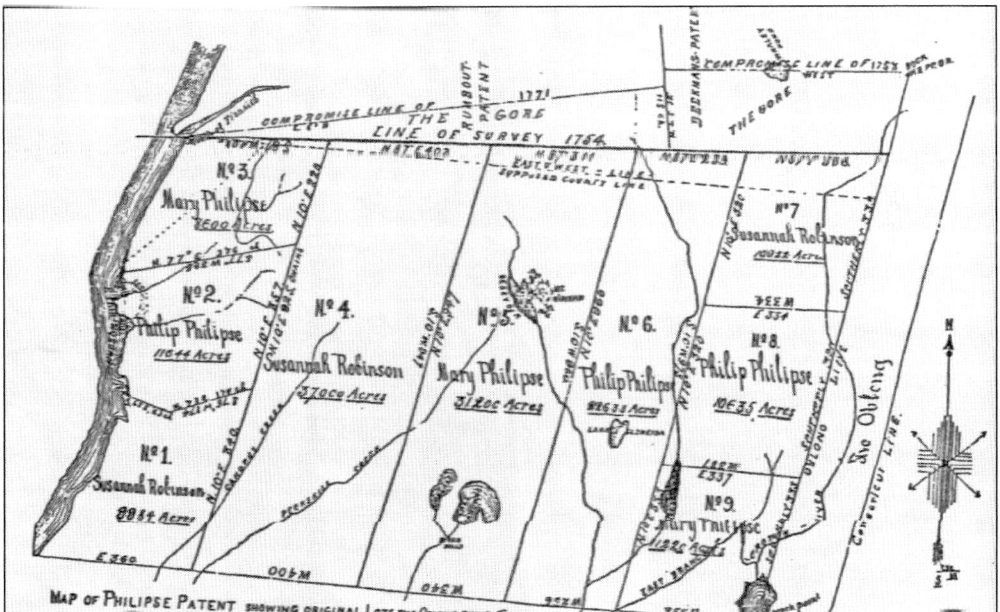

In 1697, William III of England granted land to Adolph Philipse that included all of Putnam County. This became known as Philipse Upper Patent. Philipse died in 1749, and his estate passed to his nephew Frederick Philipse. Upon Frederick's death in 1751, the land was divided among his children. What is now Mahopac was within lot five, bequeathed to Mary and her husband, Roger Morris. (Putnam County Historian's Office.)

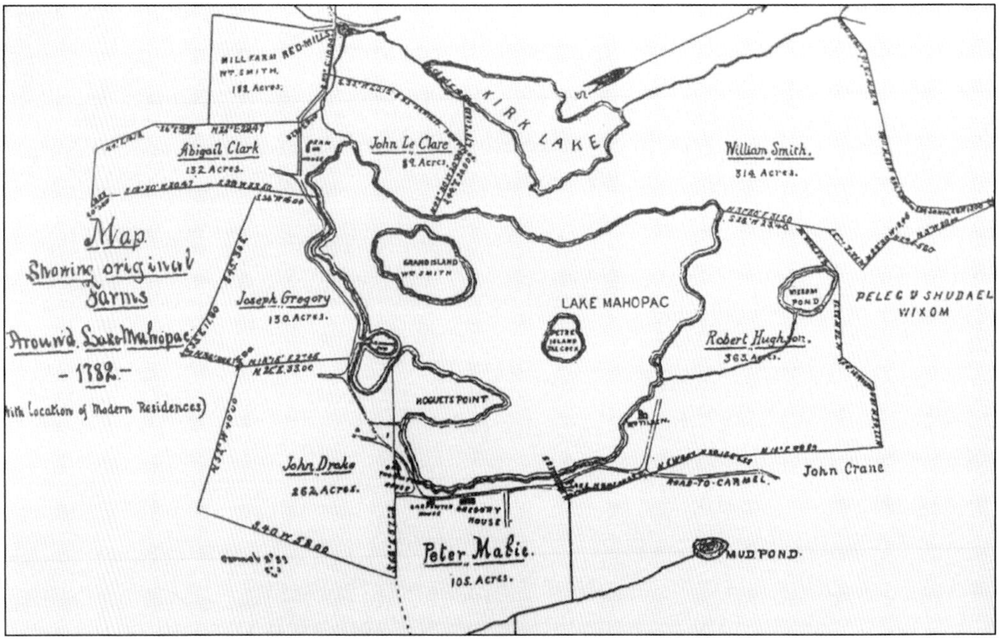

Towards the end of the Revolutionary War, New York State sold land it confiscated from British Loyalists. Most of the former tenants of Roger and Mary (Philipse) Morris, loyalists to the British cause, purchased the lands they farmed from the state by 1782. This 20th-century map indicates individuals who purchased their farms around Lake Mahopac. The map also includes the locations of some notable landmarks. (Putnam County Historian's Office.)

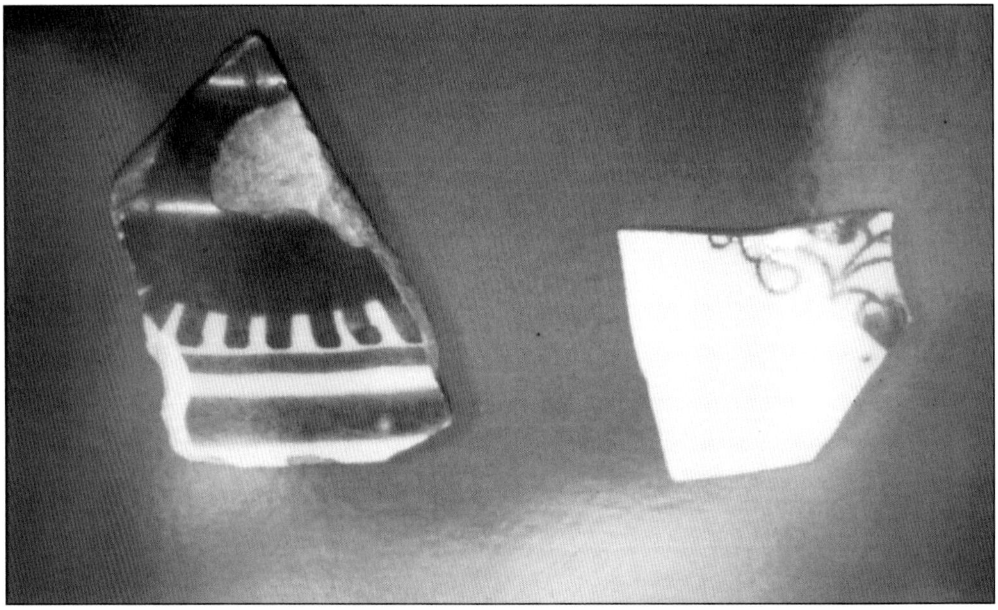

These ceramics are examples of delft and date to the 18th century. They were found near the location of the Log Mansion built for Mary and Roger Morris, and seasonally occupied, in 1760 at Mahopac Falls. The mansion was located on the knoll west of modern day Red Mills Park. Delft was fairly expensive suggesting that the Morrises brought some luxury with them to their wilderness abode. (Eugene J. Boesch.)

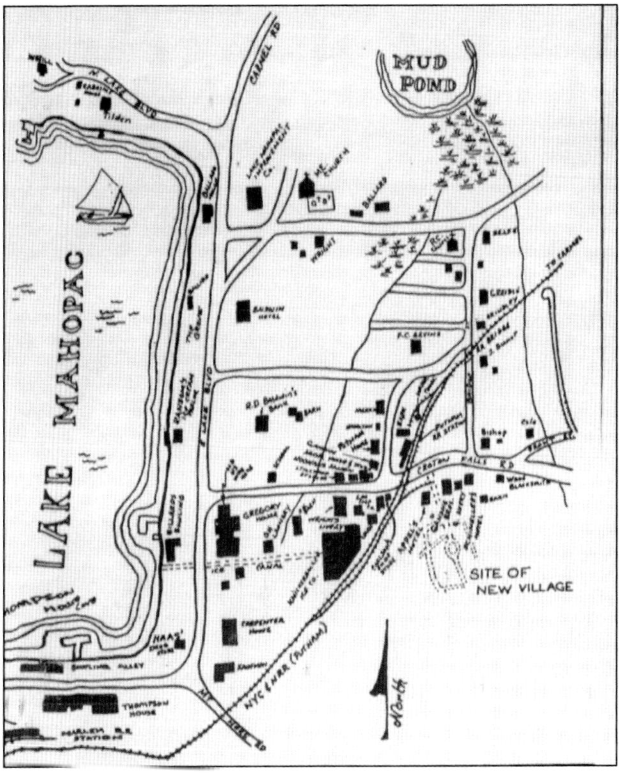

This map shows late-19th-century Mahopac. The hamlet's center was located along Croton Falls Road with residences, businesses, and other buildings in the area. New York State condemned and demolished the buildings in 1902 in order to curtail Croton River pollution. The current Carmel Town Hall is situated were a livery owned by the Ganong Brothers was located. (The Town of Carmel Historical Society.)

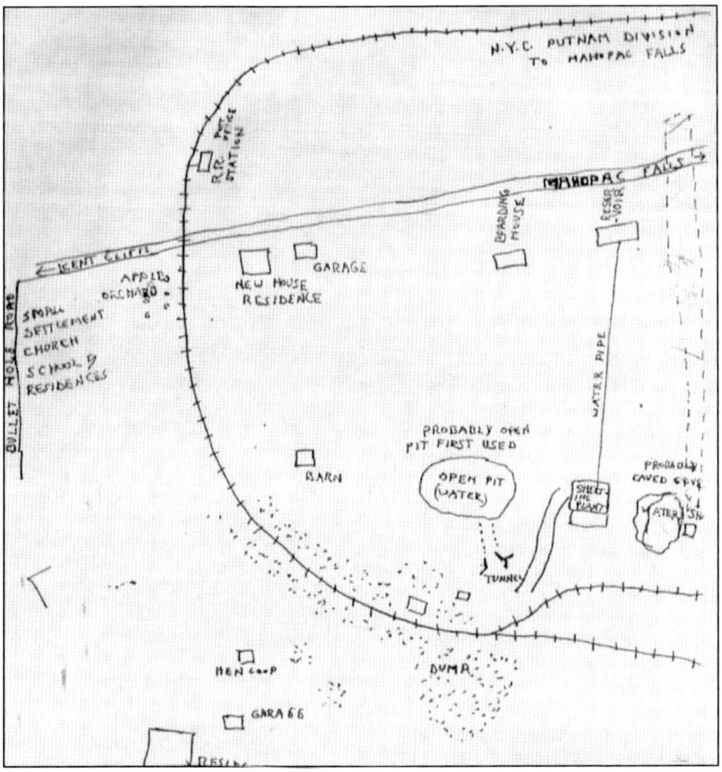

This map shows Mahopac Iron Mines near Stocum Avenue and Hill Street. The mines opened in 1879 to exploit high-grade iron ore. They were shaft type mines with some extending under Hill Street. One of the shafts collapsed in 1890 or 1892 and the mine soon closed. A village developed around the mines and the Mahopac Falls Railroad was extended from Baldwin to transport ore. (Mahopac High School Library.)

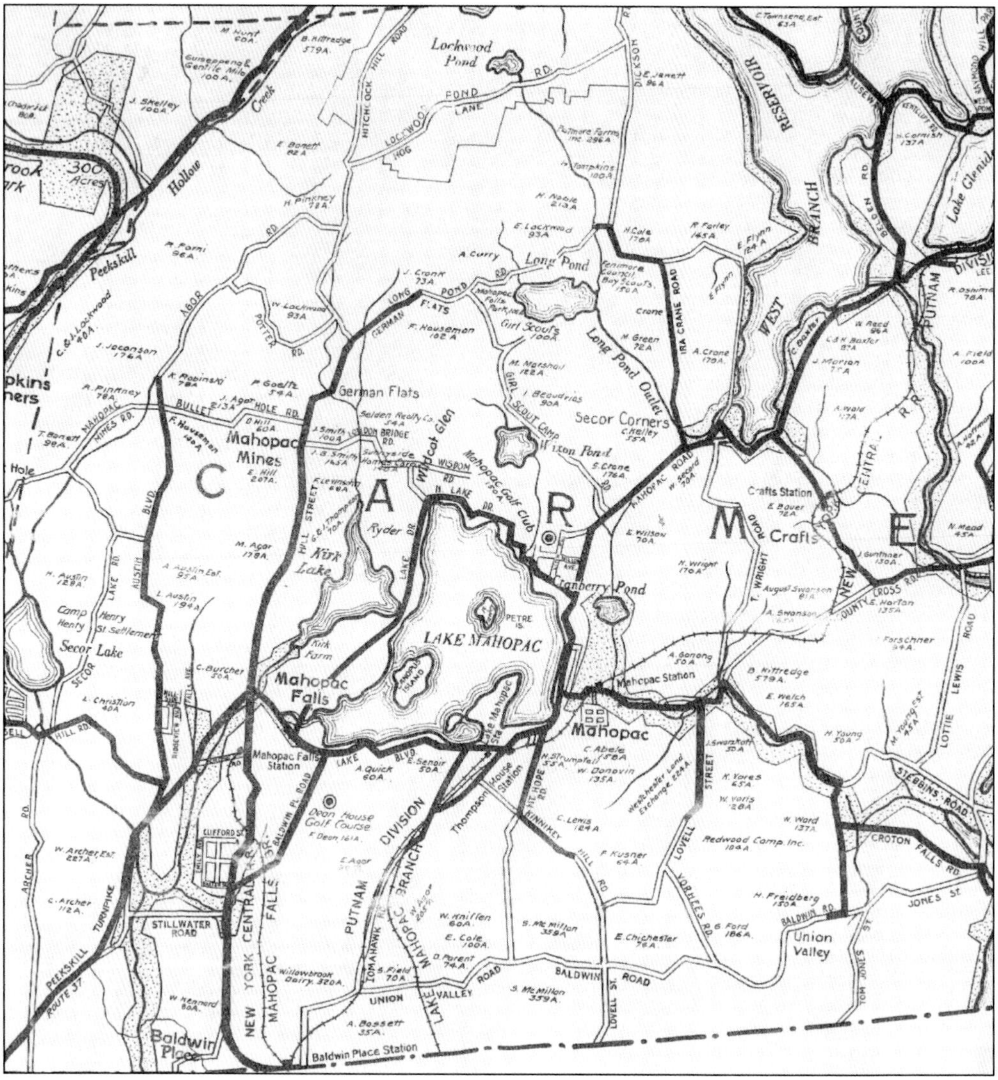

The 1931 Dolph and Steward property map indicates some of the landowners in Mahopac and how many acres they owned as of that year. Much of the acreage remained farmland at the time. The map depicts local roads and waterways, many of whose routes are recognizable today. (Putnam County Historian's Office.)

Two

HOUSES OF WORSHIP

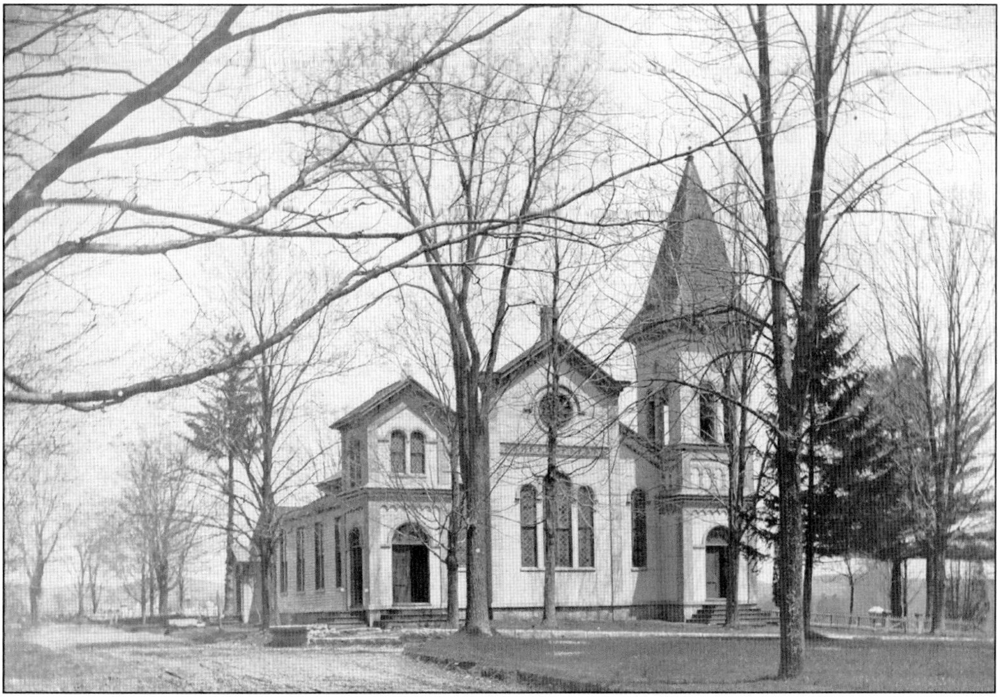

A building devoted to Presbyterian church services was constructed at the intersection of Route 6N and Secor Road in 1784. It was demolished in 1830. Another church was constructed there by 1833. It sat 300 people and was said to be one of the most attractive churches in Putnam County. In 1876, it was remodeled. This view shows the church as it appeared around 1890. (Presbyterian Church of Mahopac Falls, Rev. Kenneth Mast.)

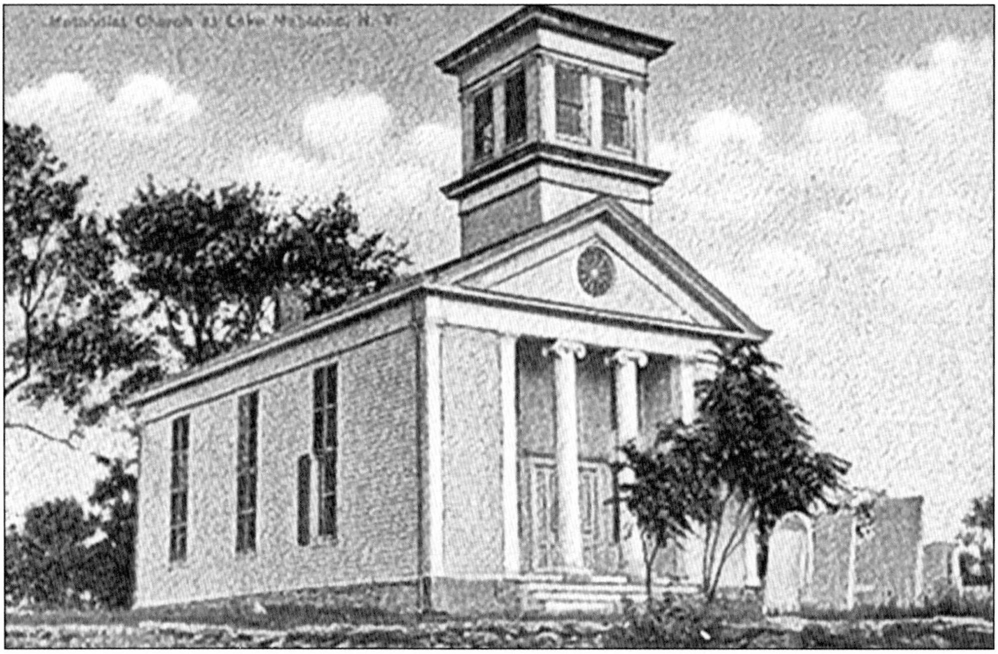

The first Methodist Episcopal church in Mahopac was constructed in 1826. The former site of the church is now the parking lot for St. John the Evangelist Roman Catholic Church. The Methodist Episcopal church was demolished in 1922 with only its cemetery remaining. The congregation moved to a new church located at the intersection of South and East Lake Boulevards and Mount Hope Road. (Greg Amato.)

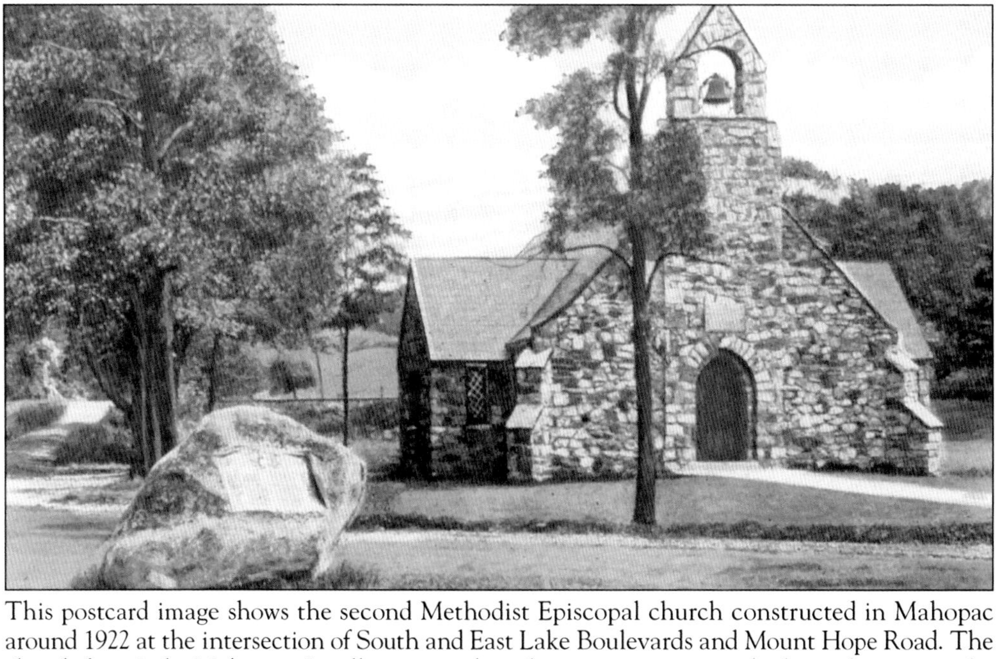

This postcard image shows the second Methodist Episcopal church constructed in Mahopac around 1922 at the intersection of South and East Lake Boulevards and Mount Hope Road. The church faces Lake Mahopac. It still exists, as does the war monument, which can be seen in the image foreground. For a short period in the 1920s, the church was known as St. John's Methodist Episcopal Church. (Greg Amato.)

This c. 1907 image shows the Methodist-Episcopal Church parsonage located near the corner of Croton Falls Road and Miller Avenue near the old Mahopac hamlet. The parsonage was bought from William Pinckney in 1867 and reportedly included 40 acres of land and 40 apple trees. It was an ideal spot near Lake Mahopac for a summer vacation. However, it was poorly insulated for the winter and located too far from the church for convenience. (Greg Amato.)

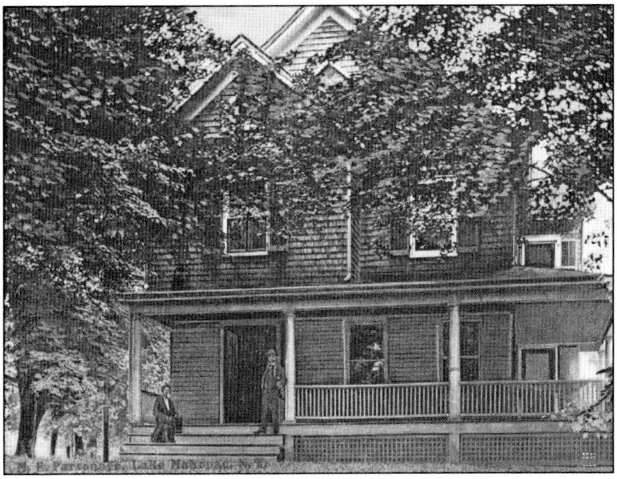

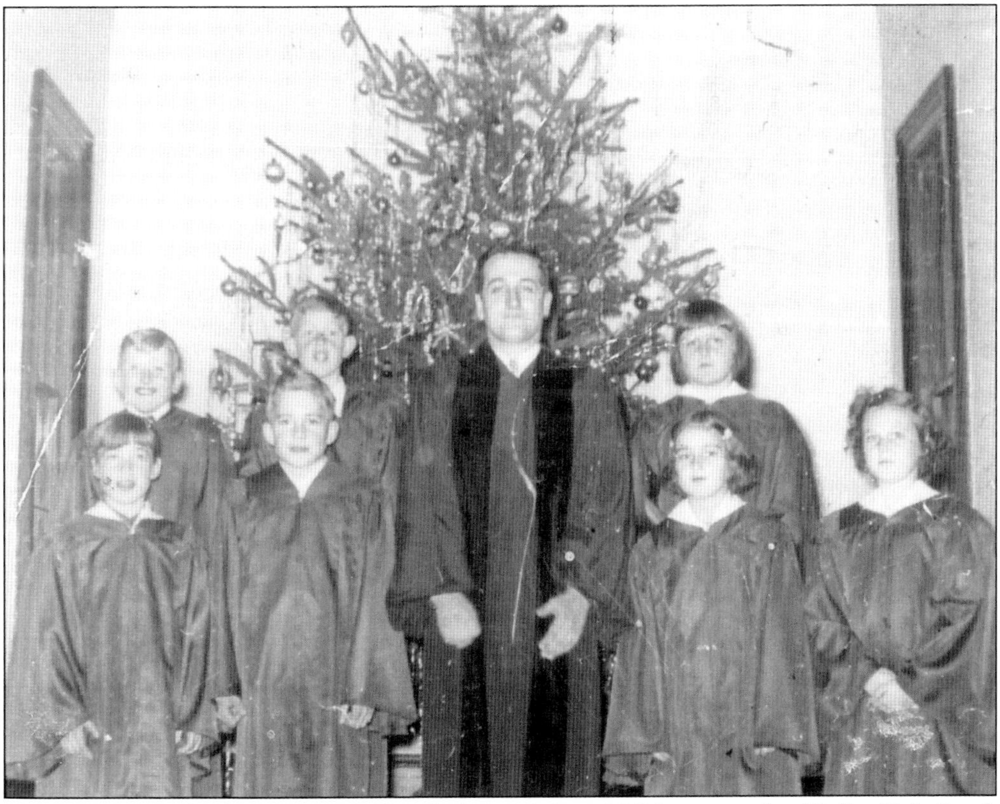

Mount Hope Methodist-Episcopal Church, located along Hill Street north of Bullet Hole Road, was constructed in 1876. This photograph shows church pastor Reverend McGongle and the children's choir on December 18, 1955. Pictured are, from left to right, (first row) M. LaPorte, J. LaPorte, Reverend McGongle, G. Sweet, and unidentified; (second row) P. Sweet, L. Sweet, and S. Williams. (Mount Hope United Methodist Church, Rev. Willett Porter.)

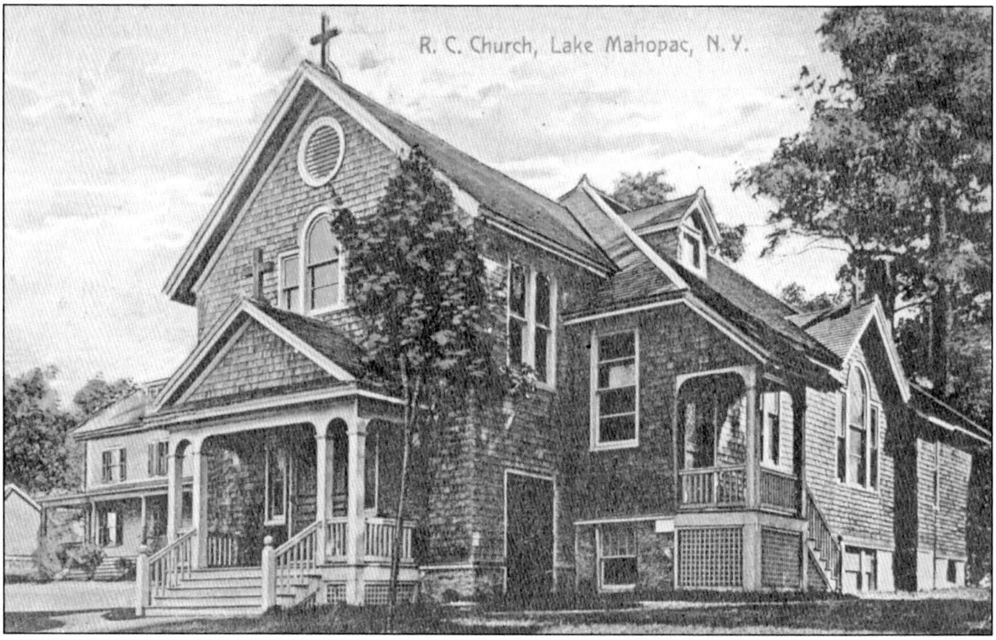

St. John the Evangelist Parish dates to 1889 with a church located in Mahopac's old hamlet. In 1902, after the hamlet's buildings were demolished to protect New York City's water supply, the parish acquired land on Lake Mahopac and built a new church in 1903. The image shows the still existing church as it appeared in 1915. (St. John the Evangelist Roman Catholic Church.)

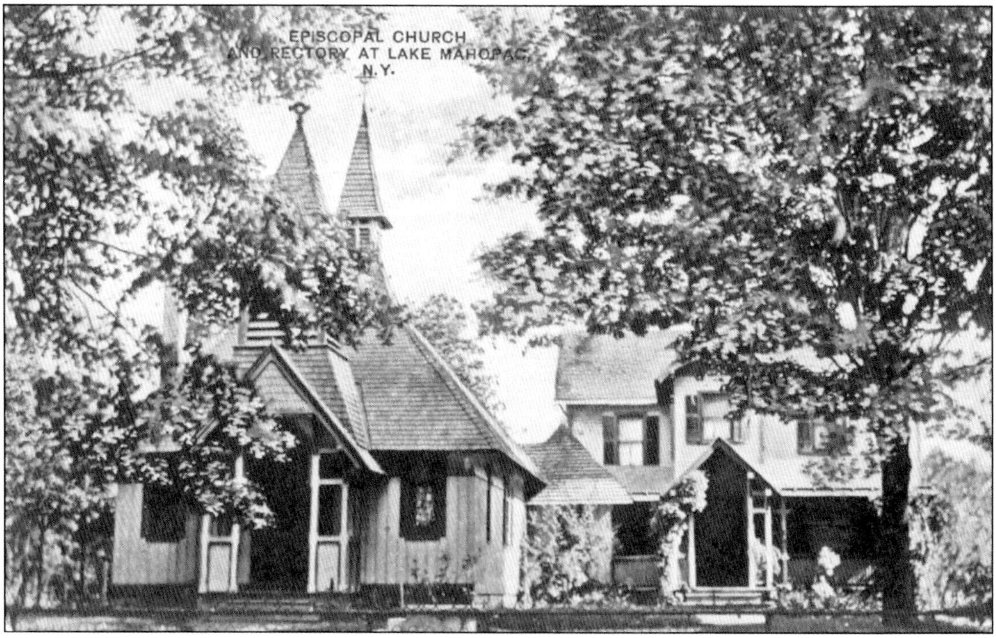

This early 20th-century image shows the Episcopal Church of the Holy Communion. It was located along East Lake Boulevard. The church was organized in 1860 with its rectory built in 1898. The chapel was donated by Egisto Fabbri, an aristocratic Italian, in memory of his brother Ernesto who passed away at Lake Mahopac in 1883. (Aaron Kass.)

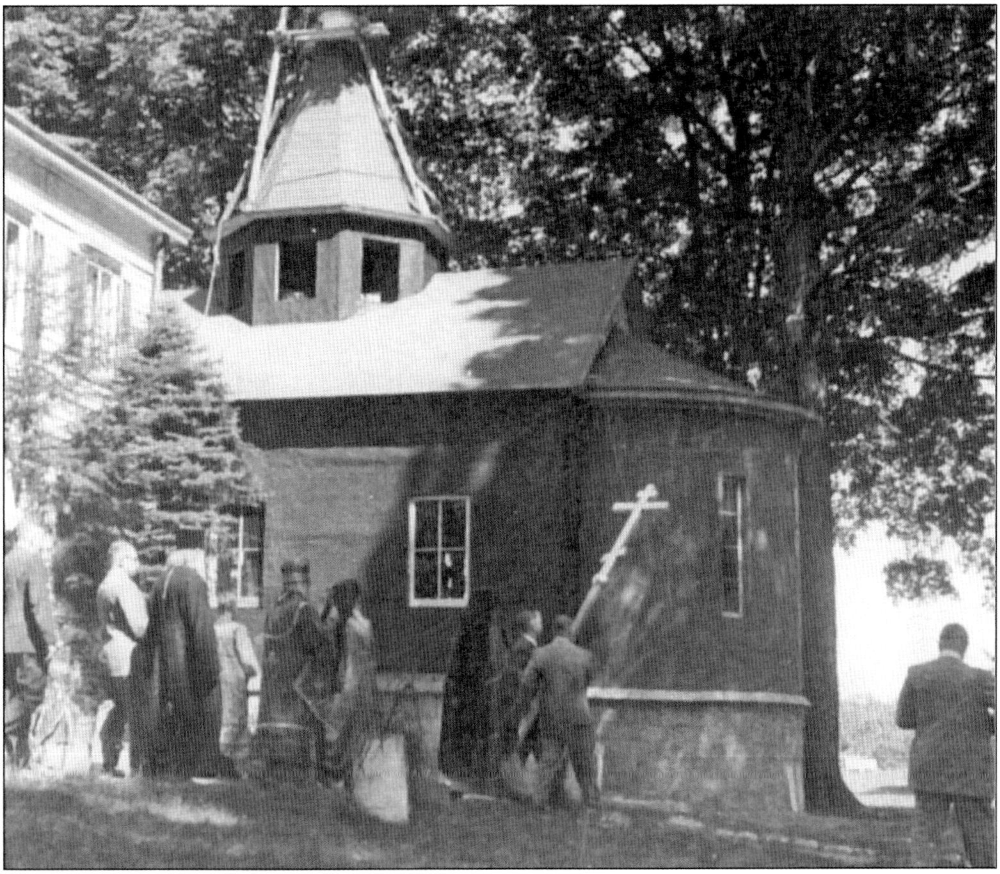

This image shows part of the dedication ceremony of the Church of the Russian Orthodox Parish of the Nativity of the Holy Mother of God in 1950. The church is located along Route 6. (The Town of Carmel Historical Society.)

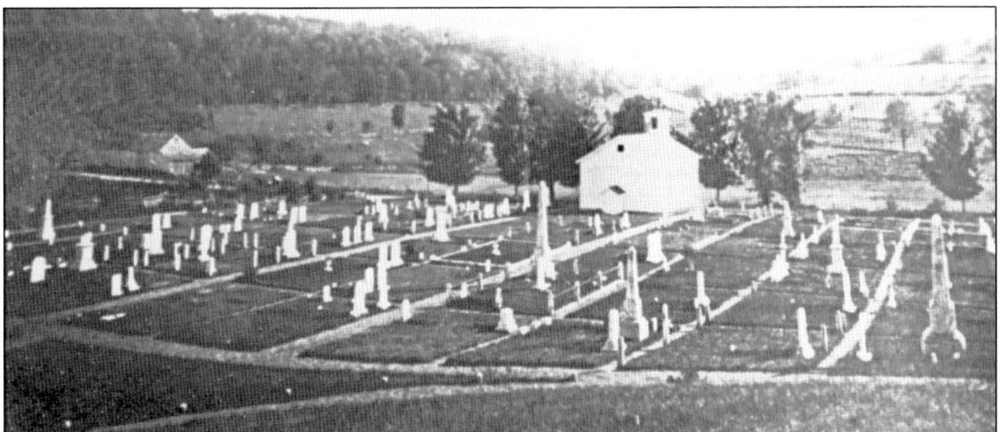

The Union Valley Chapel and Cemetery are located along Union Valley Road. The chapel was built in 1860. It is a simple New England style house of worship, seating around 100 people. The building is now maintained as a nonsectarian chapel. The image shows the Union Valley Chapel and its cemetery around 1900. (Lee and Ann Archer.)

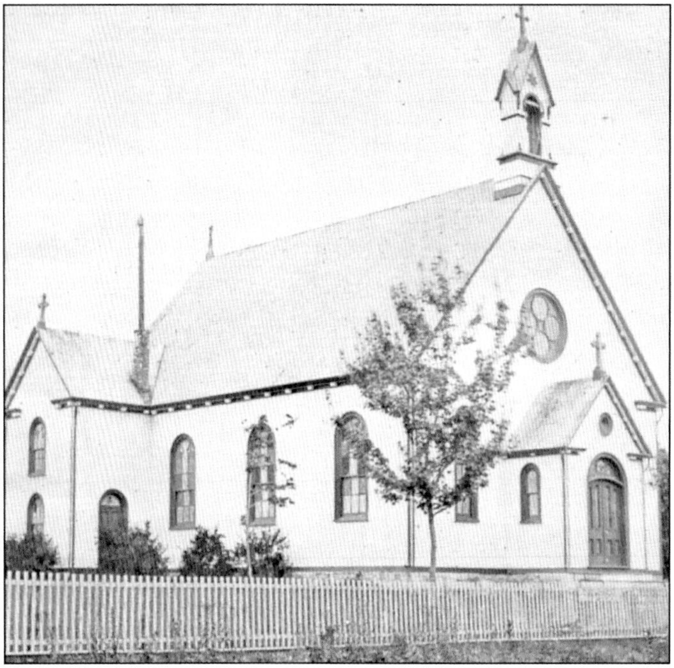

Mahopac's first Catholic church was constructed in 1869 in the old village, serving Mahopac, Carmel, and Brewster. Built on land donated in 1866 by Ruben Baldwin, the church was demolished in 1902 when the old village was condemned as part of the effort to protect the Croton watershed from pollution. The church was located near the intersection of present-day Route 6 and Lake Casse Road. A new Catholic church, now the chapel for St. John the Evangelist Parish, opened in 1903 along East Lake Boulevard. (St. John the Evangelist Roman Catholic Church.)

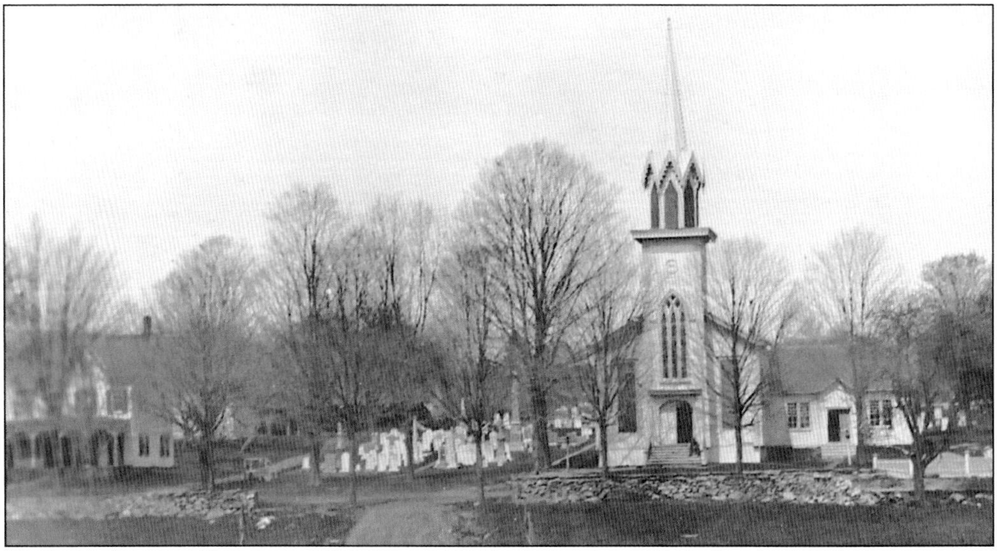

The Red Mills Baptist Church and burial ground are shown in this late-19th-century view. In 1831, some Red Mills residents decided to form a church. The original lot was sold to church trustees on August 17, 1832, and the congregation was formerly organized by Elder John Warren and 25 other members by the end of that month. The church itself was constructed shortly afterward with the first deacons being Eleazer Cole, Isaac Barrett, and Laban Cole. The front of the church originally faced south but the entire building was rotated in 1867, and a new entrance was constructed facing Peekskill Road (now Route 6N). The original entrance became the rear of the church. The Red Mills Baptist Church was demolished in 1999, and a new house of worship was constructed immediately to the south. The cemetery surrounding the original church contains the graves of many of the original members of the Red Mills Baptist Church. In 1921, the original Baptist Burial Ground was incorporated as a separate entity, the Ballard-Barrett Cemetery. (Muriel Agor Hill.)

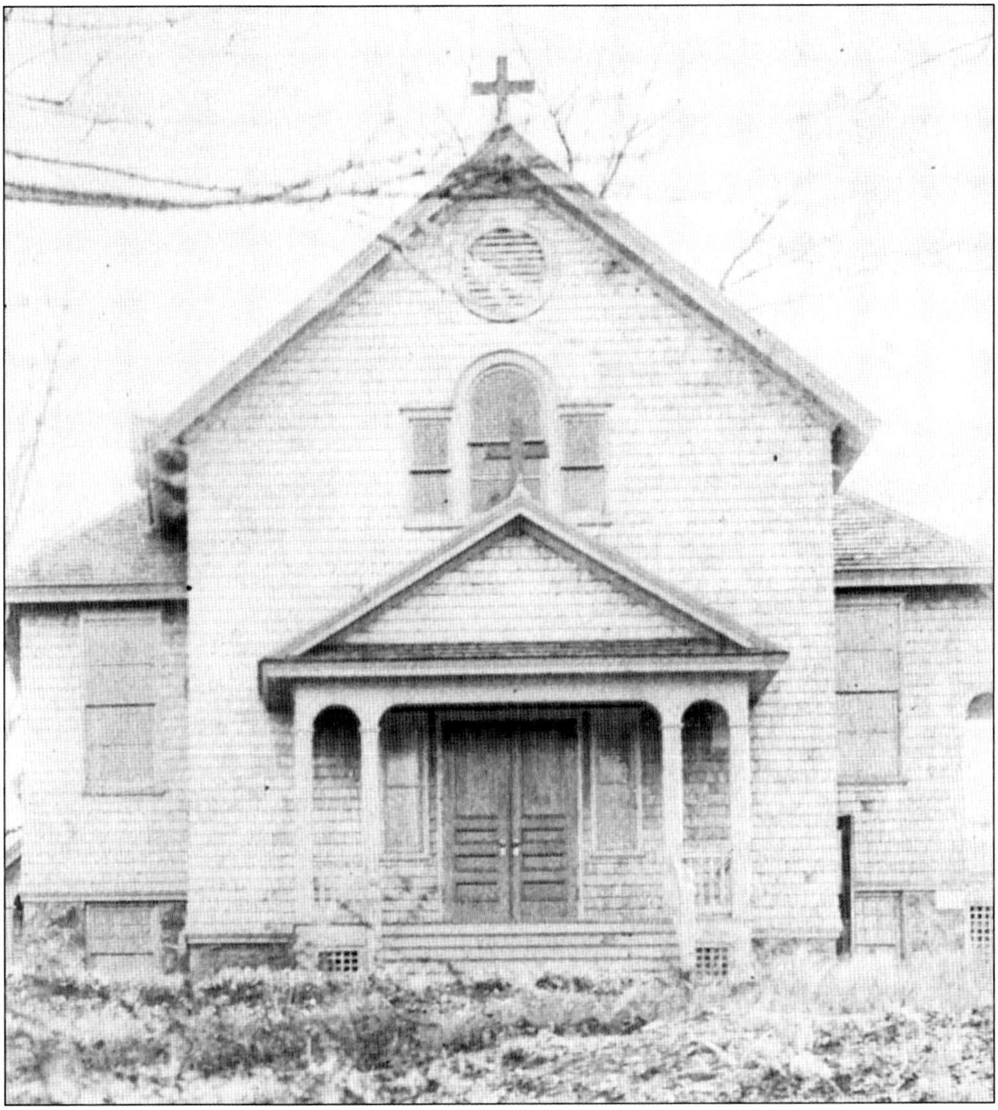

This is the front of the newly opened Catholic Chapel on East Lake Boulevard in 1903, which served Catholics of Carmel and Mahopac. It replaced Mahopac's first Catholic church, which was located in the old village of Mahopac and demolished in 1902 as part of a water pollution control effort. Carmel's Catholics raised money for their own church, which was completed in 1909 and dedicated to St. James the Apostle. (St. John the Evangelist Roman Catholic Church, Fr. Jarlath Quinn, Terri Komendowski.)

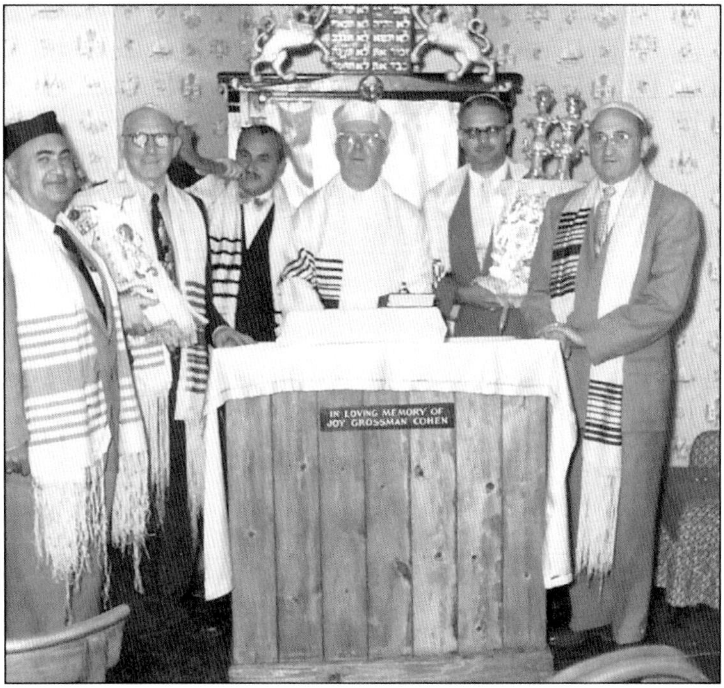

Irving Zimbarg is blowing the Shofar during Yom Kippur services around 1953 at the Jewish Center of the Mahopacs. The Jewish synagogue was located along Baldwin Road across from the current middle school. It served its congregation until around 1958 when the existing Temple Beth Shalom, located at the intersection of Croton Falls Road and Route 6, was dedicated. (Temple Beth Shalom, Rabbi Eytan Hammerman.)

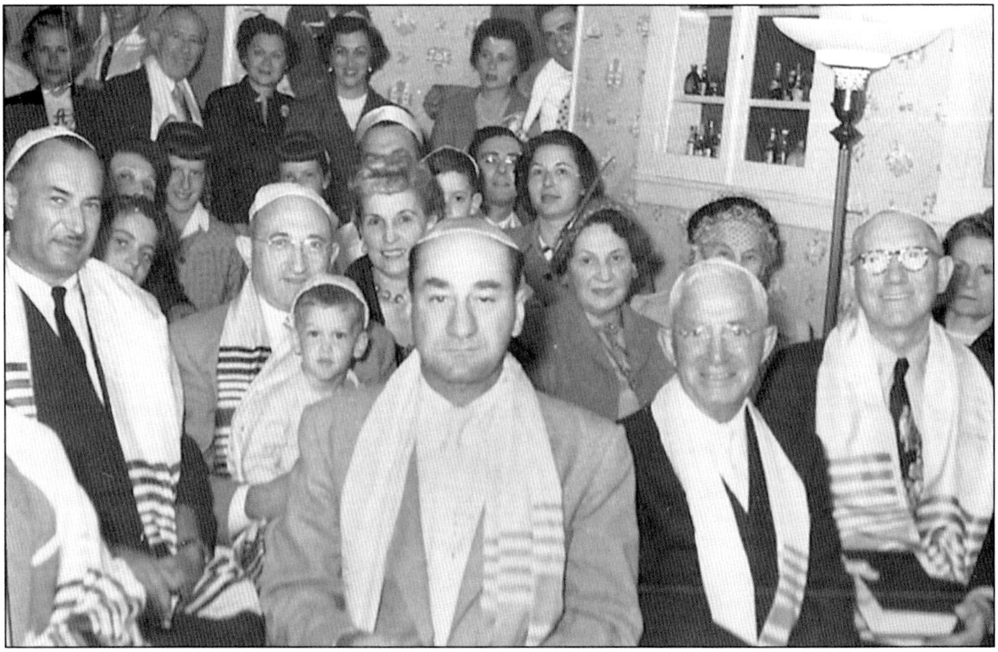

Worshipers are shown at the same Yom Kippur service around 1953 at the Jewish Center of the Mahopacs synagogue along Baldwin Road. (Temple Beth Shalom, Rabbi Eytan Hammerman.)

Three

RECREATION

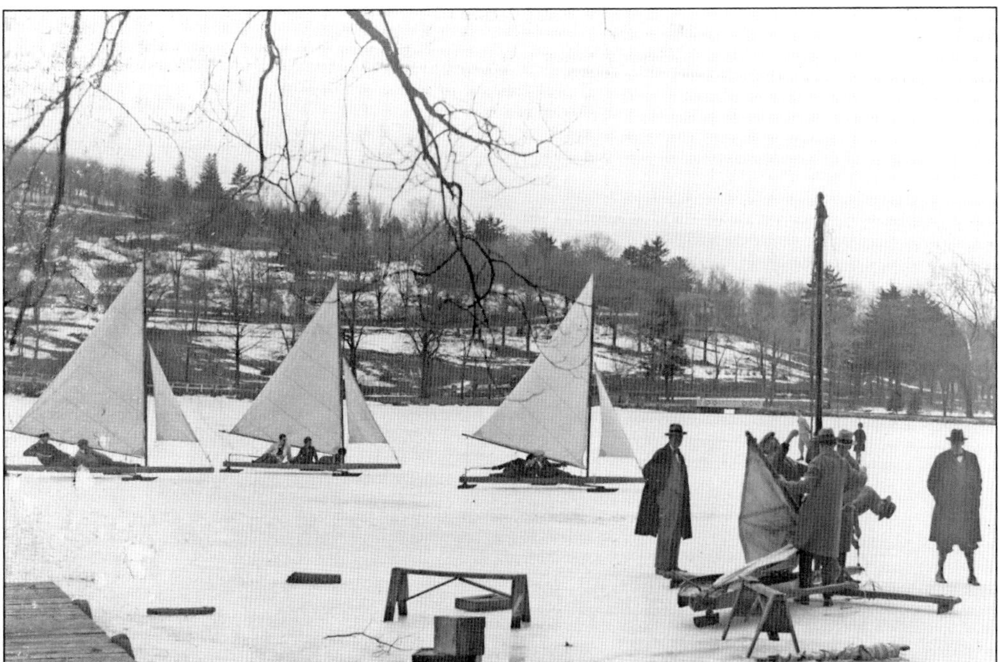

This view shows ice boaters and ice skaters in Fairy Island Cove in Lake Mahopac around 1930. The bridge to Fairy Island is seen in the distance at the right. What is now Route 6N extends along the shore's edge at the base of Indian Hill. Notice the open fields along the hill slope, areas now occupied by residences. The view was taken from the Lakeshore Club. (The Town of Carmel Historical Society.)

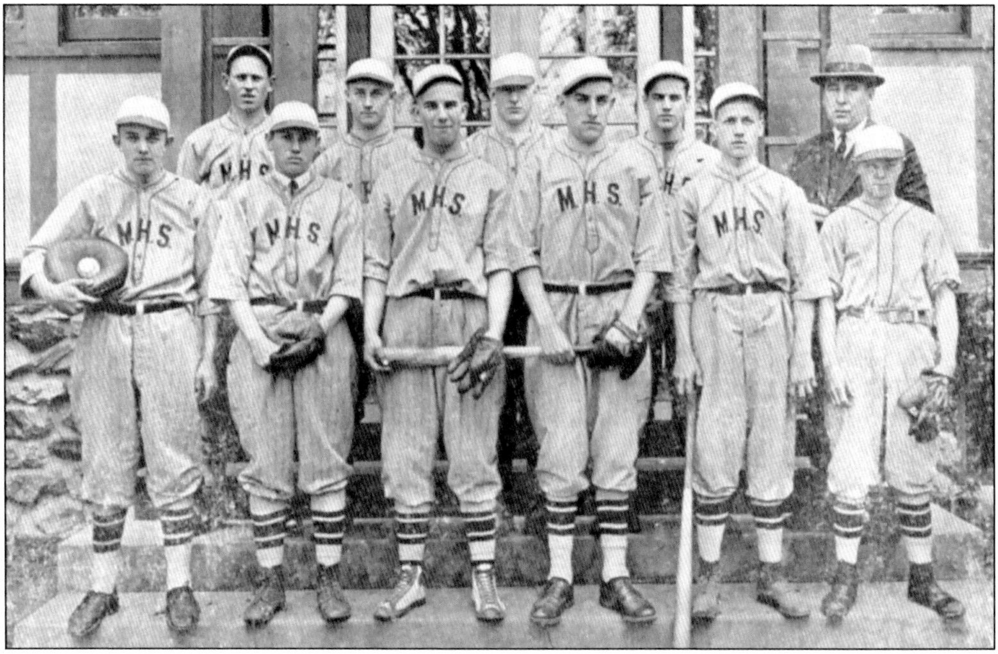

This image from the 1924 yearbook shows the nine players of the Mahopac High School baseball team. Also shown are the team's manager and ball boy. The photograph was taken at the front entrance of the Mahopac Central School on East Lake Boulevard at its intersection with Croton Falls Road. (Mahopac School District.)

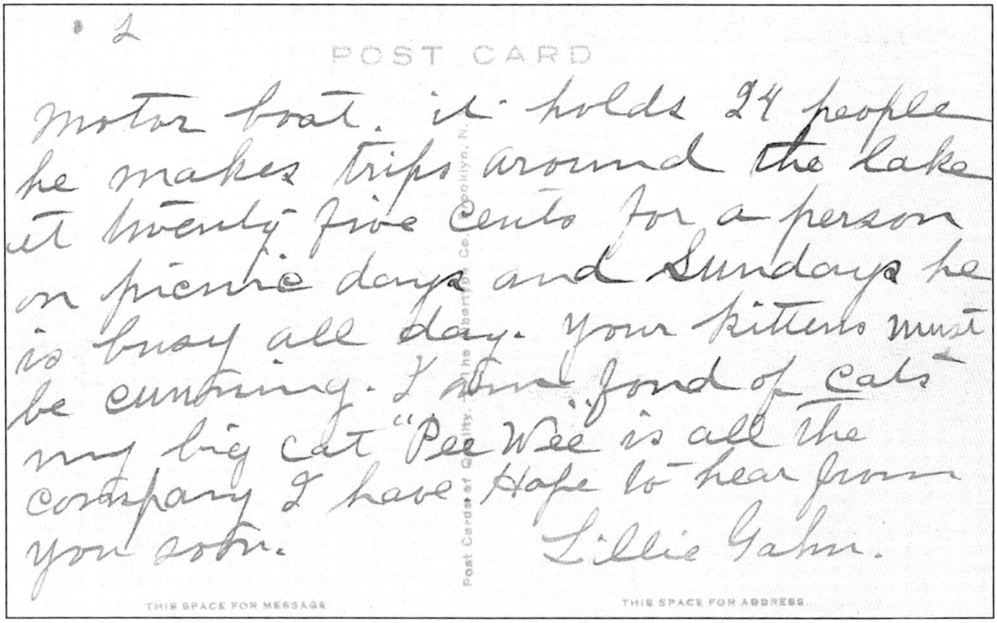

2

POST CARD

motor boat. it holds 24 people
he makes trips around the lake
at twenty-five cents for a person
on picnic days and Sundays he
is busy all day. Your kittens must
be cunning. I am fond of cats
my big cat "Pee Wee is all the
company I have Hope to hear from
you soon.

Lillie Gahn.

THIS SPACE FOR MESSAGE

THIS SPACE FOR ADDRESS

The motorboat referred to in this postcard was the *Janet*, a tour boat operating on Lake Mahopac. The launch picked up passengers at the hotel docks along the lakeshore. A postcard sent by Lillian Gahn, a Mahopac resident, indicates that the *Janet* held 24 people with excursions costing 25¢ per person. She reports that the boat was kept busy during the summer season, particularly on picnic days and Sundays. (Greg Amato.)

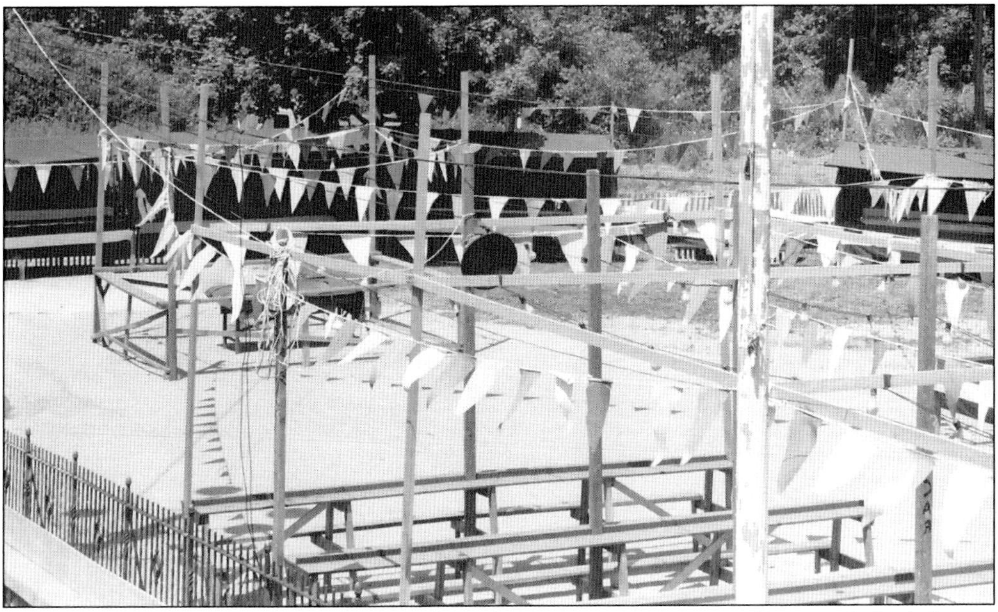

This photograph shows the Mahopac Falls Volunteer Fire Department Fair in 1940 while it is being set up. The yearly fair was a large community event attended by people from throughout Putnam and Westchester Counties and western Connecticut. The event was held in the parking lot by the firehouse. The lot is smaller today, but during the period the fair was held, it extended south to Potter Road. (Jack Casey, Mahopac Falls Volunteer Fire Department.)

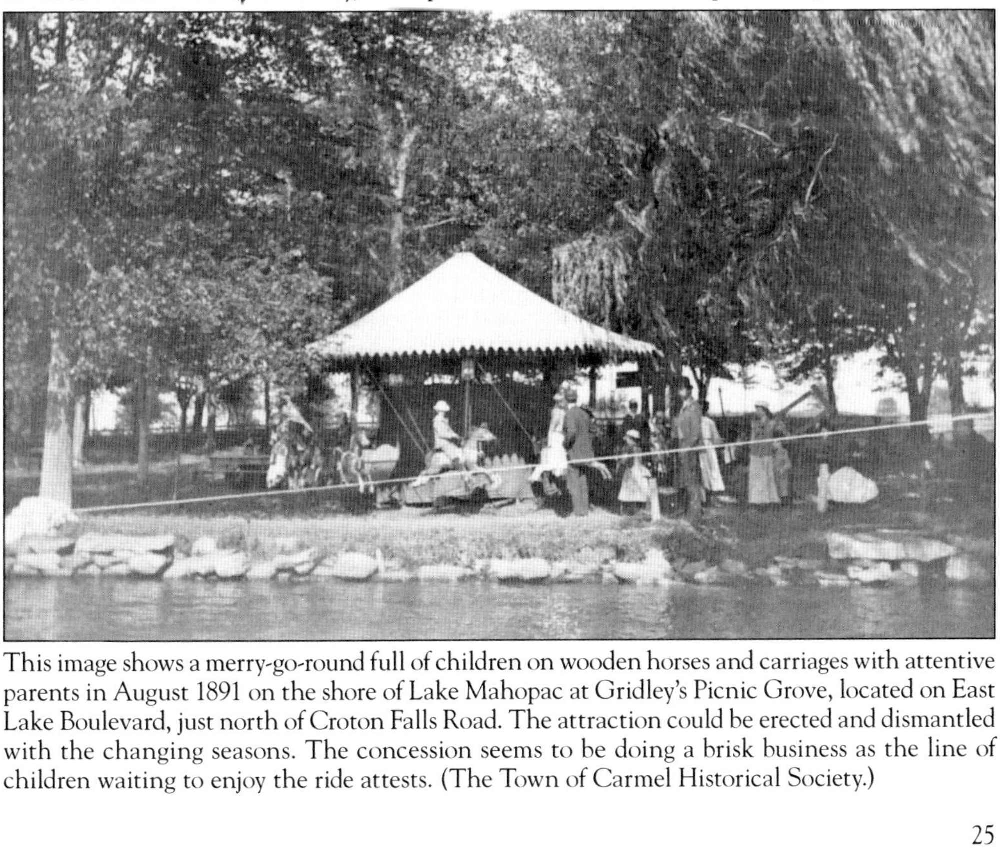

This image shows a merry-go-round full of children on wooden horses and carriages with attentive parents in August 1891 on the shore of Lake Mahopac at Gridley's Picnic Grove, located on East Lake Boulevard, just north of Croton Falls Road. The attraction could be erected and dismantled with the changing seasons. The concession seems to be doing a brisk business as the line of children waiting to enjoy the ride attests. (The Town of Carmel Historical Society.)

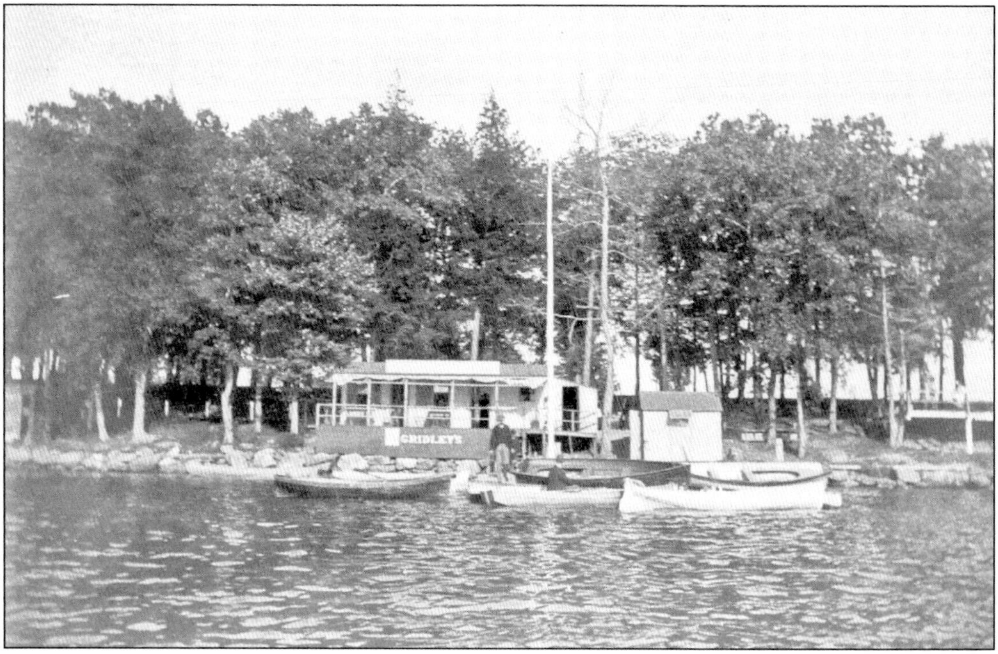

This 1891 photograph shows Gridley's livery, boathouse, and picnic grove along East Lake Boulevard on Lake Mahopac. Picnickers were local residents, but seasonal visitors and day-trippers from surrounding counties and New York City also came to enjoy an outing. Large groups from churches, sports teams, clubs, and extended families partook of Gridley's hospitality with numbers of attendees frequently reaching into the hundreds. (Greg Amato.)

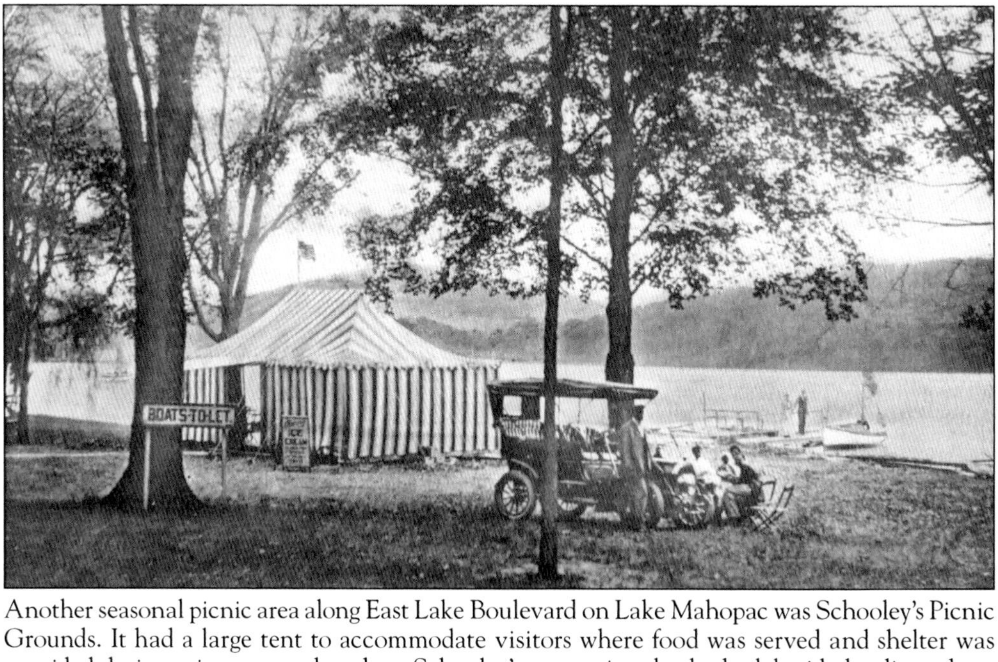

Another seasonal picnic area along East Lake Boulevard on Lake Mahopac was Schooley's Picnic Grounds. It had a large tent to accommodate visitors where food was served and shelter was provided during rainy or very hot days. Schooley's enterprise also had a lakeside landing where boats could be rented for use on the lake. As seen in the photograph, ice cream was a summertime staple with a sign imploring one to try it. (Greg Amato.)

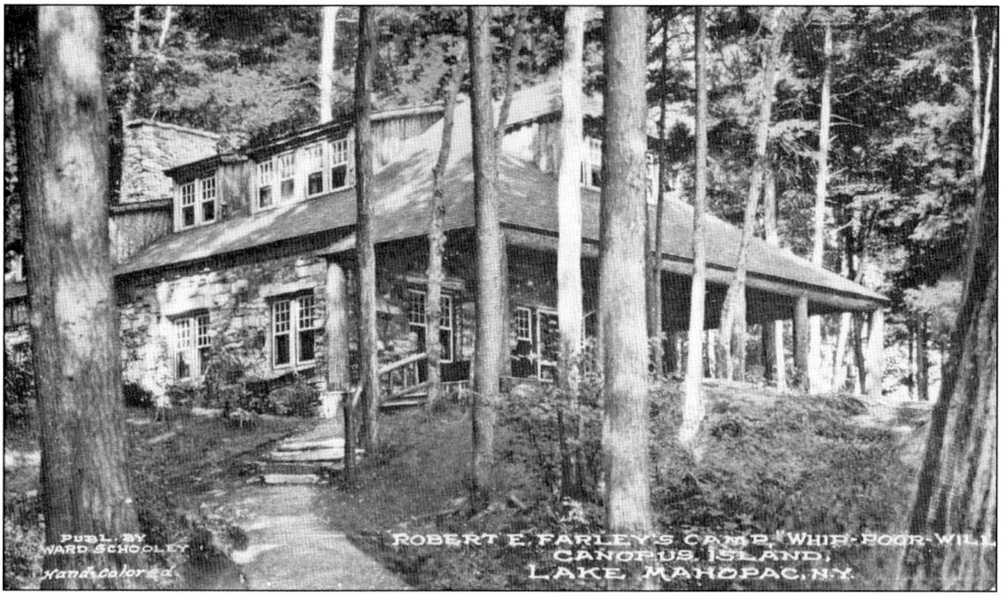

This c. 1915 postcard shows the summer cabin for Robert Farley's Camp Whip-Poor-Will on Canopus Island in Lake Mahopac. Farley also had a boathouse on the west side of the island. Visitors would come for a week or more to enjoy a rustic island experience on Lake Mahopac, rather than a large hotel stay. The cabin burned and the camp closed soon after. Farley also owned a large stone mansion along North Lake Boulevard that was known as Graymanse. (The Town of Carmel Historical Society.)

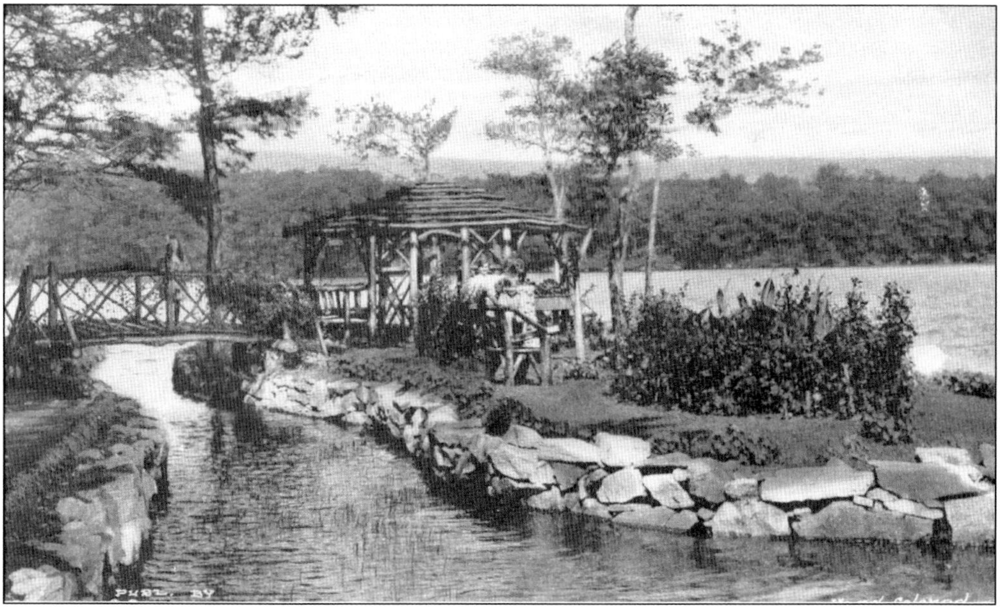

This c. 1915 photograph shows the north shoreline of Canopus Island which Robert Farley, as part of his Camp Whip-Poor-Will, had landscaped and dug a shallow passage for boats and canoes, creating a small island. The passage was crossed by a rustic, Adirondack-style wooden bridge leading to a similarly styled shelter. Farley called the area with its water passage "Little Venice." It is still present although it is now overgrown by shrubs. (The Town of Carmel Historical Society.)

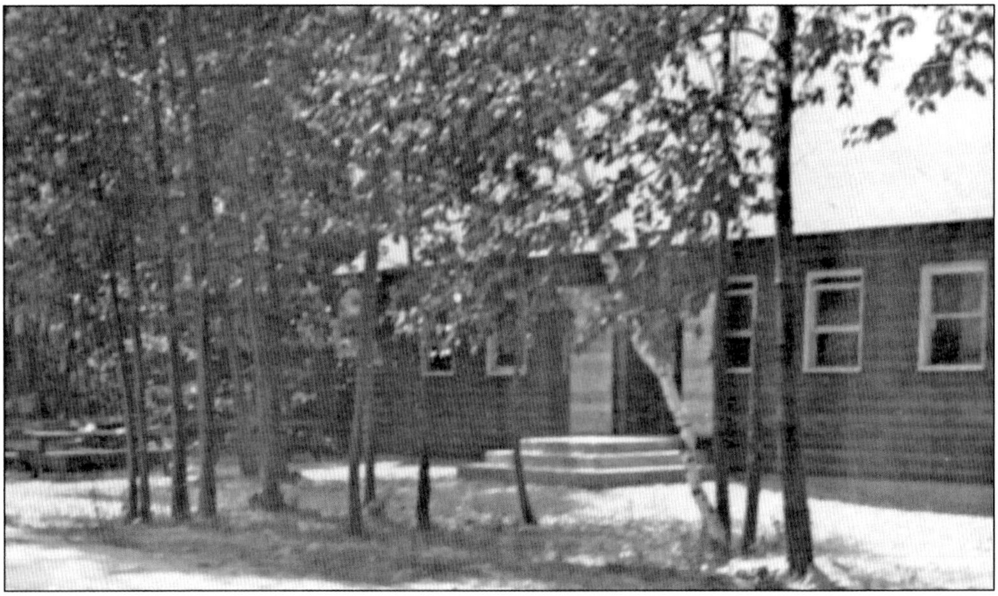

The Ossi Sport Club was founded in 1940 as a sporting club primarily by Austrian and German brewery workers from Manhattan. Land purchased along Barrett Hill Road was communally owned by members. Houses started as seasonal residences but soon became year-round dwellings. The image shows the community's Adirondack-style clubhouse around 1950, where dances and other social events were held. The community continues to exist. (Eugene J. Boesch.)

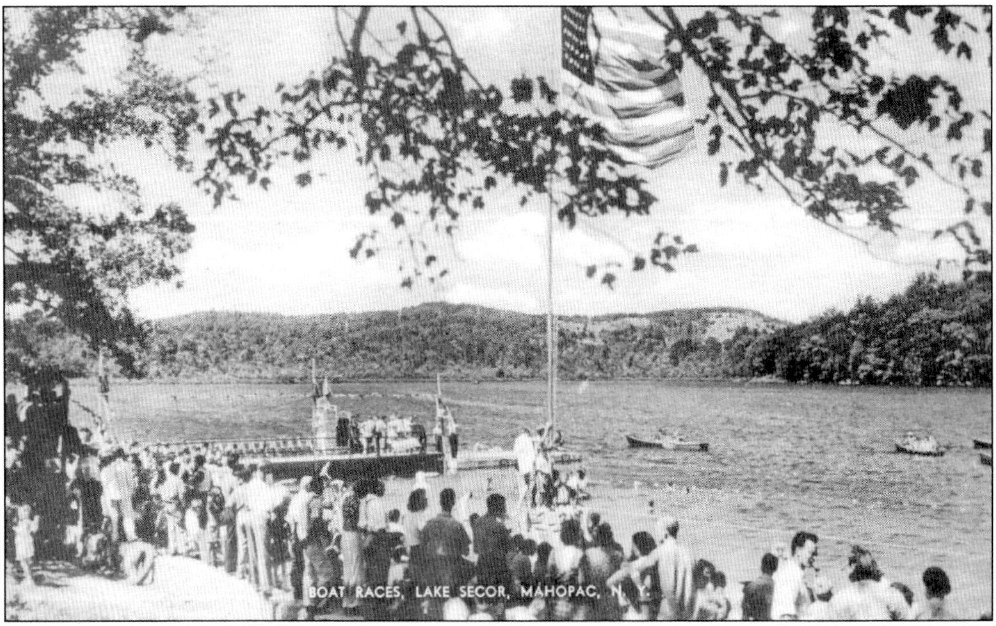

The postcard shows boat races and other activities on Lake Secor, a large residential community with over 500 families in the southwest corner of Mahopac. The community dates to the early 20th century and received its name from the Secor family, which were among the first settlers in the area. For much of its existence, the community was dominated by bungalows, where people predominantly of German heritage from New York City, spent their summer weekends. Most of the homeowners there are now year-round residents. (Bob and Claudia Stevens.)

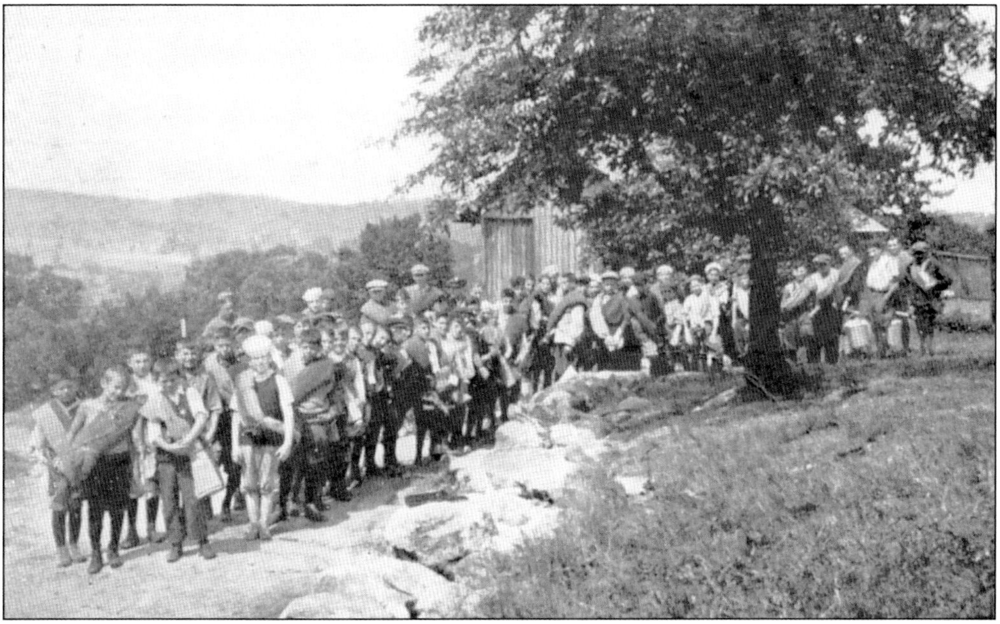

Camp Henry on Agor Lane was operated by New York City's Henry Street settlement, a nonprofit social service agency founded in 1893 by the progressive reformer Lillian Wald. Children attended the camp for extended periods, enjoying its cabins, trails, and Lake Secor. The camp played an important role during World War II by raising money for the Mahopac War Fund. (Bob and Claudia Stevens.)

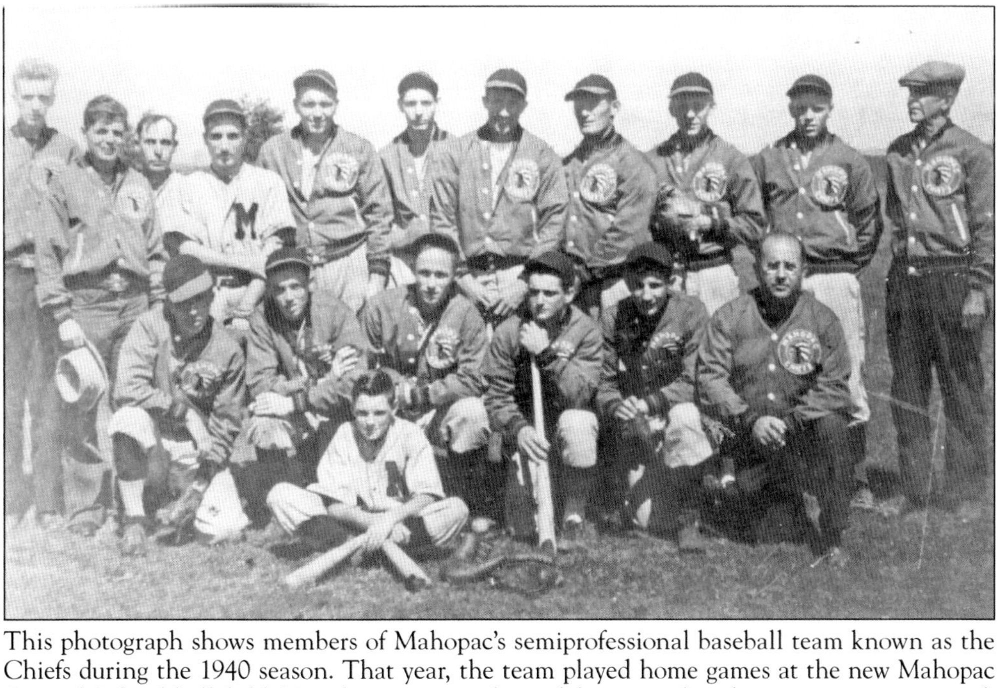

This photograph shows members of Mahopac's semiprofessional baseball team known as the Chiefs during the 1940 season. That year, the team played home games at the new Mahopac Central School ball field. No admission was charged for games but donations were requested. Unique to this team was that each player was under 22 years old. Team members included Ward Mead, DeLong "Bud" Kellogg, and Joseph Butironi. (Ted Dwyer.)

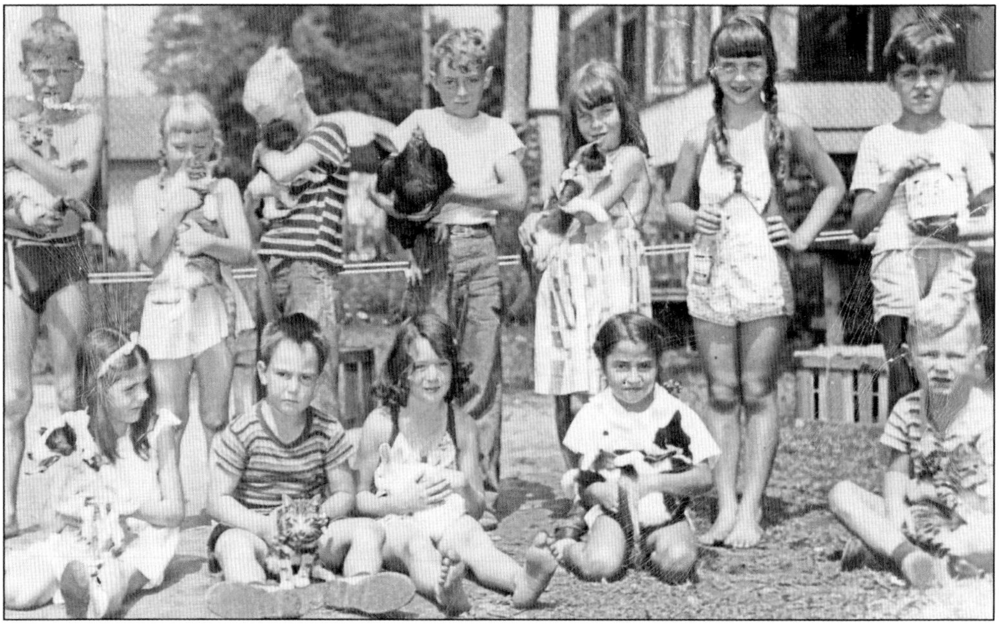

“Bring a pet day” at the Mahopac Central School District playground on Lake Mahopac during the summer of 1947 was a special treat for the children. Chickens, cats, dogs, and other pets brought fun to the kids. The playground served as a day camp with swimming, climbing, running, games, and special activities occurring. The camp was opened to all and continued until around 1960. Barbara Lacina is shown standing second from right. (Barbara Lacina Bosch.)

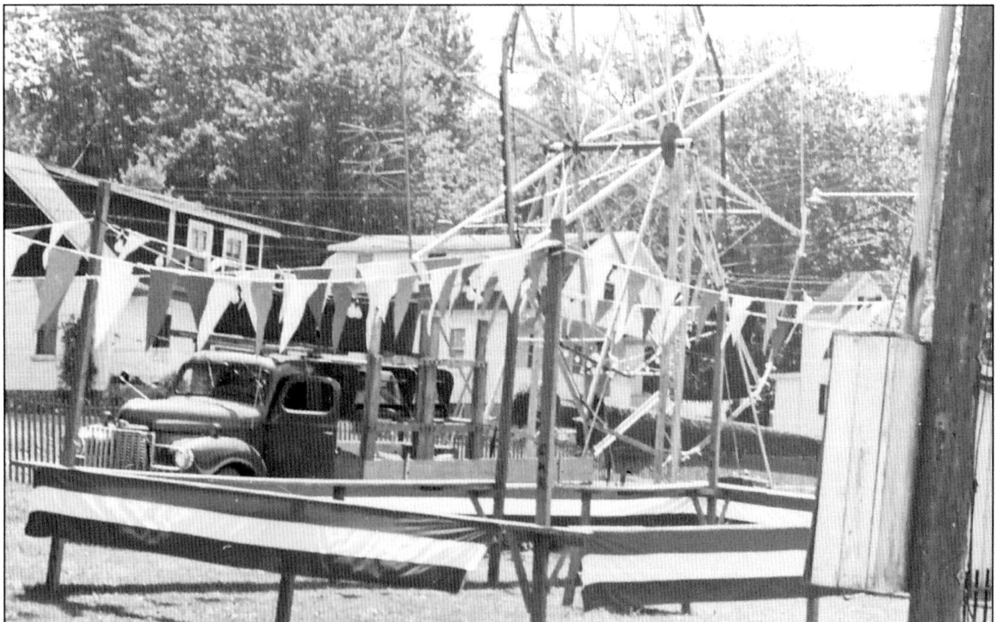

This is another photograph showing the Mahopac Falls Volunteer Fire Department Fair in 1940. The annual fair was held in the current parking lot for the fire department. The image shows a Ferris wheel being erected. What look like seats for the attraction are in the bed of the truck. (Jack Casey, Mahopac Falls Volunteer Fire Department.)

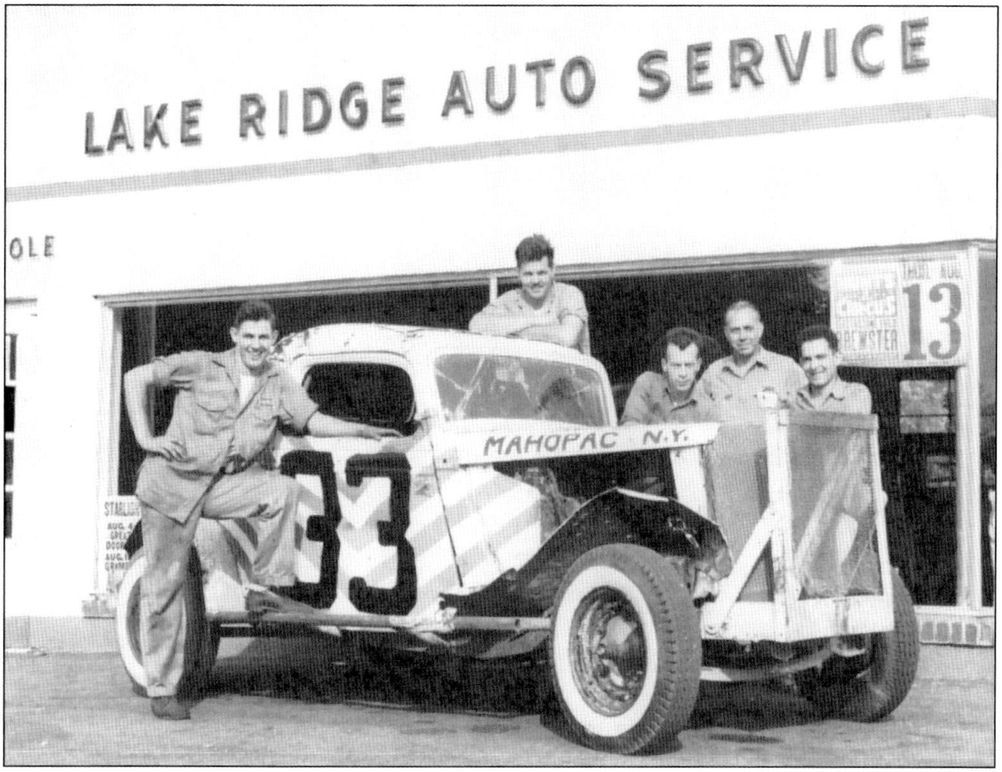

This image shows Bill Crew's Car No. 33, a racing stock car at Cole's Lake Ridge Auto Service on Route 6 around 1953. Pictured are, from left to right, Howard Beach, Bill Depp, Jimmy Curry, Paul Cole, and Rick Pegoli. (Ted Dwyer.)

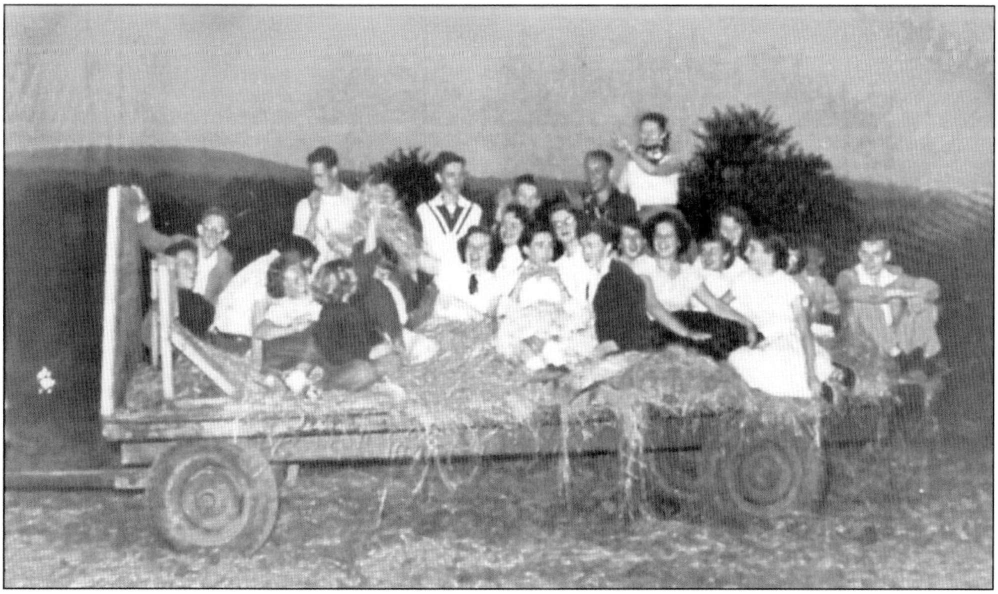
Barn dancing and hayrides for local youth were a frequent occurrence at the Agor Farm, the home of Jessie and Ruth Crane Agor and their children, located along Hill Street in Mahopac. The hayride photograph shown here dates to around 1960. (John Agor.)

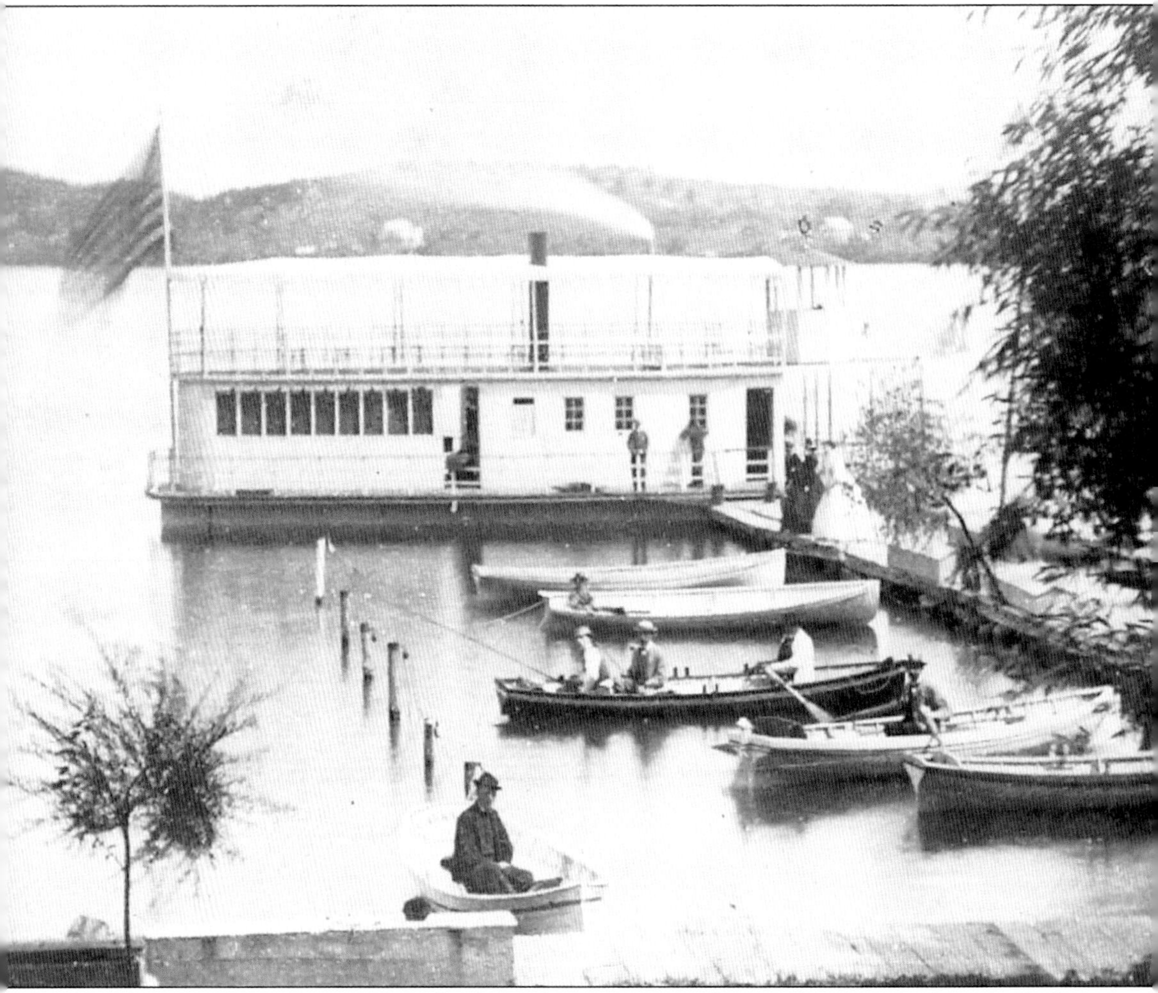

The *Dew Drop*, a stream-powered Lake Mahopac excursion boat, is shown around 1885. The boat was purchased and transported to Lake Mahopac by a Mr. North in 1869. It made daily trips from Thompson's Hotel to other places around the lake when signaled. Fares were 35¢ for adults and 20¢ each for children and their nurses. The boat could also be chartered for private parties, picnics, and fishing. After the tourist industry decreased, the boat reportedly was sunk in Lake Mahopac at Thompson's Cove. (Greg Amato.)

Four

Schools

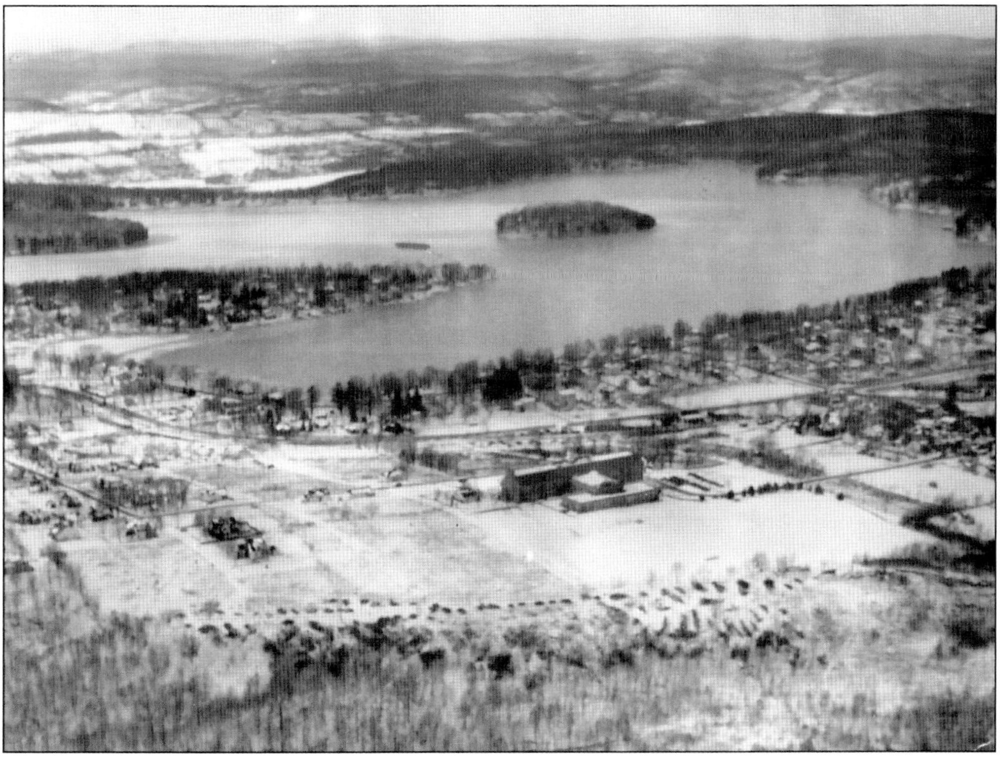

This aerial view shows a winter panoramic of Lake Mahopac and the hamlet's Route 6 corridor around 1940. Mahopac Point and Petre Island are seen in the image. The building on the hill is Mahopac Central School, now Lakeview Elementary School. The land below the school was used by the Carpenter House as its vegetable garden. The area eventually became the Mahopac Ridge development. (The Town of Carmel Historical Society.)

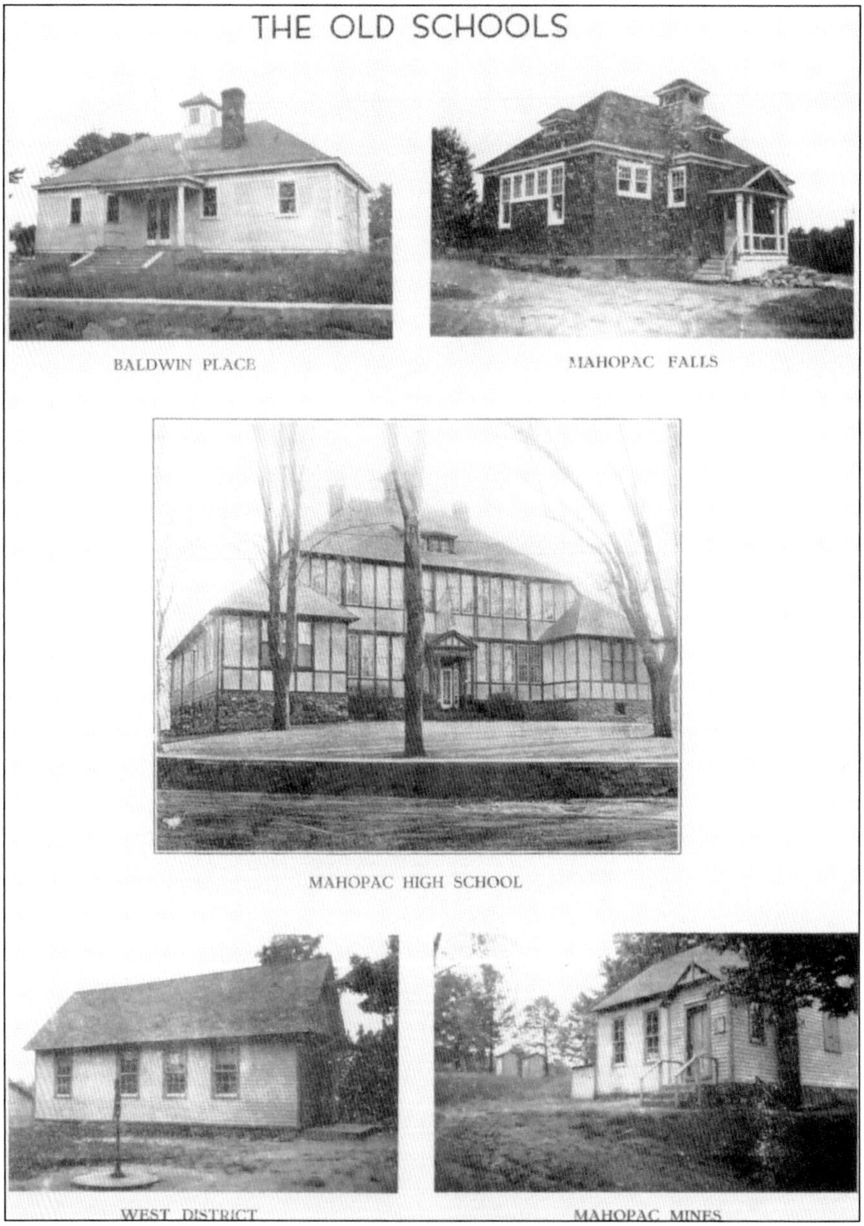

This poster shows the old Mahopac schools around 1920. The school in the center is the Mahopac High School (also known as the Mahopac Central School), formerly located at the corner of Croton Falls Road and East Lake Boulevard. The school was used for kindergarten through high school. The other schools shown were one- or two-room schoolhouses. The Mahopac Mines School was located along Bullet Hole Road. It still exists as a private residence. The West District No. 5 School was located on Secor Road and later served as the Lake Secor Community House. The Baldwin Place School was located on Route 118, where the HSBC Bank is currently located. The Mahopac Falls School later served as the Mahopac Falls Volunteer Fire Department headquarters and was located at the intersection of Brook Road and School Street. It was demolished to make way for the existing fire department headquarters. (Mahopac Central School District.)

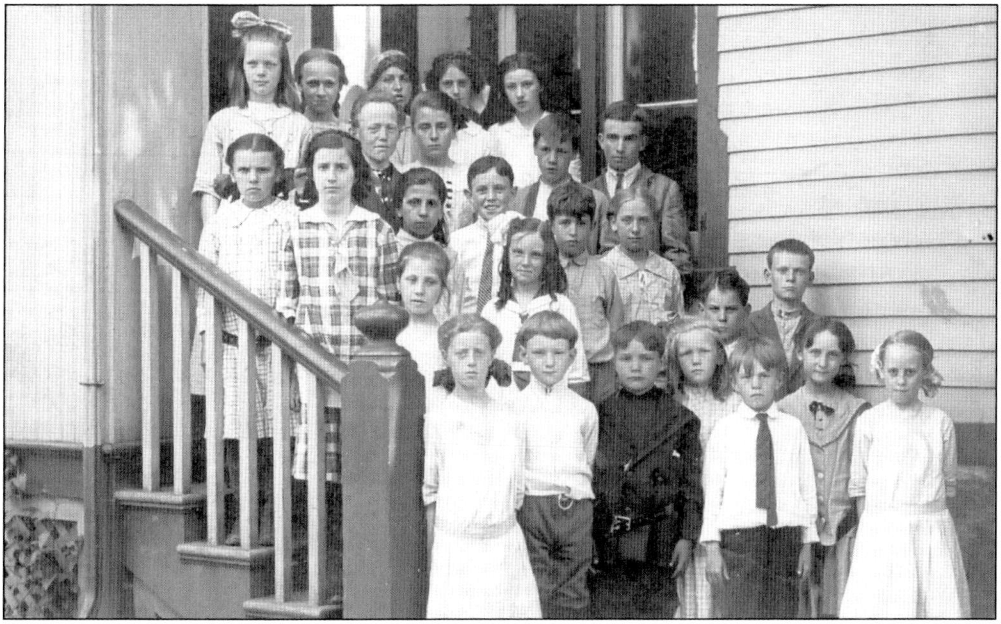

These Mahopac Falls school students of various ages show a mixture of smiles and frowns in this c. 1910s image. The two-room schoolhouse was located on School Street, within what is now the parking lot for the Mahopac Falls Volunteer Fire Department. Note the bows and tight braids extending over the heads of some of the girls, particular the older three in the back. (Muriel Agor Hill, Darlene Hill Lampe, Karen Hill Czysz.)

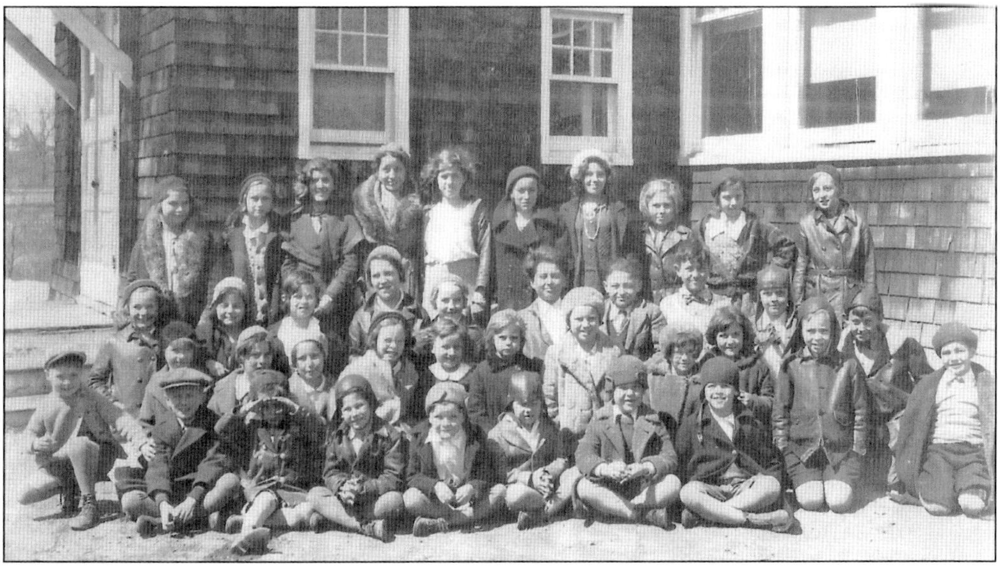

This is a late-1920s photograph of Mahopac Falls students. Pictured are, from left to right, (first row) four unidentified, Abel Hunt, unidentified, Earl Benjamin, and Hugo Hunt; (second row) George Field, three unidentified, Barbara Field, ? Siskorsky, unidentified, Betty Hadden, two unidentified, Ralph George, and unidentified; (third row) Muriel Agor (Hill), Bernice Beach, John Hunt, Lois Agor, Virginia Agor, Donald Blissard, unidentified, Donald Benjamin, and Donald Hill; (fourth row) Florence Townsend, Marion Warnecke, ? Puroy, unidentified Dorothy Frome, unidentified, Marjorie Hill, Eunice Walworth, and Betty Kohlbergen. (Muriel Agor Hill.)

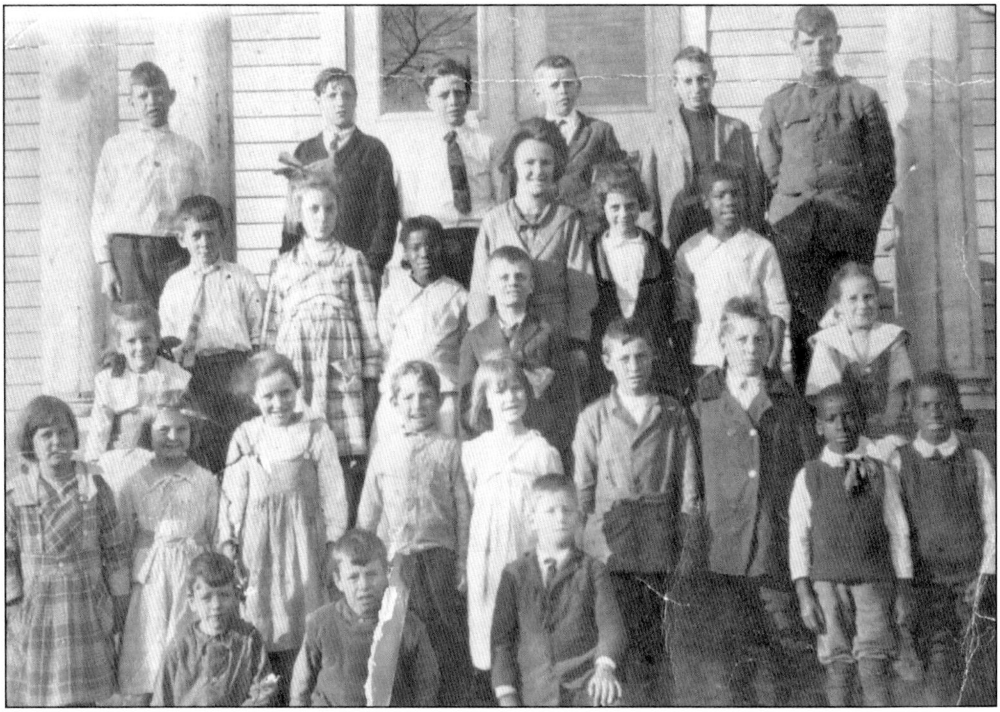

These students and their teacher stand on the steps of the Baldwin Place School around 1920. The older boy on the right in the top row may be set to join the military. (Margaret Head Neary.)

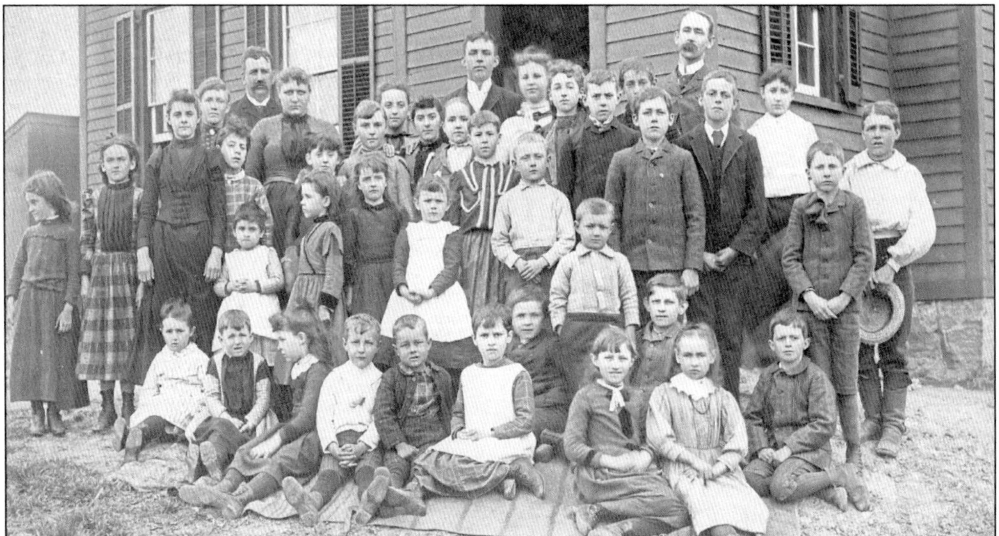

This group of students, their teacher, and other adults are at the Mahopac Mines School around 1900. Something is occurring to the left of the photograph, which has caught the attention of some of them. The community of Mahopac Mines, centered at the intersections of Hill Street with Bullet Hole Road and Stocum Avenue near German Flats, was a vibrant community during the late 19th century with its economy primarily centered on the nearby iron mine. Farms and orchards also were part of the community. For a while, mink was also commercially raised. Their pelts were sold to fur dealers in New York City. (Loretta Post Billington.)

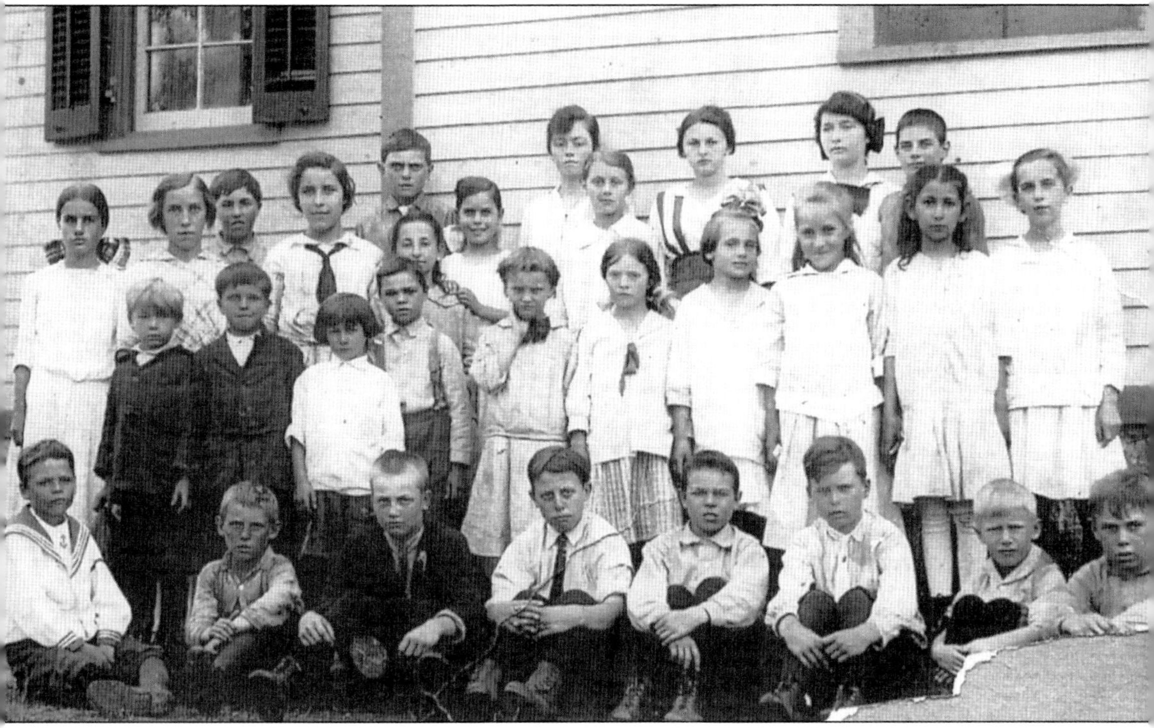

These girls and boys stand for their class photograph outside of the Mahopac Mines schoolhouse around 1917. It still stands as a private residence along Bullet Hole Road. The boy with the longer hair, third from the left in the second row, is Simon Amsterdam, whose father, Samuel, ran a boardinghouse along Long Pond Road. His older sisters Bess and Rose also are in the photograph as is Glynis Lockwood. Lockwood later ran a dairy farm in a nearby valley where Craescot Way now runs. (Karen and Gerry Levitis.)

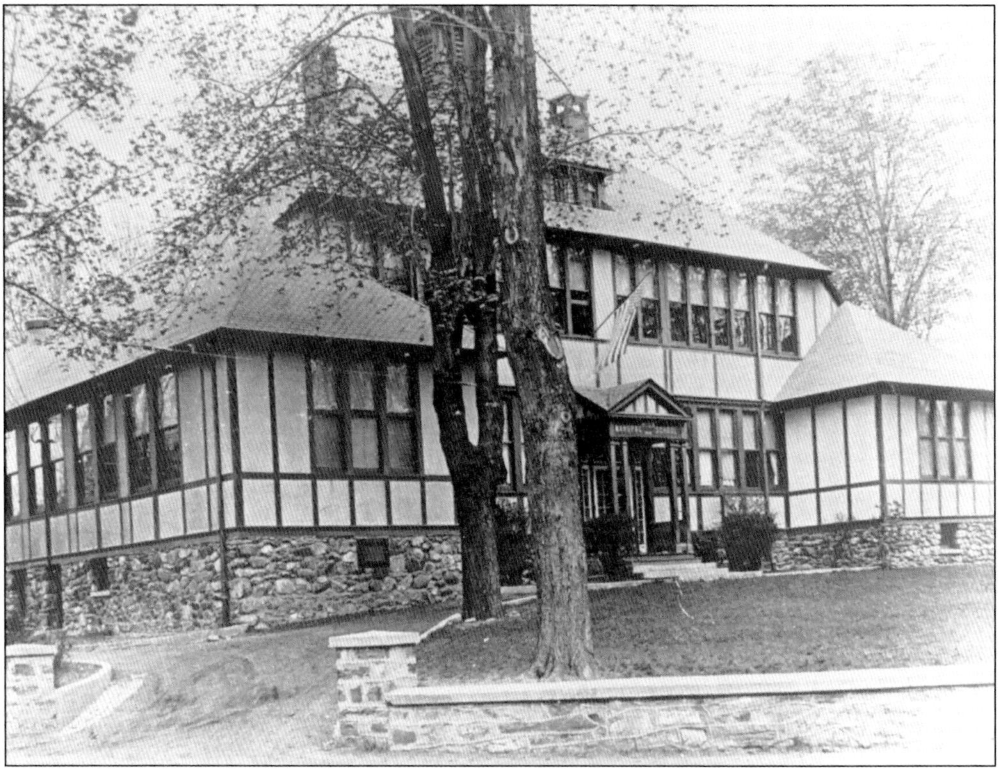

This is the old Mahopac High School, which opened near the intersection of Croton Falls Road and East Lake Boulevard in September 1918. It was also known as the Mahopac Central School and taught children from kindergarten through high school. It closed in June 1936 and was demolished when the new school (Lakeview School) was constructed on Mahopac Ridge. Stone pillars and the stone wall associated with the central school along East Lake Boulevard are all that remain. (Mahopac School District.)

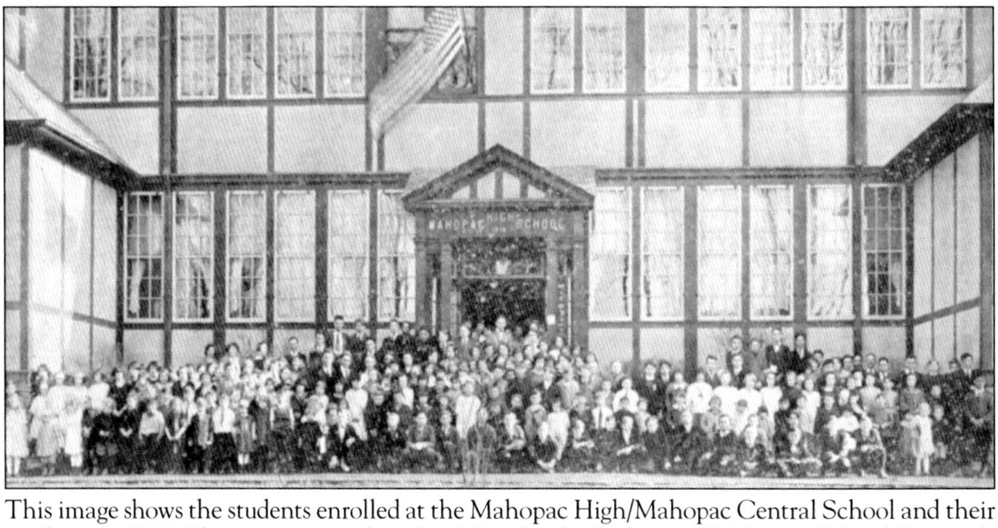

This image shows the students enrolled at the Mahopac High/Mahopac Central School and their teachers in 1924. The entrance to the school faced Lake Mahopac. (Mahopac School District.)

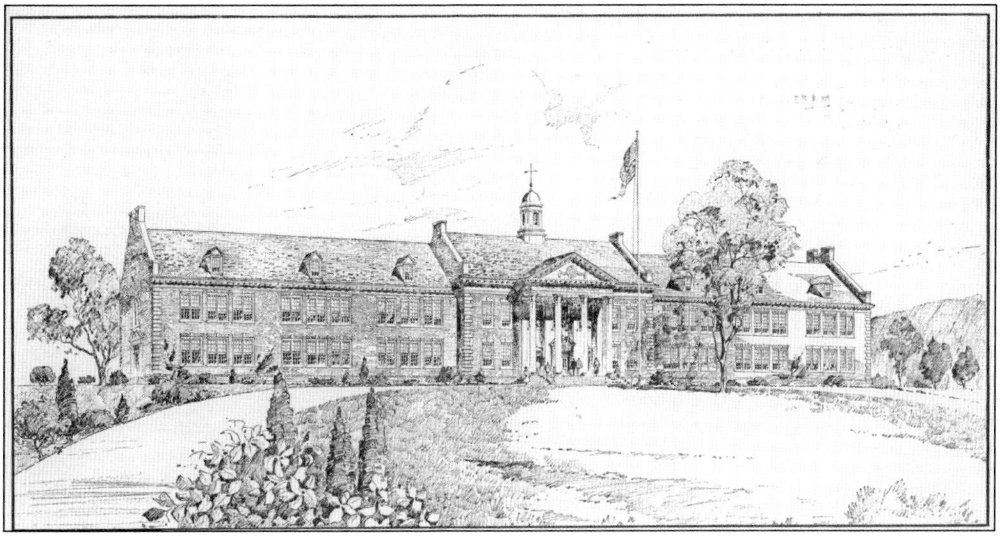

This architectural elevation image dated 1937 shows the front of the planned new Mahopac Central School. The school opened in 1939. The building is now the Lakeview Elementary School. (Mahopac School District.)

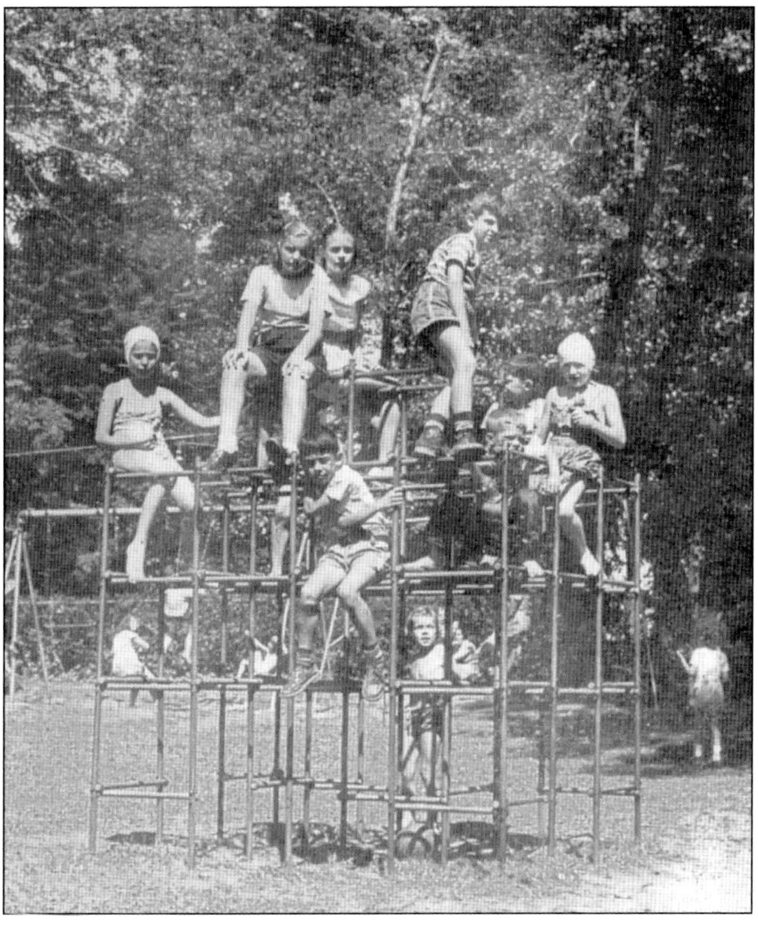

The playground across from the Mahopac Central School along East Lake Boulevard provided excitement and fun for kids for many years. The image shows the playground during the summer of 1947 with children on the jungle gym. Children who lived locally as well as those who came to Mahopac seasonally shared summer fun and friendship there. (Greg Amato.)

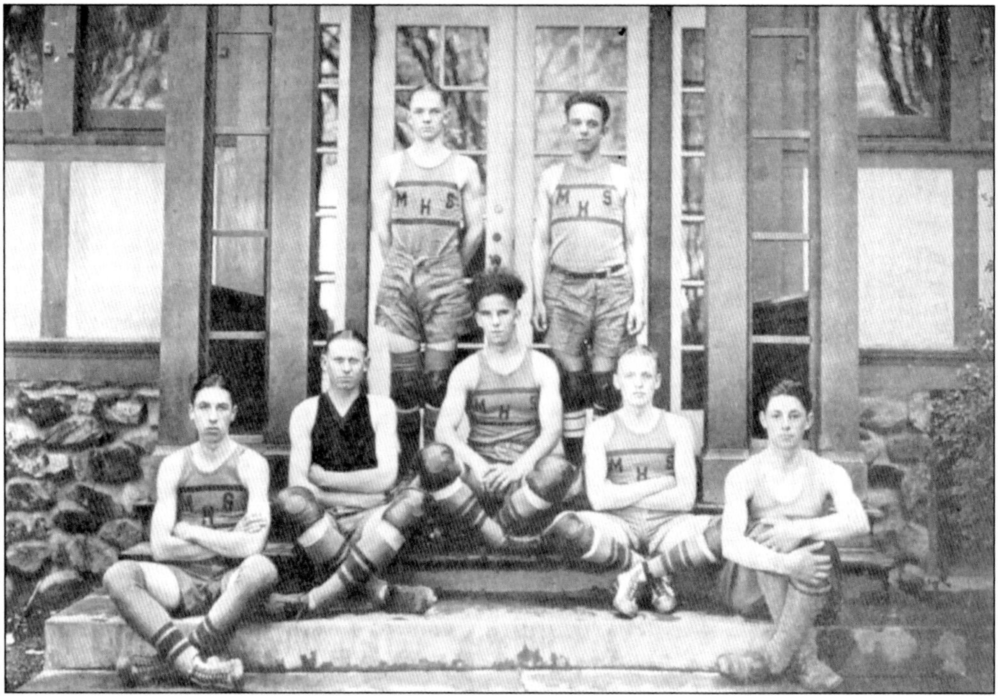

These young men comprised the Mahopac High School basketball team in 1925. This photograph comes from the school yearbook. Many of the players wear protective pads on their knees suggesting the rough and tumble nature of the game they played. (Mahopac Central School District.)

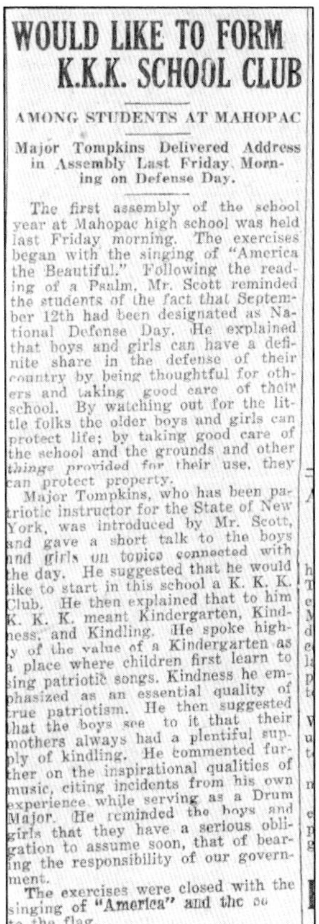

WOULD LIKE TO FORM K.K.K. SCHOOL CLUB

AMONG STUDENTS AT MAHOPAC

Major Tompkins Delivered Address in Assembly Last Friday Morning on Defense Day.

The first assembly of the school year at Mahopac high school was held last Friday morning. The exercises began with the singing of "America the Beautiful." Following the reading of a Psalm, Mr. Scott reminded the students of the fact that September 12th had been designated as National Defense Day. He explained that boys and girls can have a definite share in the defense of their country by being thoughtful for others and taking good care of their school. By watching out for the little folks the older boys and girls can protect life; by taking good care of the school and the grounds and other things provided for their use, they can protect property.

Major Tompkins, who has been patriotic instructor for the State of New York, was introduced by Mr. Scott, and gave a short talk to the boys and girls on topics connected with the day. He suggested that he would like to start in this school a K. K. K. Club. He then explained that to him K. K. K. meant Kindergarten, Kindness, and Kindling. He spoke highly of the value of a Kindergarten as a place where children first learn to sing patriotic songs. Kindness he emphasized as an essential quality of true patriotism. He then suggested that the boys see to it that their mothers always had a plentiful supply of kindling. He commented further on the inspirational qualities of music, citing incidents from his own experience while serving as a Drum Major. He reminded the boys and girls that they have a serious obligation to assume soon, that of bearing the responsibility of our government.

The exercises were closed with the singing of "America" and the sa to the flag.

Post–World War I patriotism was exhibited in September 1924, when guest speaker Major Tompkins spoke to students of Mahopac High School about forming a KKK Club by which he meant kindergarten, kindness, and kindling. Tompkins explained that it is in kindergarten that students first learned to sing patriotic songs, that kindness was an essential part of true patriotism, and that boys always supply their mothers with a plentiful supply of kindling. (The *Putnam County Courier*, 1924.)

Five

Mahopac Falls and Red Mills

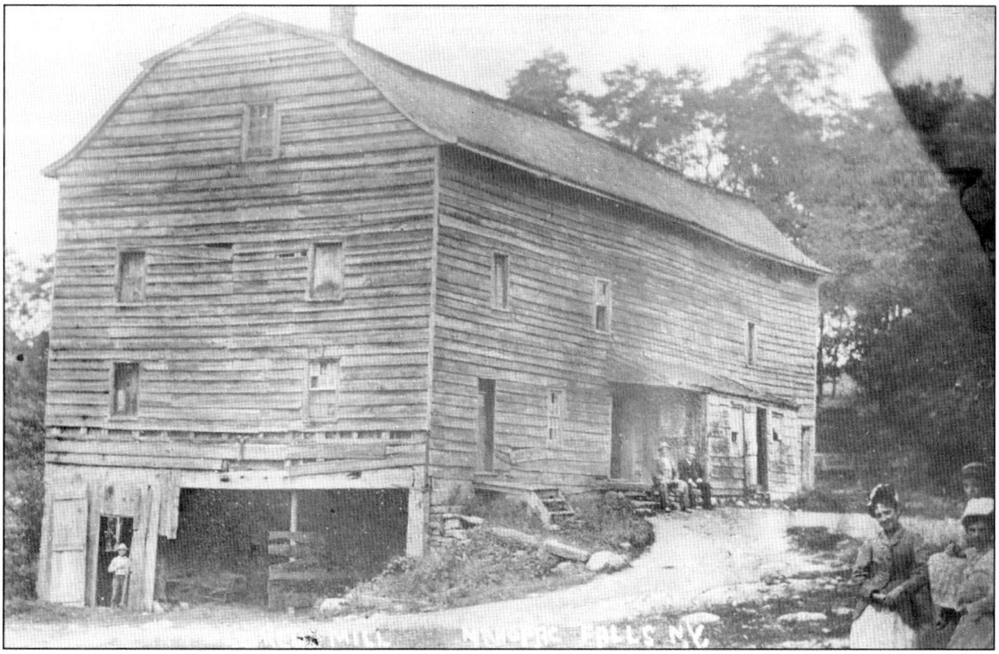

This mid-19th century image shows the Red Mill that was constructed in 1756 to grind flour. It used Lake Mahopac's water for power. The mill was important during the Revolutionary War, producing supplies for the Continental Army. Painted red, the mill soon became known as the Red Mill. The building was located north of what is now Route 6N and east of Hill Street. It was demolished around 1881. (The Town of Carmel Historical Society.)

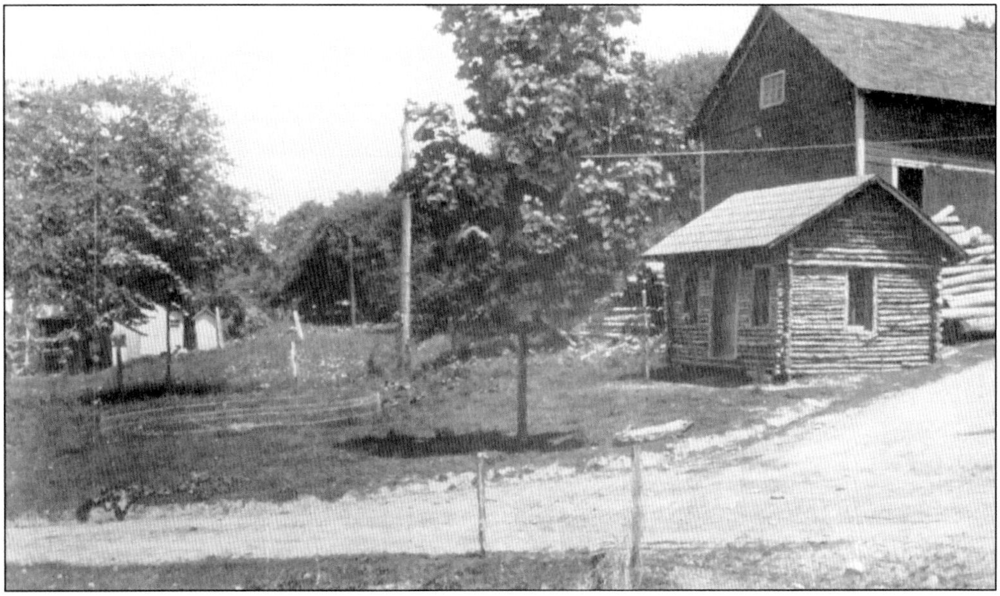

This log cabin just west of Myrtle Avenue was actually the playhouse of Ruben Barrett, whose father, Henry, owned the lumberyard and barn behind it. The photograph dates to around 1918. (Carol and Randy Tompkins.)

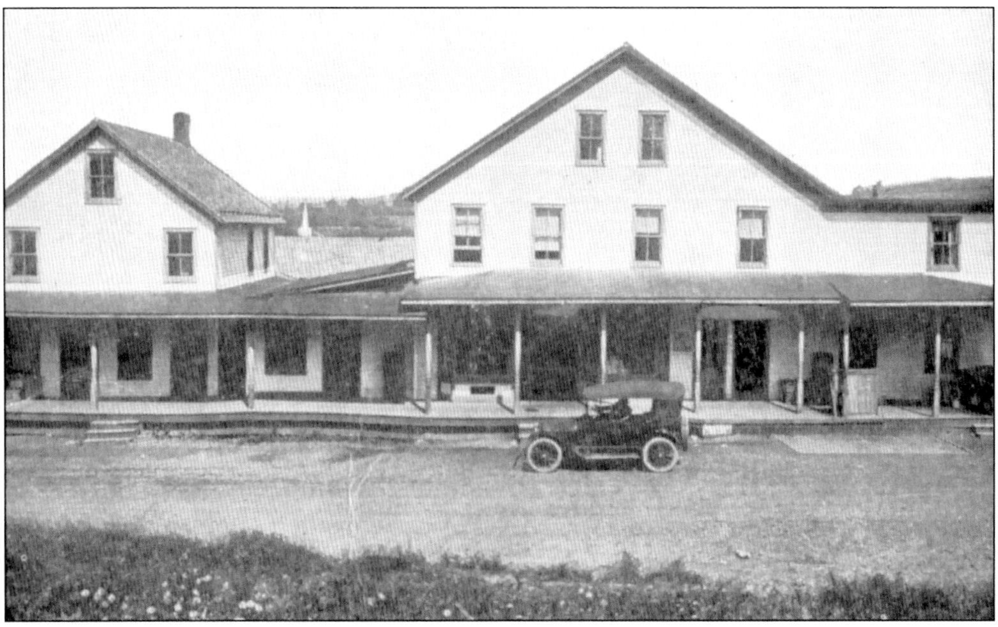

This was the general store on Railroad Avenue in Mahopac Falls owned by either Henry Barrett or the Agor Bros. when this 1914 photograph was taken. The great Mahopac Falls fire destroyed the building on November 7, 1919. The fire demolished much of the area's business section. Note the steeple for the Red Mills Baptist Church in the background. (Carol and Randy Tompkins.)

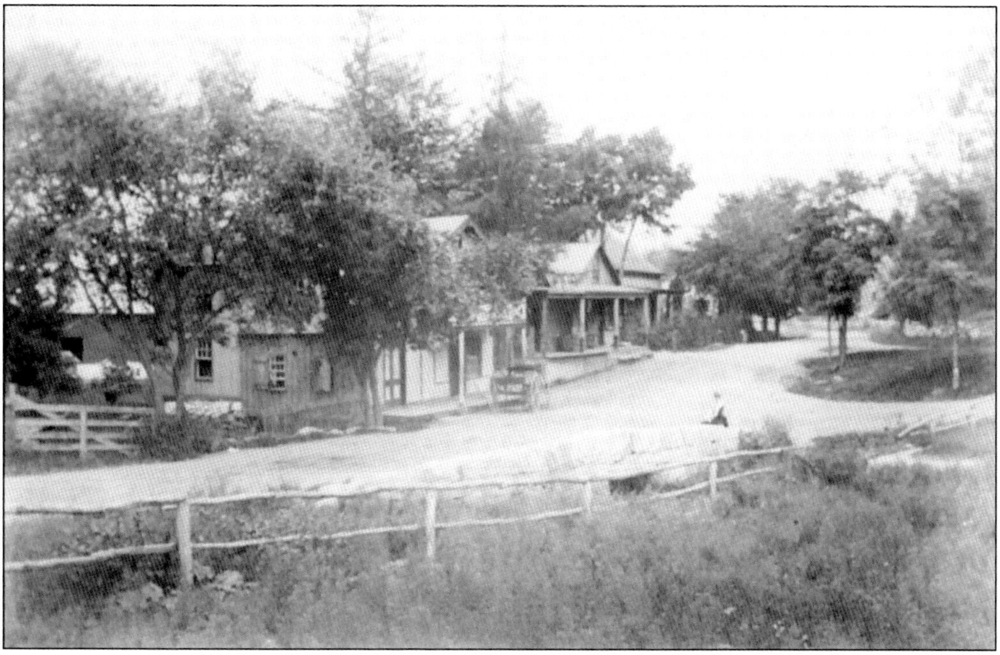

This image shows the intersection of today's Hill Street and Route 6N at Red Mills in 1885. Commercial buildings line the road to the south. They were demolished as part of New York City's efforts to protect its watershed from pollution. The old Red Mill was demolished around four years before this photograph was taken. The mill had been located immediately behind the photographer. (The Town of Carmel Historical Society.)

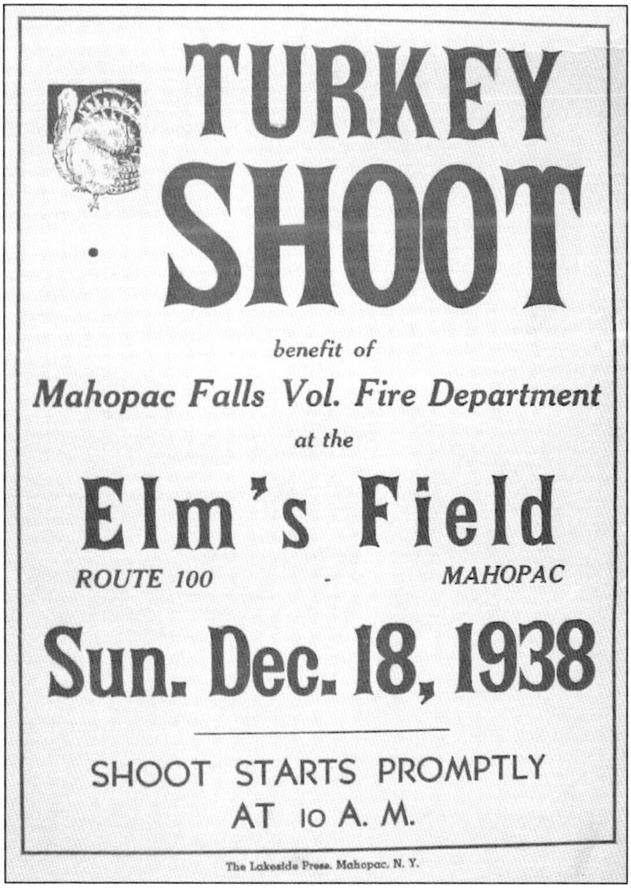

The 1934 flyer from the Mahopac Falls Fire Department advertises a turkey shoot fundraiser at Elm's Field, located on Baldwin Place Road just north of Myrtle Avenue. The Elm's was a restaurant from around the 1920s, and during Prohibition it was reported to be a speakeasy. (Carol and Randy Tompkins.)

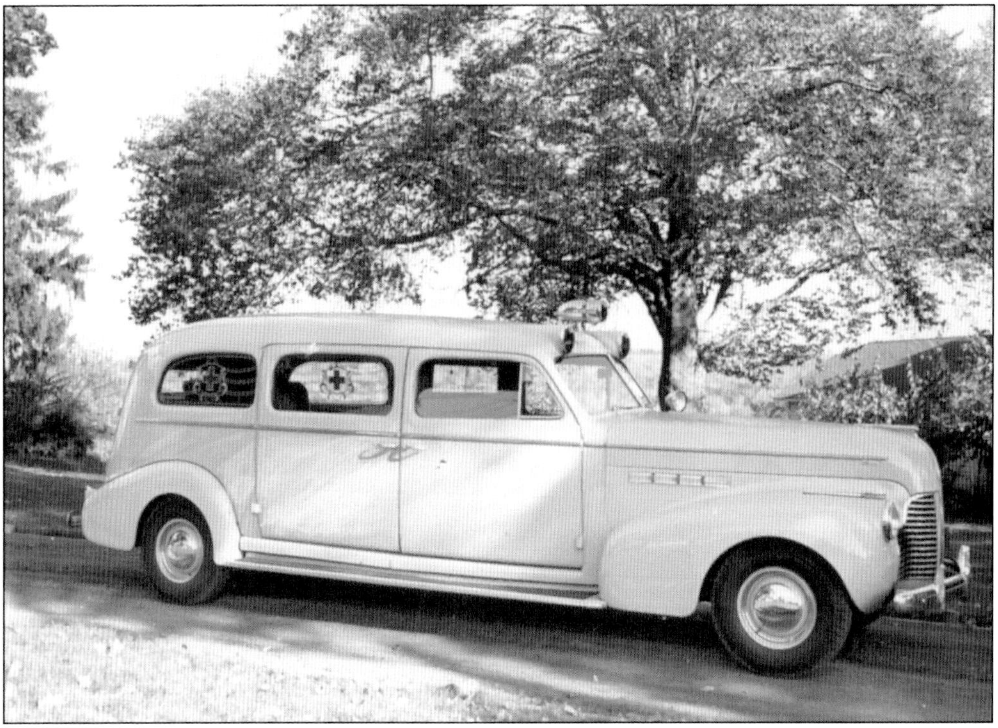

This automobile was the ambulance used by the Mahopac Volunteer Fire Department in 1940. The ambulance would take patients to the first aid station in town or to other area hospitals as needed. (Putnam County Historian's Office.)

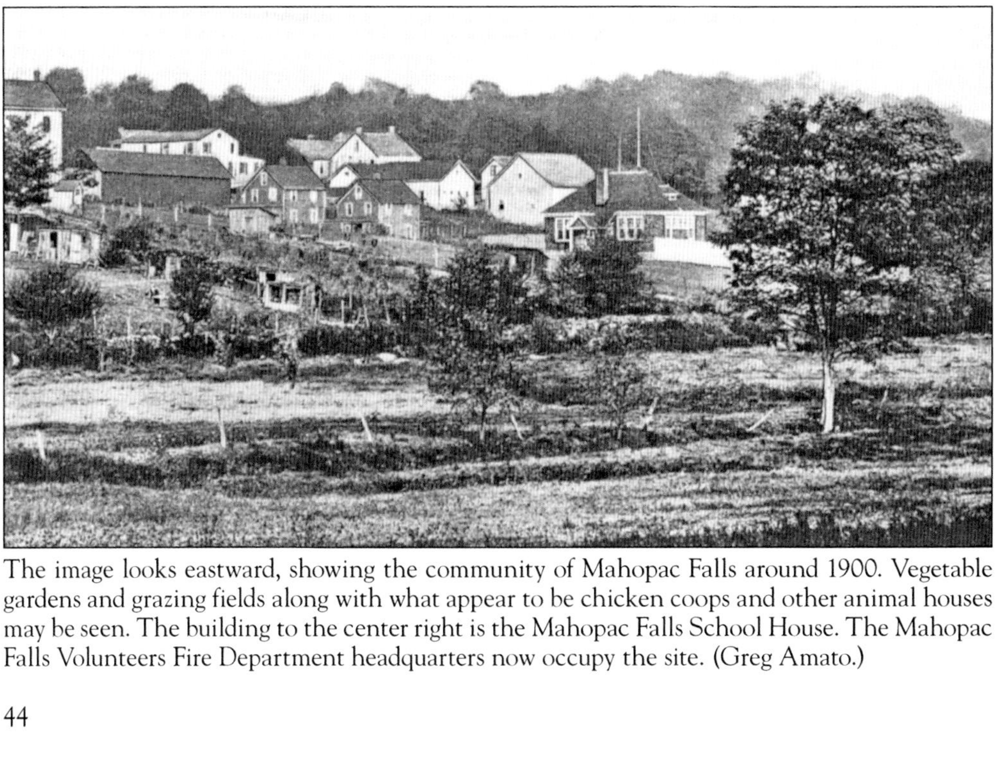

The image looks eastward, showing the community of Mahopac Falls around 1900. Vegetable gardens and grazing fields along with what appear to be chicken coops and other animal houses may be seen. The building to the center right is the Mahopac Falls School House. The Mahopac Falls Volunteers Fire Department headquarters now occupy the site. (Greg Amato.)

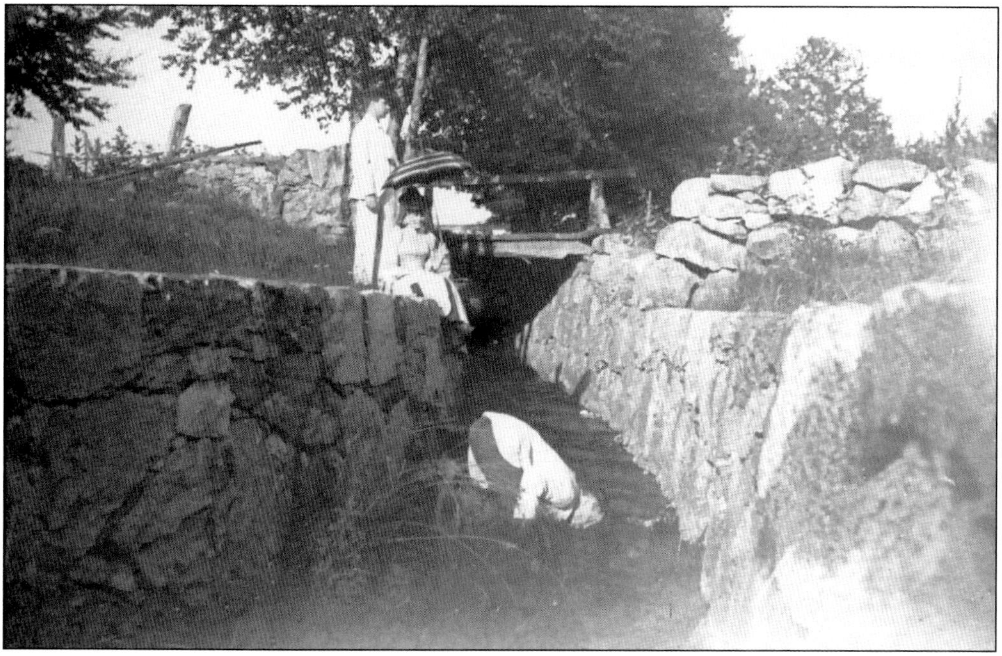

The outlet for Lake Mahopac apparently served as an ideal location for this gentleman to quench his thirst on what must have been a warm summer day during August 1891. Note the light-colored clothes and the woman shading herself with a parasol. Water flowed down the outlet to supply power to Red Mills. (The Town of Carmel Historical Society.)

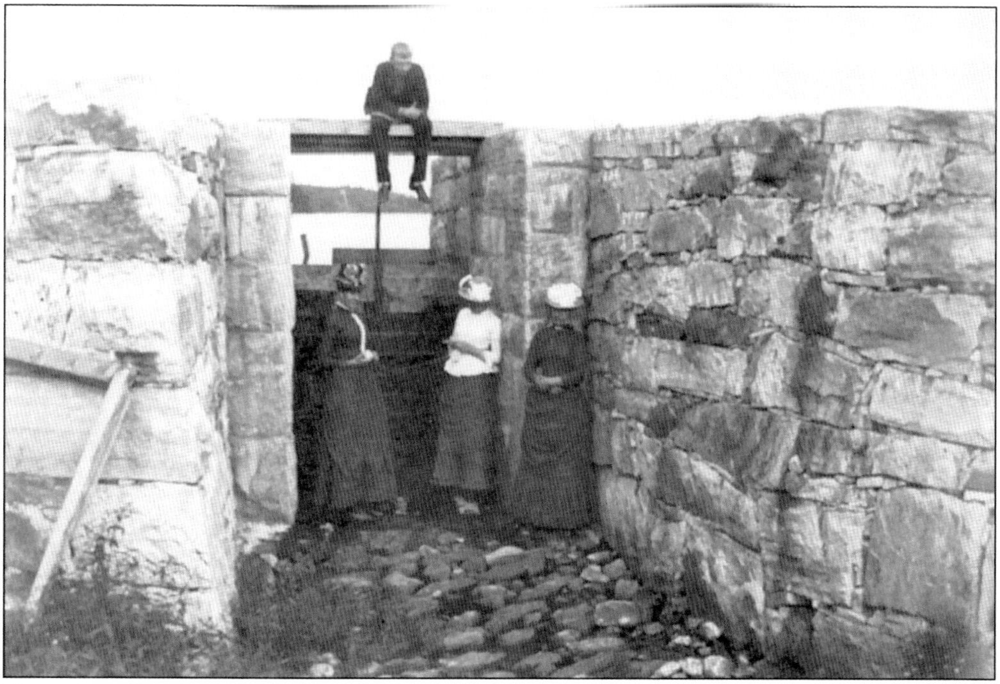

These three ladies stand at Lake Mahopac's wooden sluice gate for the outlet in 1885 as a young man towers over them while seated. The stonework was completed by New York City after it acquired the rights to the water as part of its watershed. (The Town of Carmel Historical Society.)

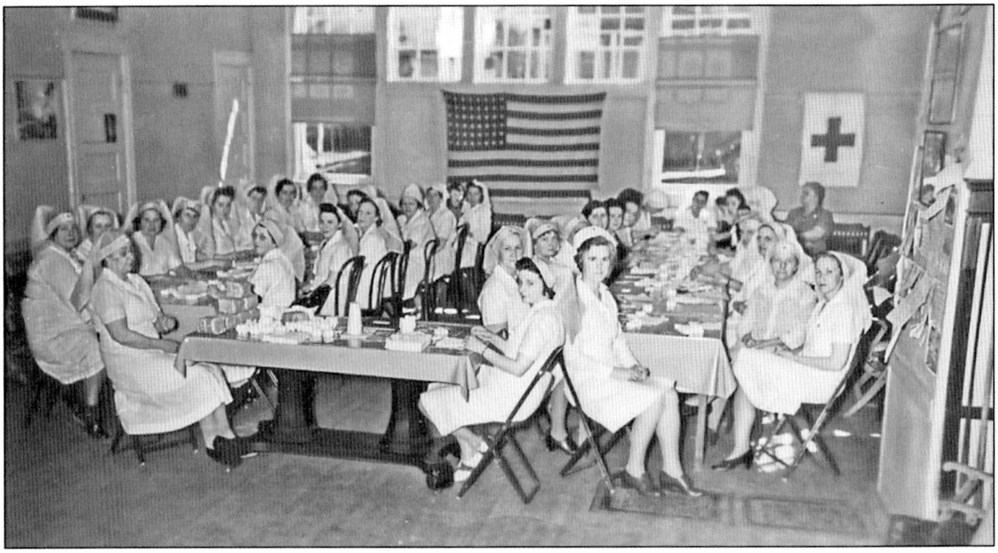

This image shows Red Cross volunteers packing bandages and other medical dressings at the Mahopac Falls two-room schoolhouse during World War II. (Putnam County Historian's Office.)

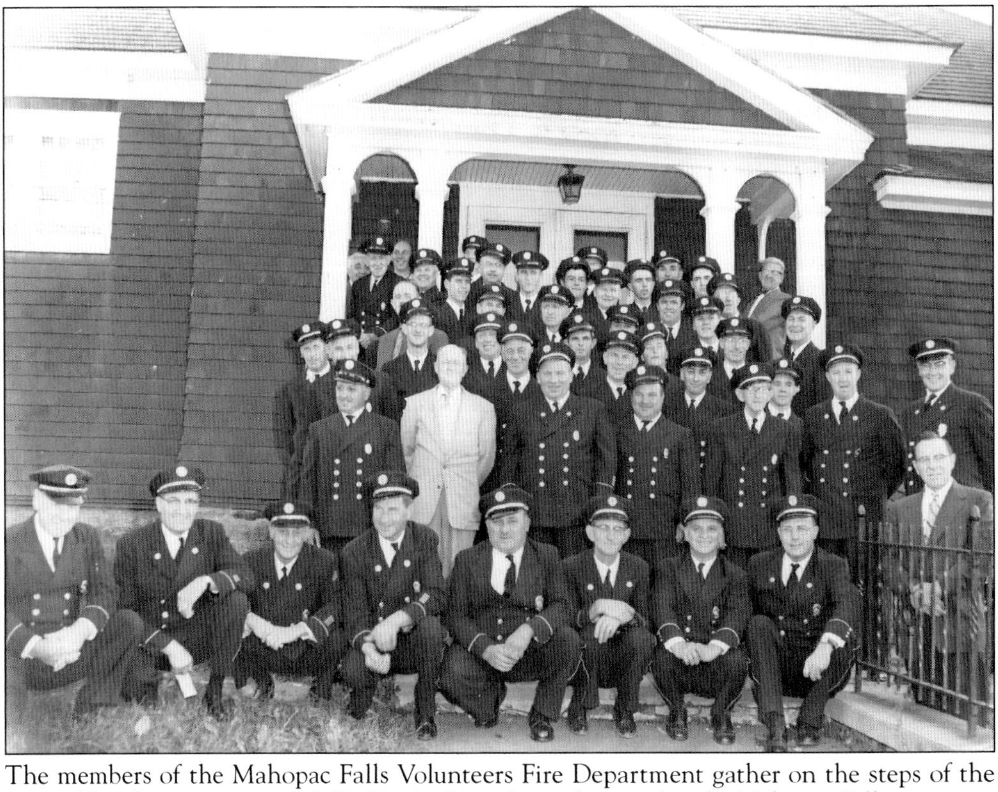

The members of the Mahopac Falls Volunteers Fire Department gather on the steps of the original headquarters around 1950. The building formerly served as the Mahopac Falls two-room schoolhouse. (Mahopac Falls Volunteer Fire Department, Chipper Swarm.)

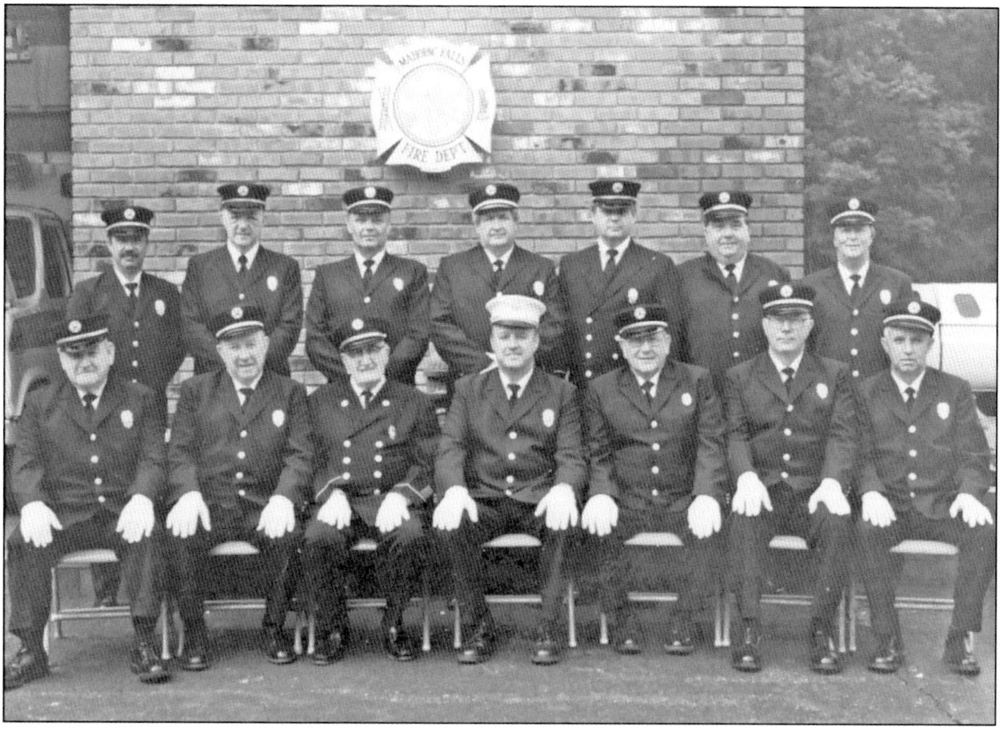

This gathering is of the chiefs of the Mahopac Falls Volunteer Fire Department. The photograph was taken around 1970. (Mahopac Falls Volunteer Fire Department, Jack Casey.)

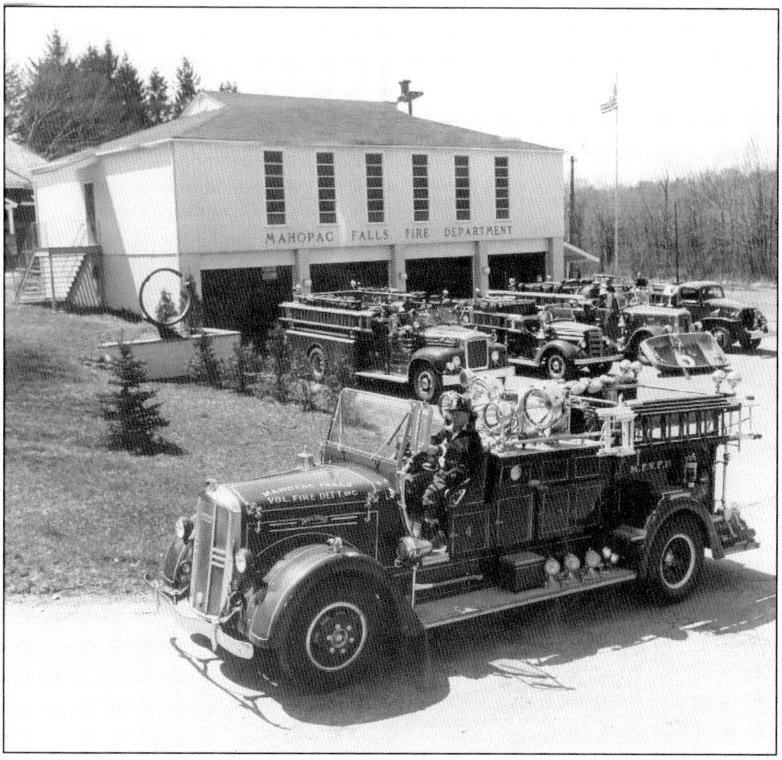

This 1966 photograph shows the new fire truck purchased by the Mahopac Falls Volunteer Fire Department. Other equipment is shown behind the pumper next to the firehouse. (Putnam County Historian's Office.)

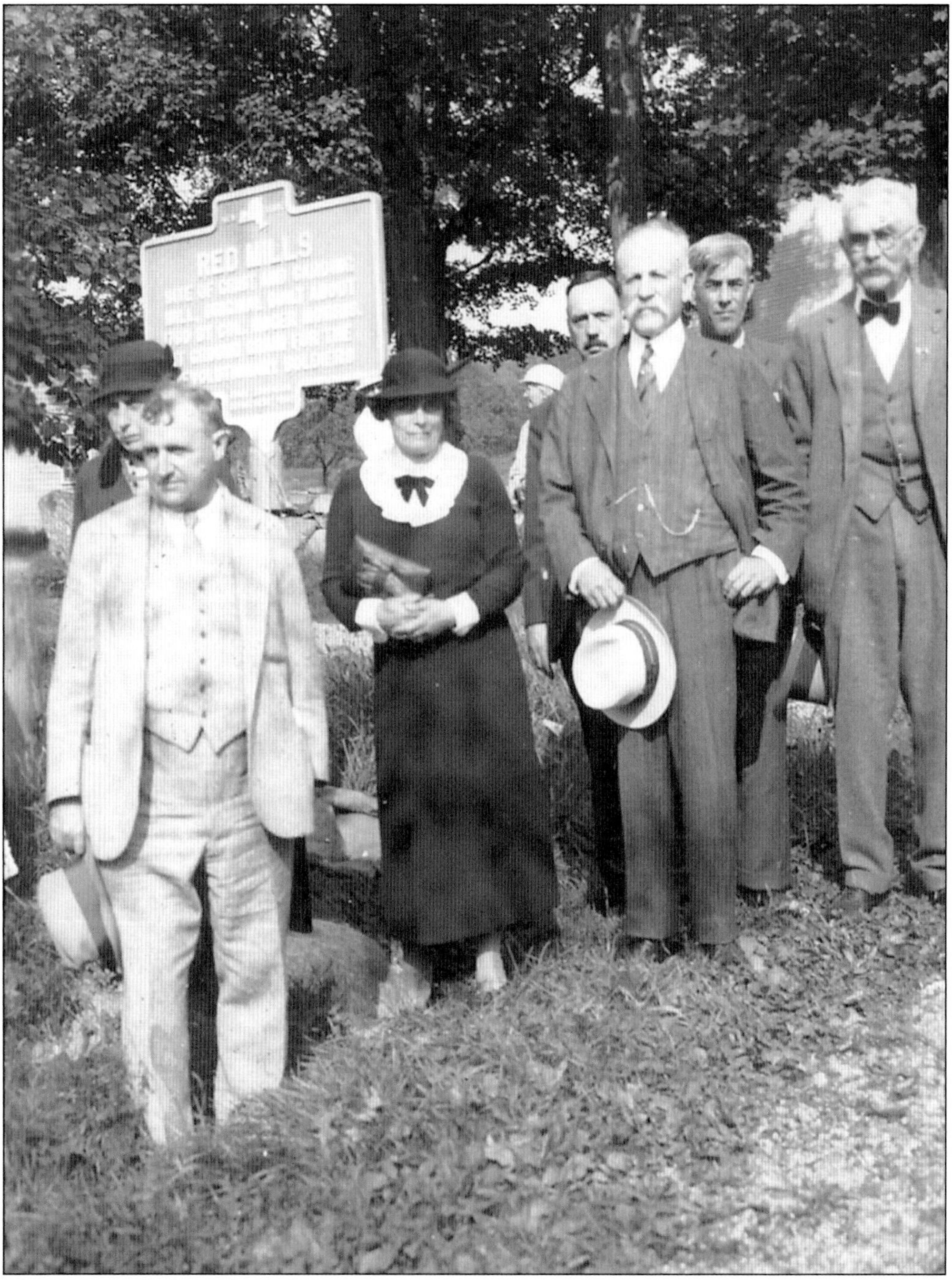

The photograph shows the dedication ceremony for the placement of the Red Mills Historic Marker around 1925. The marker still stands at Red Mills. In the photograph are Chester Pugsley (left) and Mahopac Falls residents Miss Blake (center) and George Turner. The rest are unidentified. (Putnam County Historian's Office.)

Six

Lake Mahopac

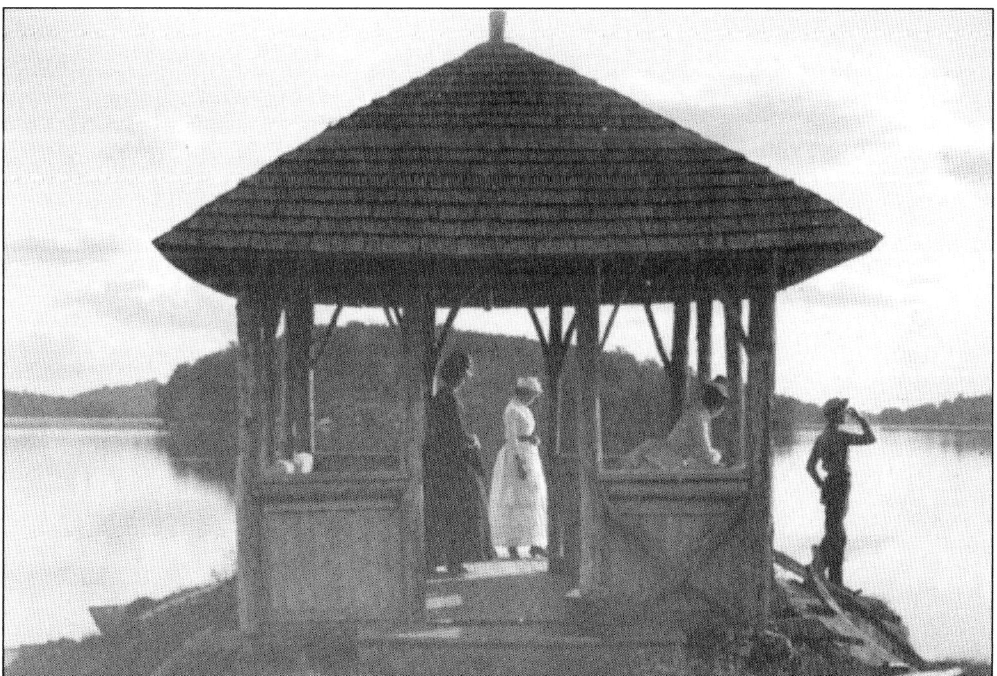

The romantic image of three young women and one young man gazing out toward Lake Mahopac on a summer morning is enchanting. It was taken at the lakeshore from Bradley's Summer House along West Lake Boulevard in 1885. Petre Island is in the background. (Greg Amato.)

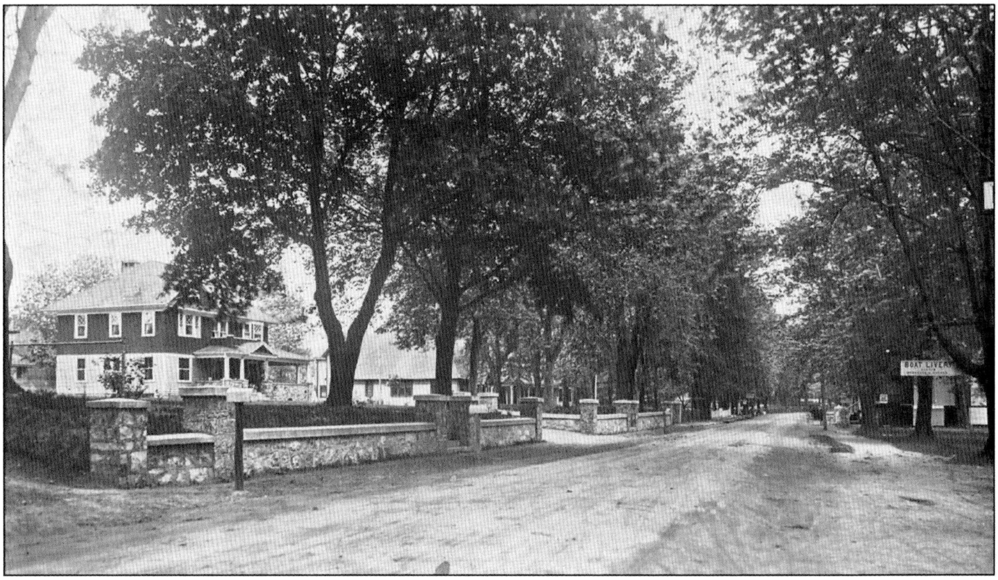

These two photographs show similar sections along East Lake Boulevard near its intersection with Croton Falls Road. The top image, taken around 1910, shows the unpaved road looking south towards what is now Route 6. A horse, wagon, and driver are seen by the side of the road in front of the Schooley's Boat Livery Service. The houses on the left were built by Mrs. Ganung for herself and her daughter Mrs. Ward Schooley. The houses and stone walls are still there. The bottom image, taken around the same time period, clearly shows the intersection of Croton Falls Road and East Lake Boulevard on the right. (Both, Randy and Carol Tompkins.)

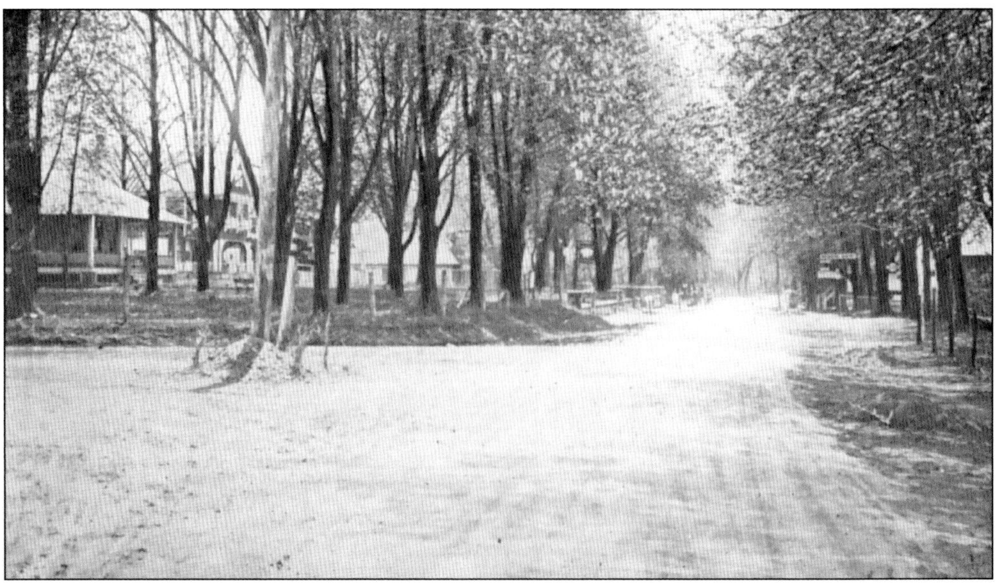

The poster advertises the planned public auction of 800 waterfront bungalow sites near the Dean House on Saturday, August 18, 1923. Bryan L. Kennelly, Inc., of New York City, was scheduled to run the auction. Lake Mahopac is described on the poster as the finest mountain lake resort near New York City. Note the simplicity of the telephone number to call for information. (The Town of Carmel Historical Society.)

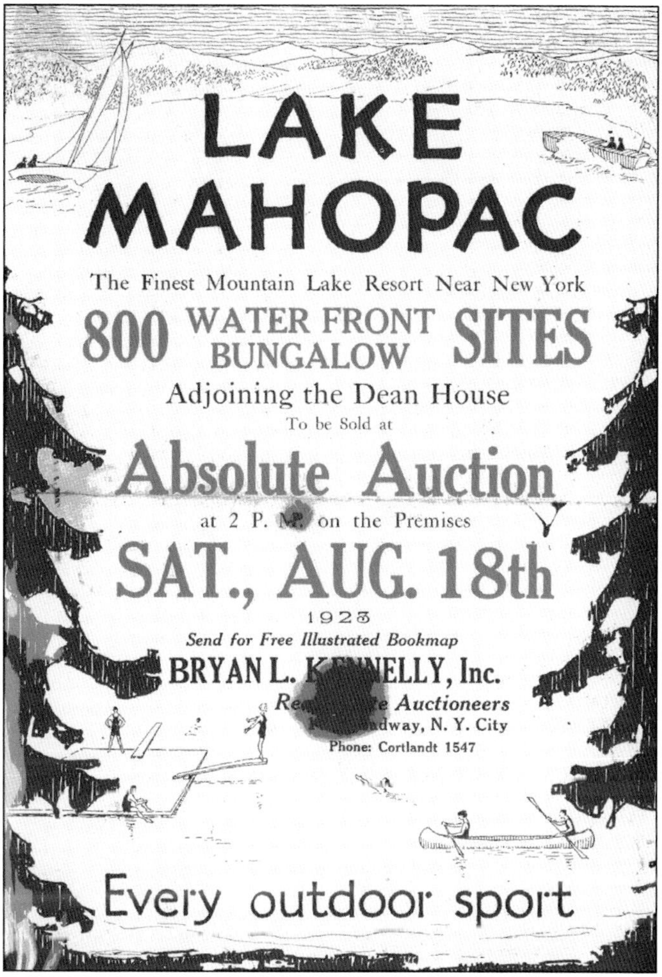

Erickson's Restaurant and Ice Cream Parlor, located across from Erickson's Boat Livery on East Lake Boulevard, was a well-known place for area residents to get the best and largest ice cream cones. During the 1950s, the Mahopac Library Association rented space on the parlor's second floor. In 1967, the association purchased the entire building from the Erickson family for use as the Mahopac Public Library. (Aaron Kass.)

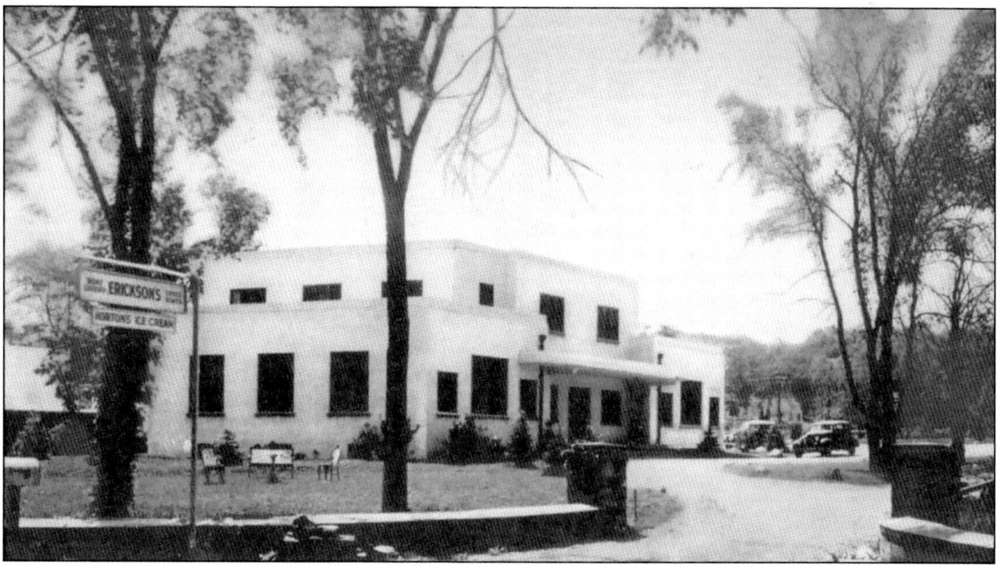

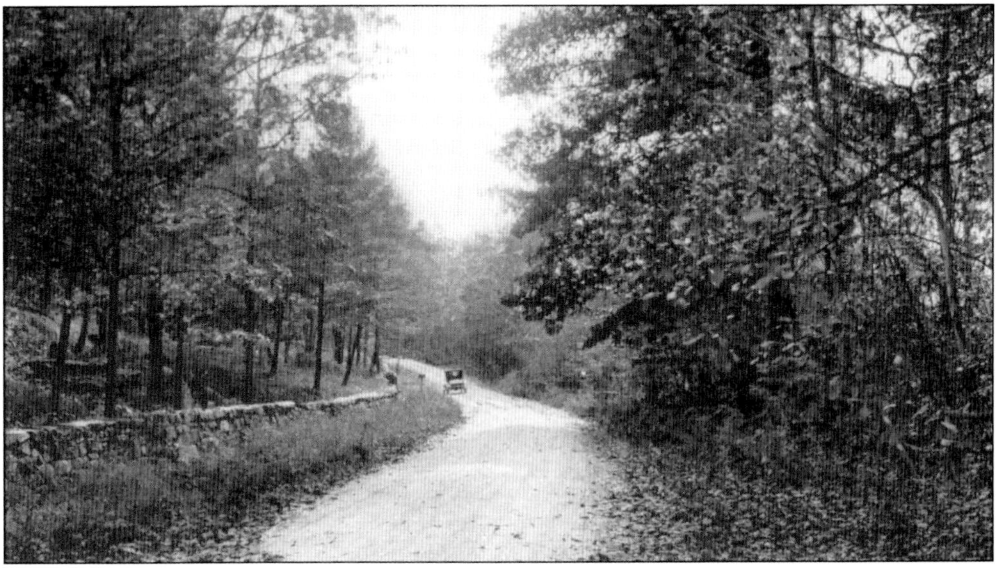

This bucolic scene shows an unpaved West Lake Boulevard and surrounding woodlands, as it appeared around 1915. What seems to be a Model T Ford is heading away from the viewer in the direction of the Forest House. (Aaron Kass.)

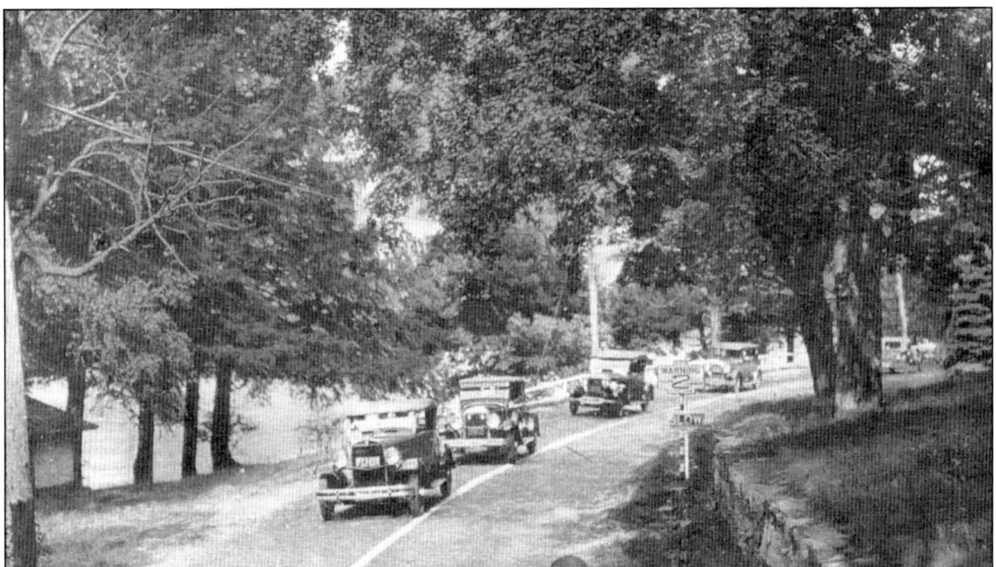

Jung's Corner along South Lake Boulevard was a distinctive S-shaped section of the roadway that became a local landmark. Here, it looks like a line of Model A Fords are negotiating a part of the curve. The photograph dates to around 1930. (Mark Fraser.)

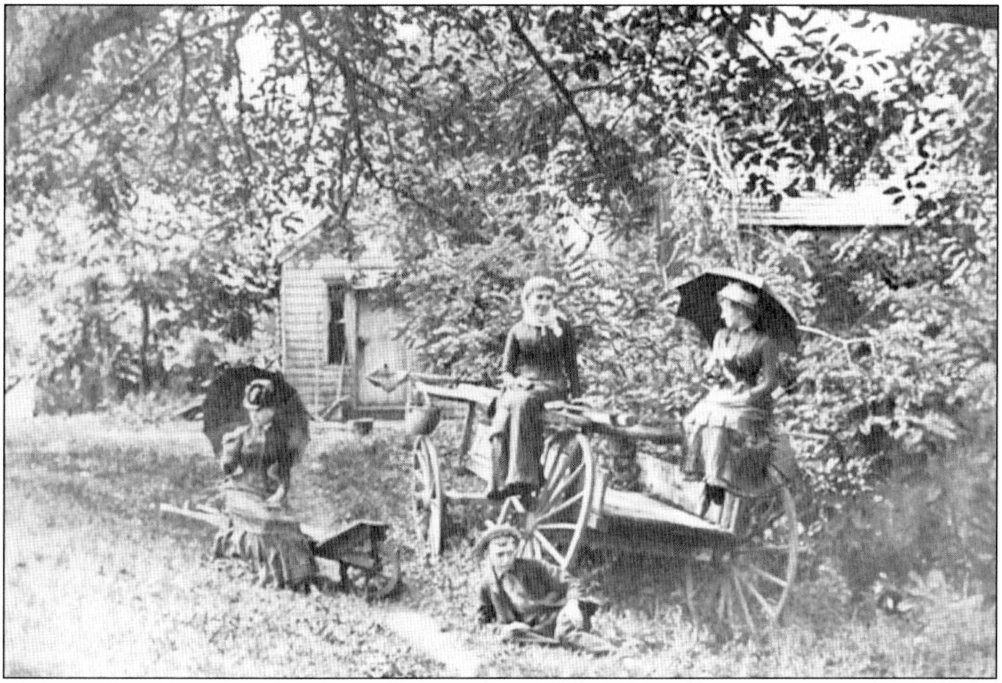

This photograph of three ladies and a young boy at ease was taken on September 11, 1885. It comes from a photograph album of a guest at the Dean House. Information on the photograph identifies the grounds as belonging to a Mrs. Carmen. (The Town of Carmel Historical Society.)

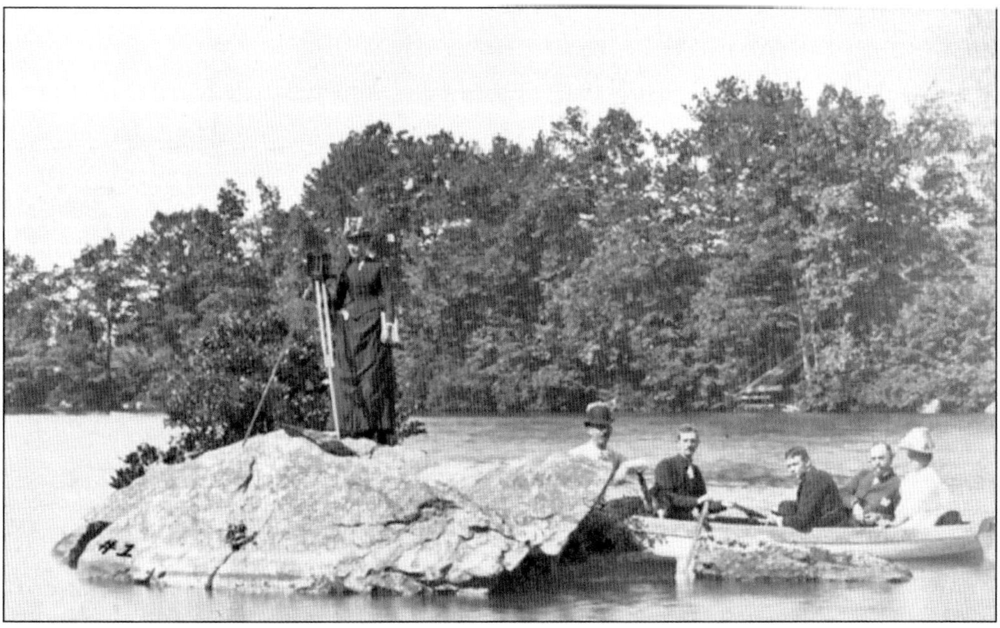

A photographer, identified on the back of the original image only as Miss Maggie, has set up equipment on Hummingbird Island along the west side of Canopus Island within Lake Mahopac around 1870. It is actually little more than an exposed rock peeking up from the lake. What her subject was is unknown. Her companions wait patiently in the boat for her to finish. One wonders who was taking a photograph of the photographer? (The Town of Carmel Historical Society.)

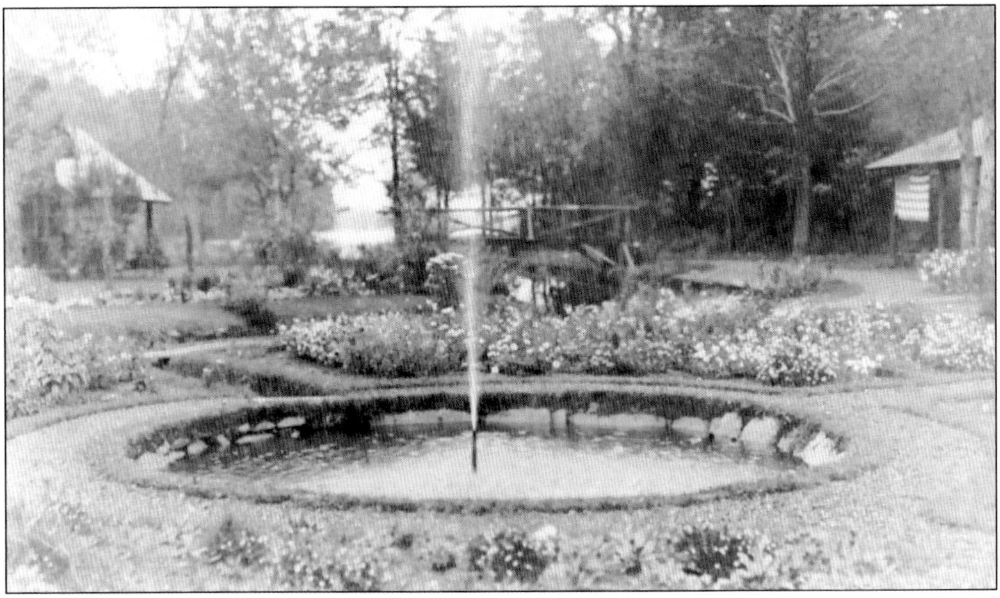

These two images show different views of Turtle Creek, which enters Lake Mahopac just to the west of what is today the Mahopac National Bank Community Center and just east of Mahopac Point (Hoguet's Point). The creek flows through what is today Chamber Park, separating the park from the community bank building. The above image shows the area near the creek sometime around 1915. A fountain, gazebos, flower beds, and a wooden bridge beautify the area. Coincidentally, the Town of Carmel recently installed another fountain in almost the same spot shown in the photograph. The below image shows the same general area at an unspecified earlier date, prior to landscaping and beautification. (Both, Putnam County Historian's Office.)

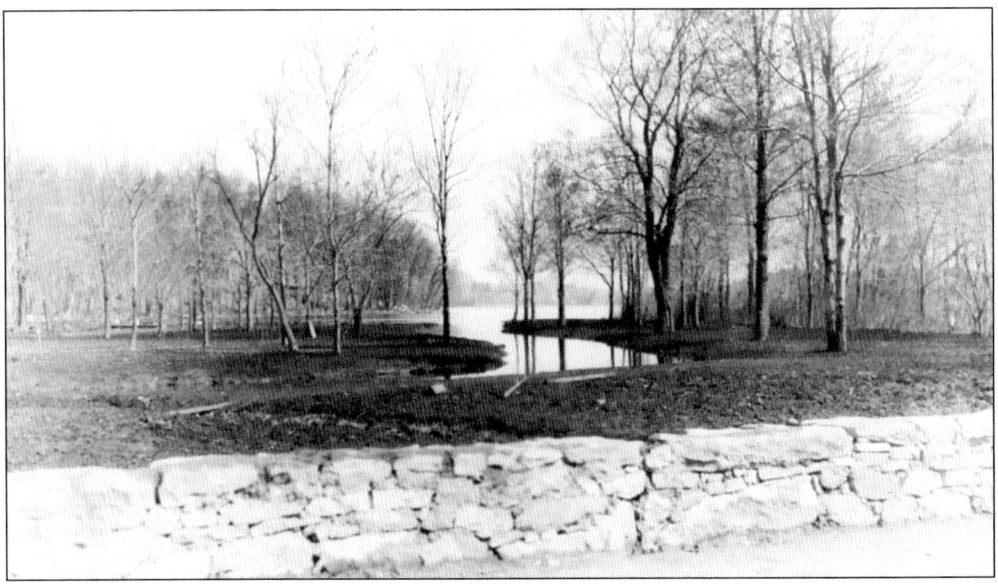

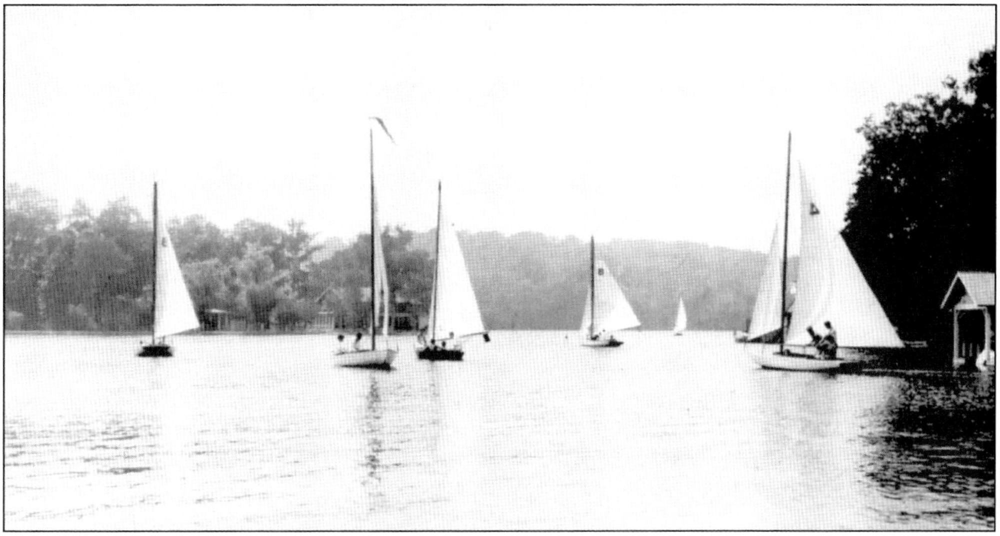

Fairy Island is the littlest island in Lake Mahopac and the only one with a bridge. It was developed by Thaddeus Ganong in 1859. He enlarged the island by filling along the lakeshore. The island's soil was composed of thick compost and when Ganong cleared the island's vegetation by burning, the ground caught fire. His home still stands on the east side of the island. (The Town of Carmel Historical Society.)

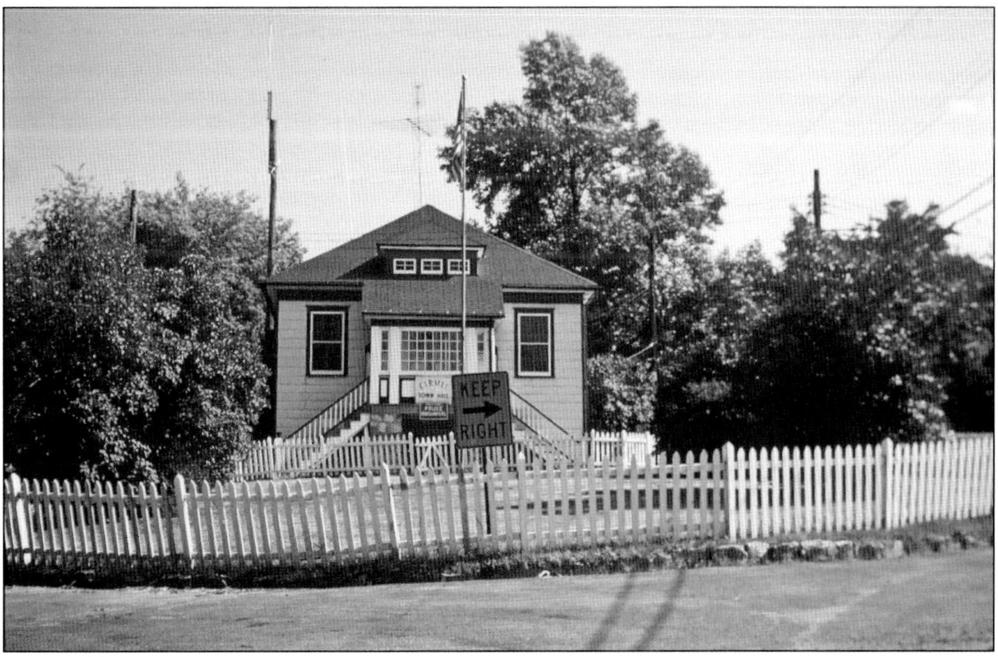

This building served as the police headquarters and town hall for the Town of Carmel in 1968. The building, located on McAlpin Avenue, reportedly dates to 1903. In 1976, the current town hall and police headquarters were constructed about a quarter mile to the north, fronting onto Croton Falls Road. The former town hall now serves as the Carmel Historical Society. (The Town of Carmel Historical Society.)

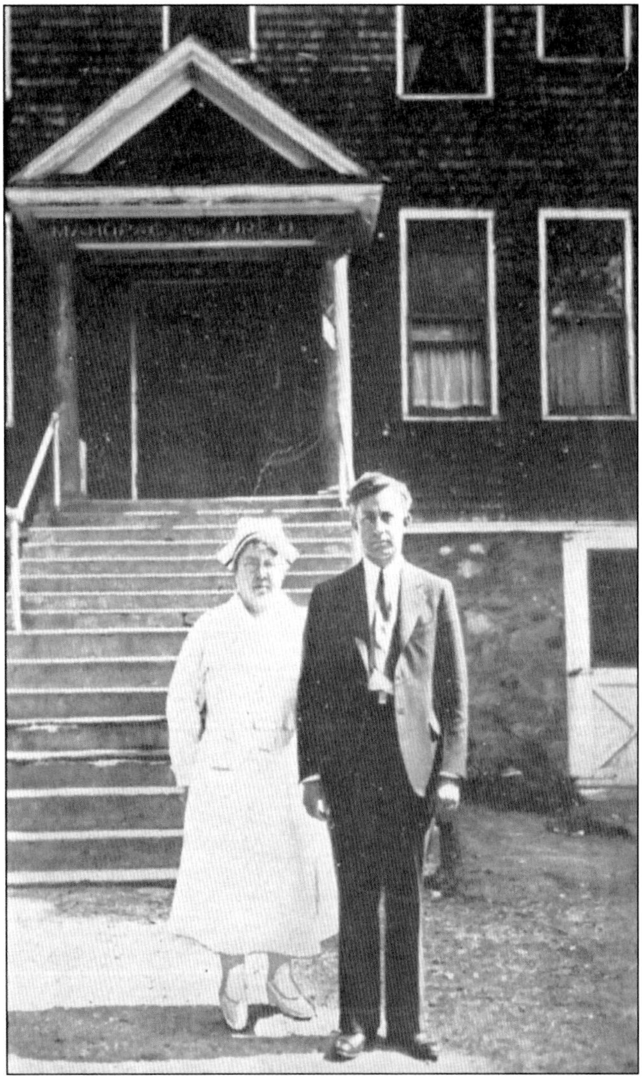

A first aid station was started in Mahopac after two young people died in motor vehicle accidents. Had an emergency treatment center been available, it was thought that their lives might have been saved. As a result, the New Emergency First Aid Station of the Putnam Community Hospital was begun on the second floor of the Mahopac Volunteer Firehouse in 1928. A sign over the front door in the photograph notes the location along East Lake Boulevard. The station initially employed Dr. George Steacy and nurse Hetta Alexander, shown in this 1933 photograph. The first aid station served the needs of emergency care in Mahopac until the establishment of the Mahopac Emergency Hospital (below), which served the community until the Putnam Community Hospital was established in the 1960s. (Kenneth Schmidt and the Town of Carmel Historical Society.)

MEMBER OF ASSOCIATED HOSPITAL SERVICE OF NEW YORK

MAHOPAC HOSPITAL - Mahopac, New York

1953 Fund Drive

MEMBER OF AMERICAN HOSPITAL ASSOCIATION

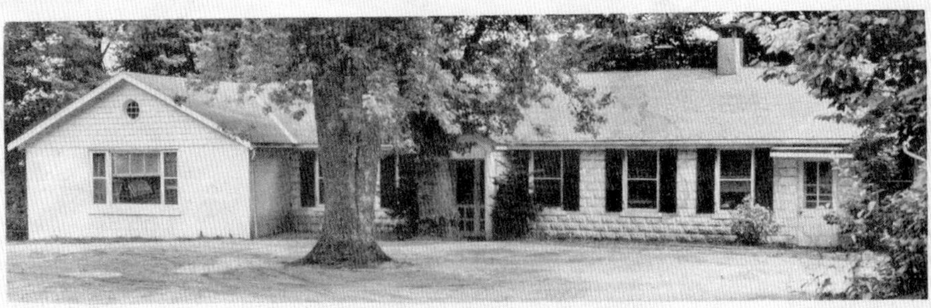

A hospital is the most important building in any community. So be generous and help make yours one to be proud of.

Seven

Hotels and Boardinghouses

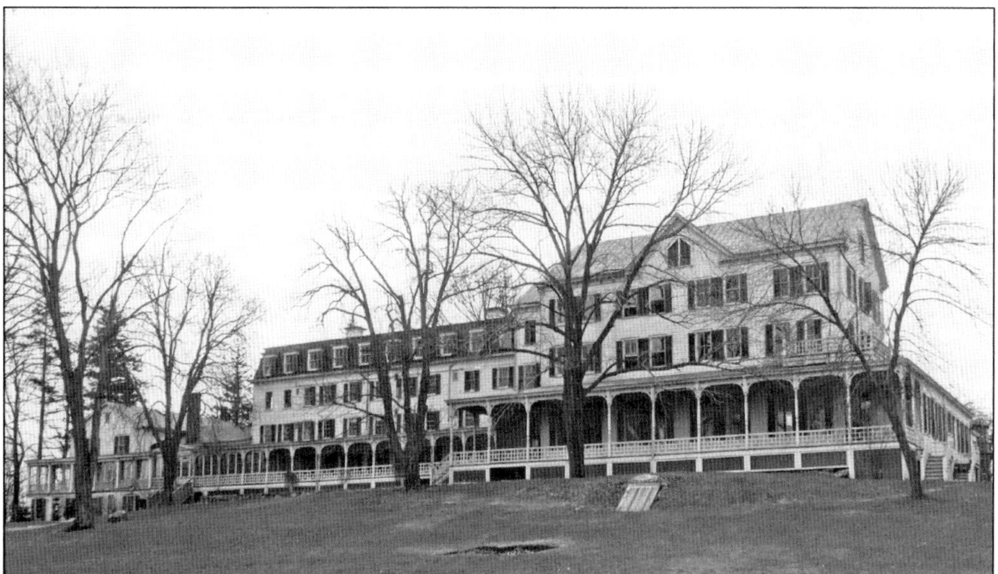

The Dean House, first constructed in 1852, was located near the intersection of West Lake Boulevard and Route 6N. It became one of the largest hotels on Lake Mahopac by the early 20th century. This image shows the Dean House as it appeared around 1937. The complex included the hotel, Bailey Cottage, a golf course, a boathouse, and a swimming beach. The complex closed around 1970. (The Town of Carmel Historical Society.)

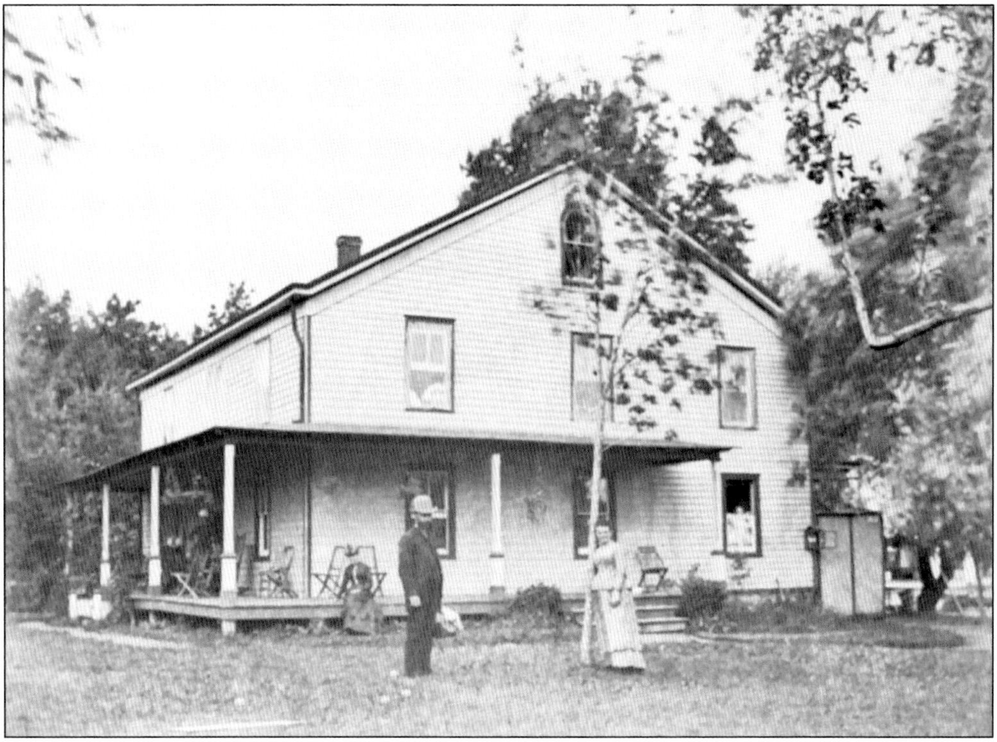

Bailey Cottage was a visitor's cottage for the Dean House. Tourists could stay there for a week or more. The image shows the cottage as it appeared in 1885. It was located at the intersection of Baldwin Road and Route 6N. The building has been recently renovated. (The Town of Carmel Historical Society.)

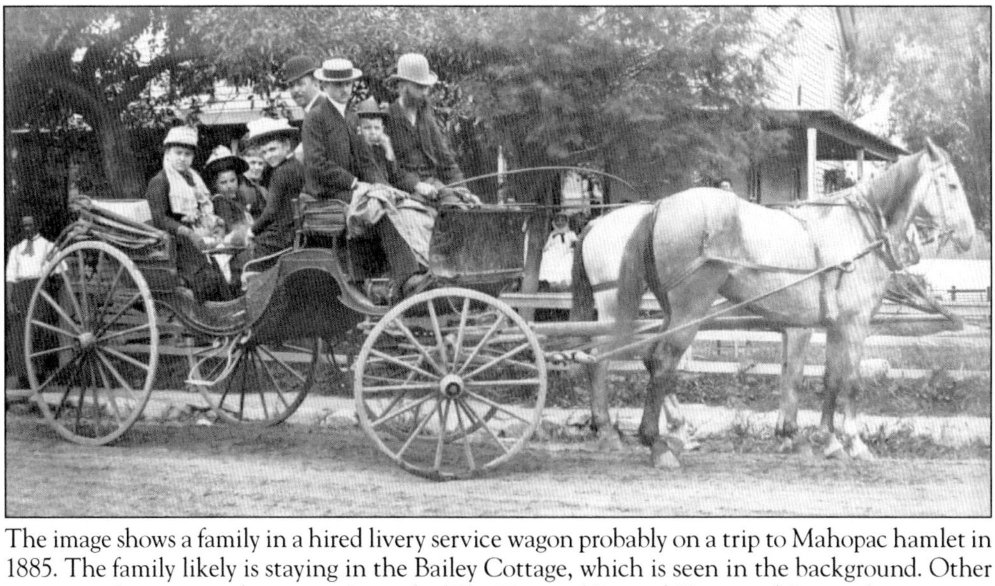

The image shows a family in a hired livery service wagon probably on a trip to Mahopac hamlet in 1885. The family likely is staying in the Bailey Cottage, which is seen in the background. Other guests can be seen on the cottage's porch. (The Town of Carmel Historical Society.)

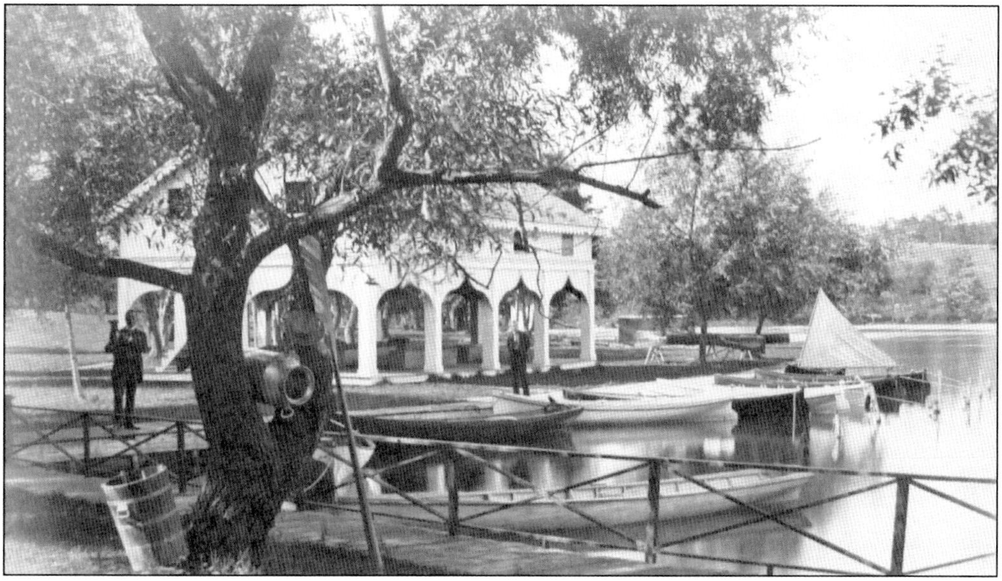

This is the wooden boathouse associated with the Dean House as it appeared in 1885. Canoes, sail boats, and other boats are shown along the shoreline. (The Town of Carmel Historical Society.)

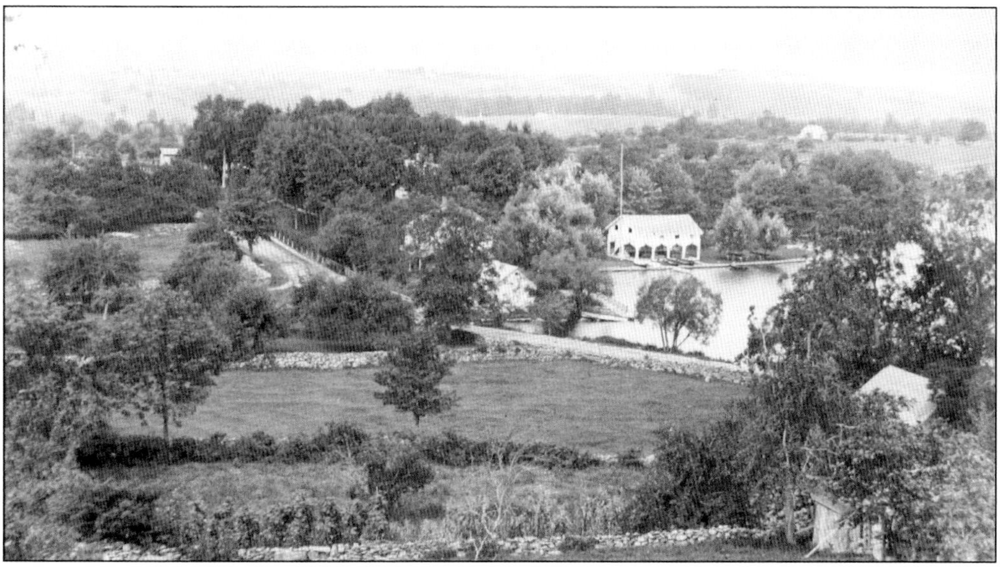

This view shows the rural landscape along the south edge of Lake Mahopac, taken from atop Indian Hill around 1885. What is now Route 6N extends past the lake on the right with its modern-day intersection with Baldwin Road at center. Across from the intersection is the Bailey Cottage, part of the Dean House complex. The large structure beyond visible between the trees is the Dean House. The open white structure to the right of the Bailey House is the hotel's boathouse. (The Town of Carmel Historical Society.)

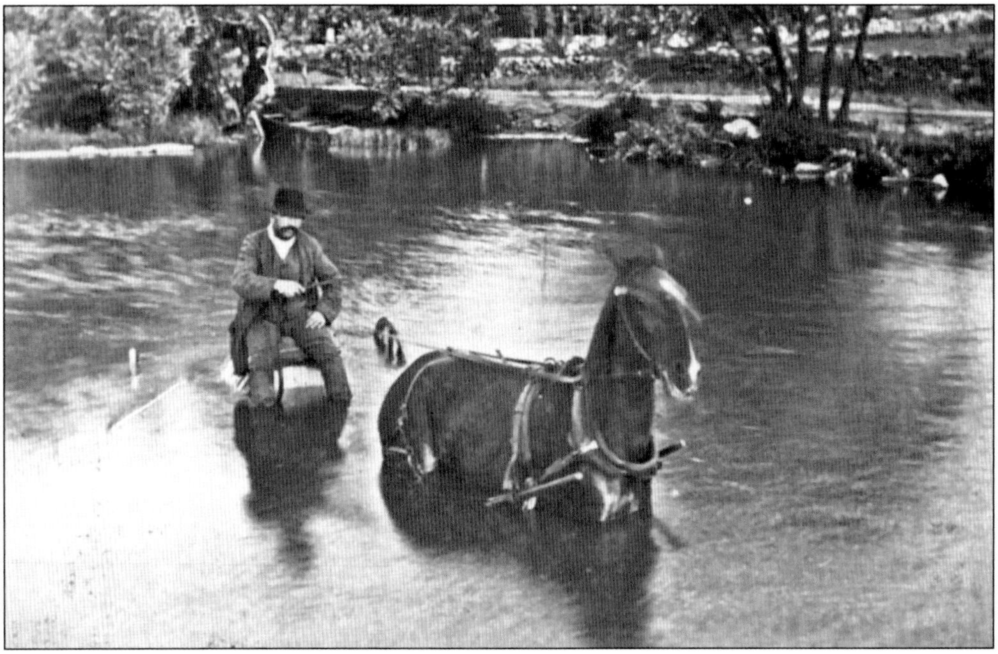

A horse-drawn cart containing a barrel fixed to its bed was used to collect water for use at the Dean House. The horse cart and driver would enter the shallows of Lake Mahopac near the hotel and open the barrel, filling it with lake water. It is assumed that the water was not used for drinking or bathing. The image dates to around 1885. (The Town of Carmel Historical Society.)

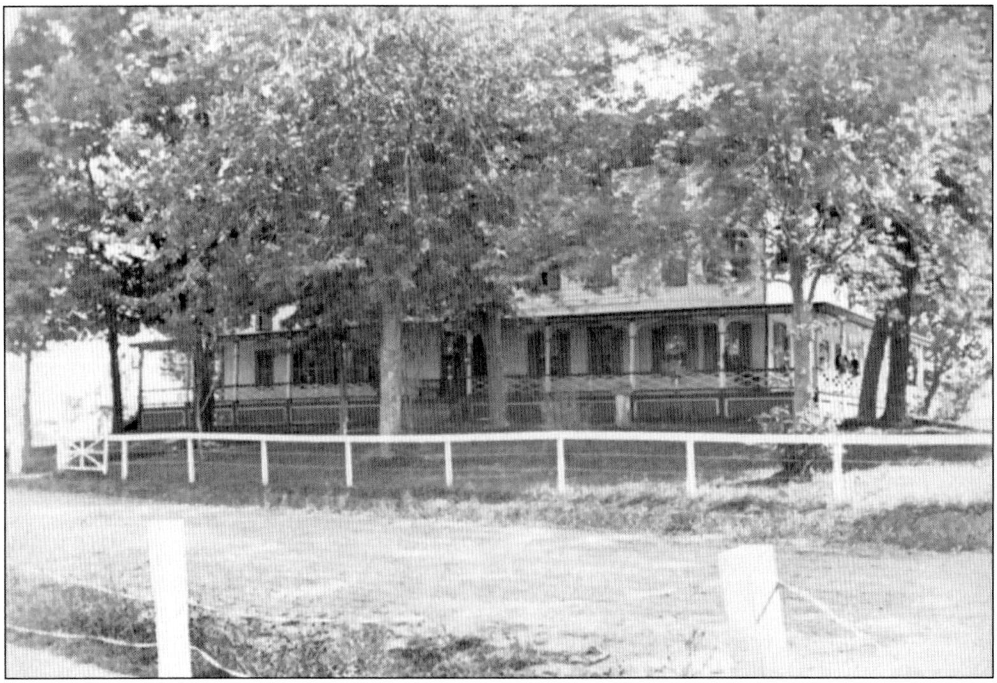

This view shows the front of the Carpenter House and its shady lawn along East Lake Boulevard on September 19, 1885. The image was taken from the hotel's boathouse along the Lake Mahopac shoreline. (The Town of Carmel Historical Society.)

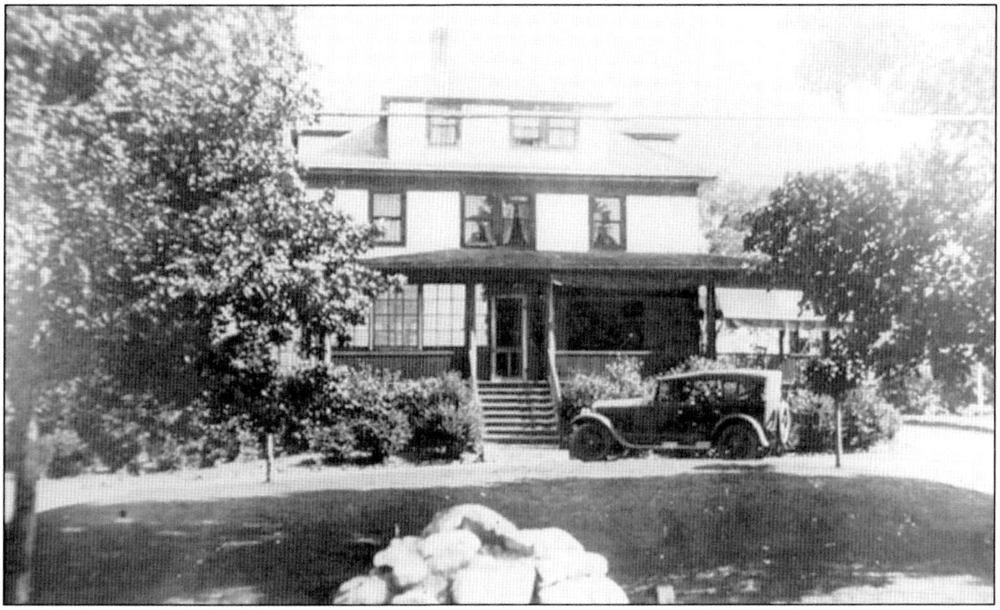

Ney-a-Ki was a spacious boardinghouse located on the high ground west of Route 6N, overlooking Fairy Island Cove in Lake Mahopac. It had a dock in the cove. The boardinghouse opened around 1920 and operated until the 1940s. The original owners were the Condon family, who operated a successful landscaping and tree service in White Plains. The building still exists as an apartment building. (Ed and Ann Dazi.)

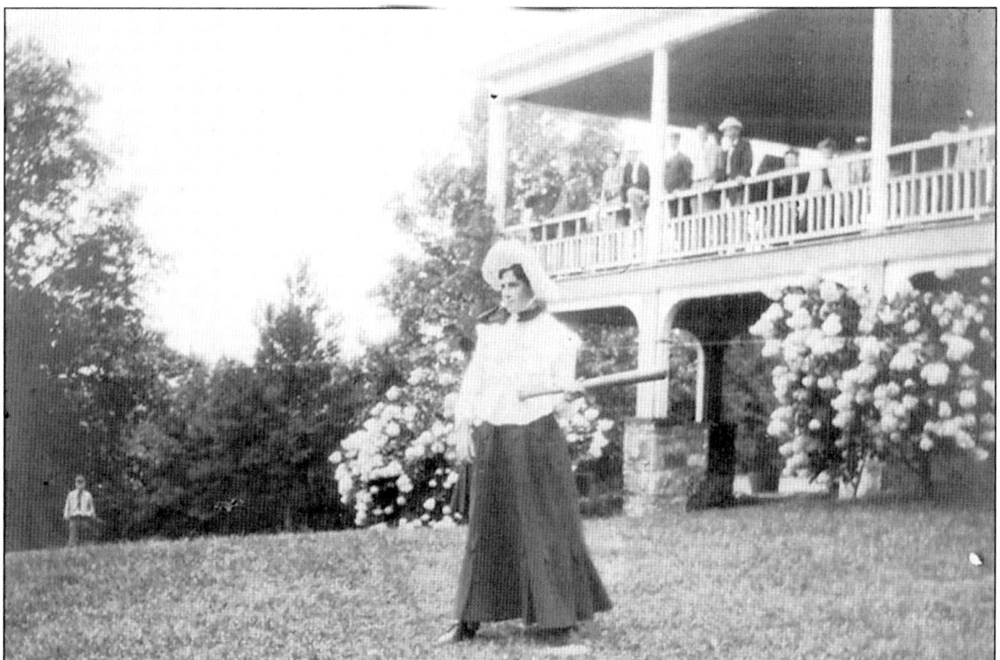

A young woman of the Julius DeLong family is shown playing baseball at the Forest House in this 1905 image while admirers and family members look on. The right fielder in the distance has a nonchalant pose, perhaps not expecting too much from the batter. (Susan Brady Mauldin.)

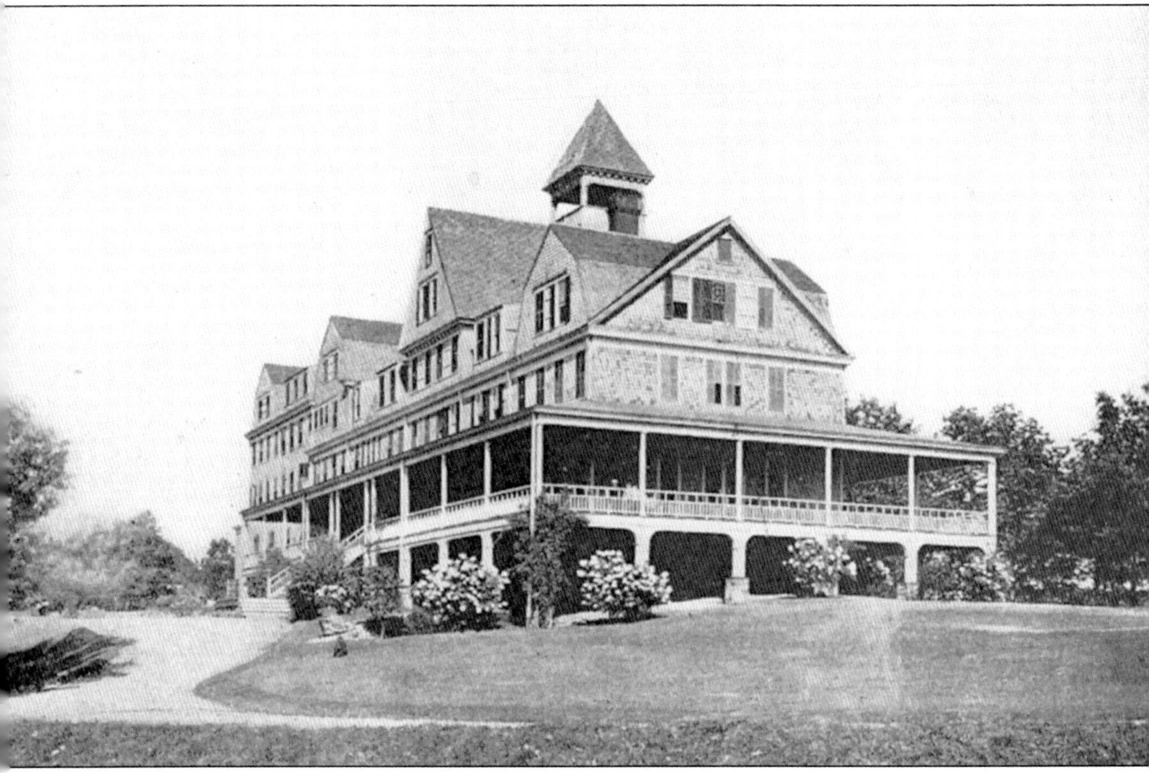

The first Forest House was constructed in 1893 by J. Prior Rorke on 27 acres of land on a ridge separating Lake Mahopac and Kirk Lake. It was the first substantial development along the western edge of Lake Mahopac. The hotel was a large structure, having 100 rooms to serve at least 125 guests. It also had a series of trails and rest areas in the surrounding woodlands as well as a natural spring. The image shows the Forest House as it looked in 1905. Louis Dean (Dean House) purchased the hotel in 1935. The Forest House burnt down in January 1940. (Greg Amato.)

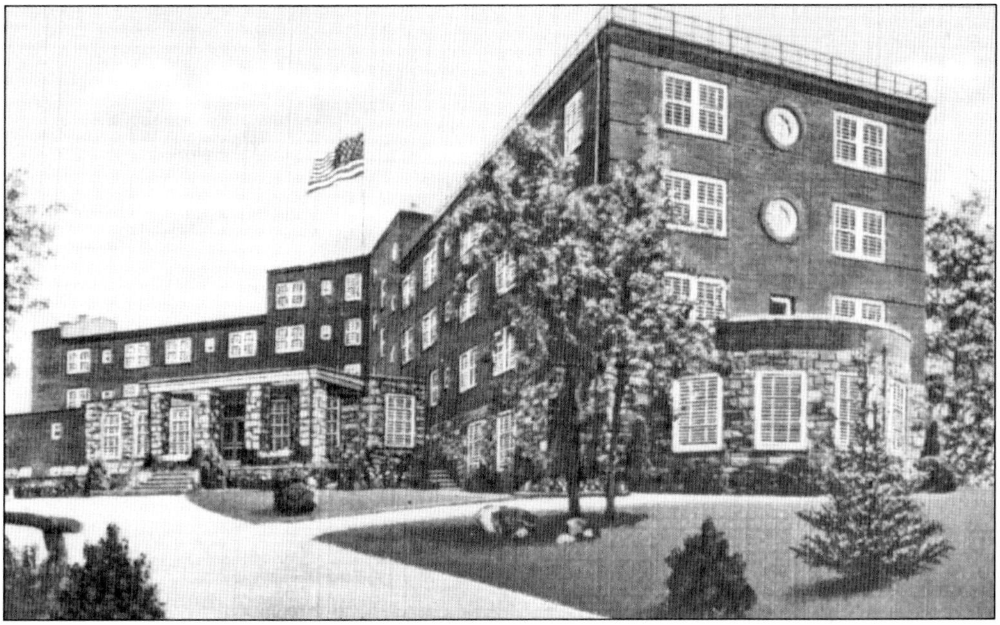

The second Forest House was rebuilt soon after the original Forest House burned in 1940. The new structure was a three-story brick building, which operated year-round. It was demolished in the late 1980s. Private homes are now located at the former hotel site. (Mark Fraser.)

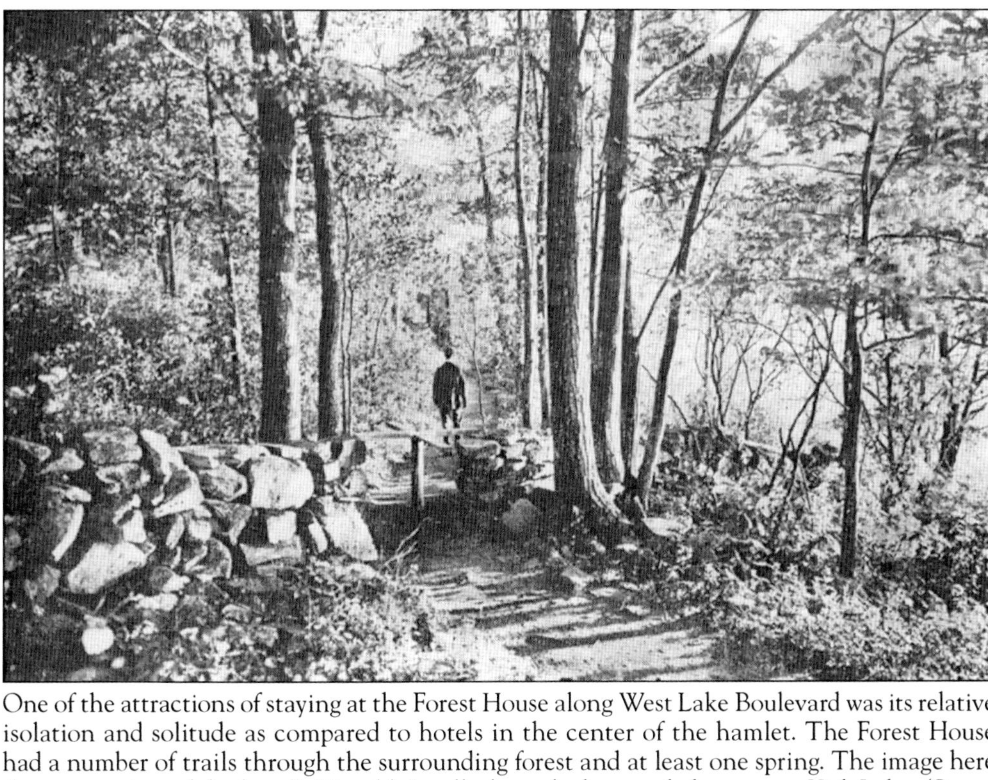

One of the attractions of staying at the Forest House along West Lake Boulevard was its relative isolation and solitude as compared to hotels in the center of the hamlet. The Forest House had a number of trails through the surrounding forest and at least one spring. The image here shows a section of the hotel's "Ramble" walk through the wooded area near Kirk Lake. (Susan Brady Mauldin.)

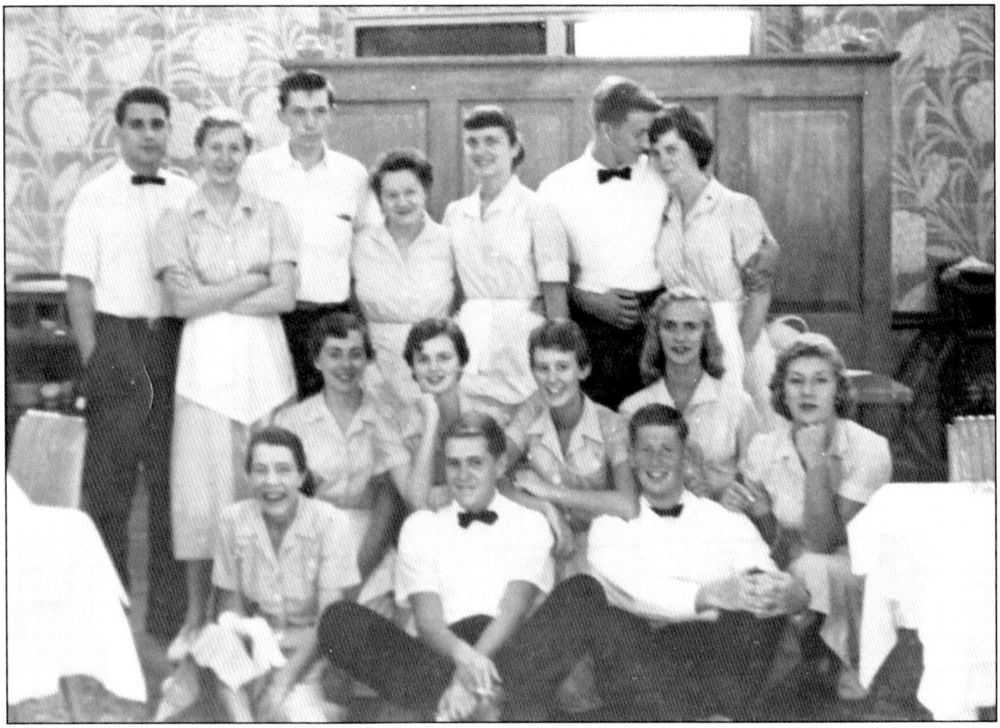

This image shows some of the Forest House waitresses and bus boys in 1957. They included college students that were employed seasonally in addition to year-round residents. The staff was required to work seven days a week throughout the summer but was allowed to use the hotel's facilities after work. Barbara (Lacina) Bosch is shown in the top row, third from the right. (Barbara Lacina Bosch.)

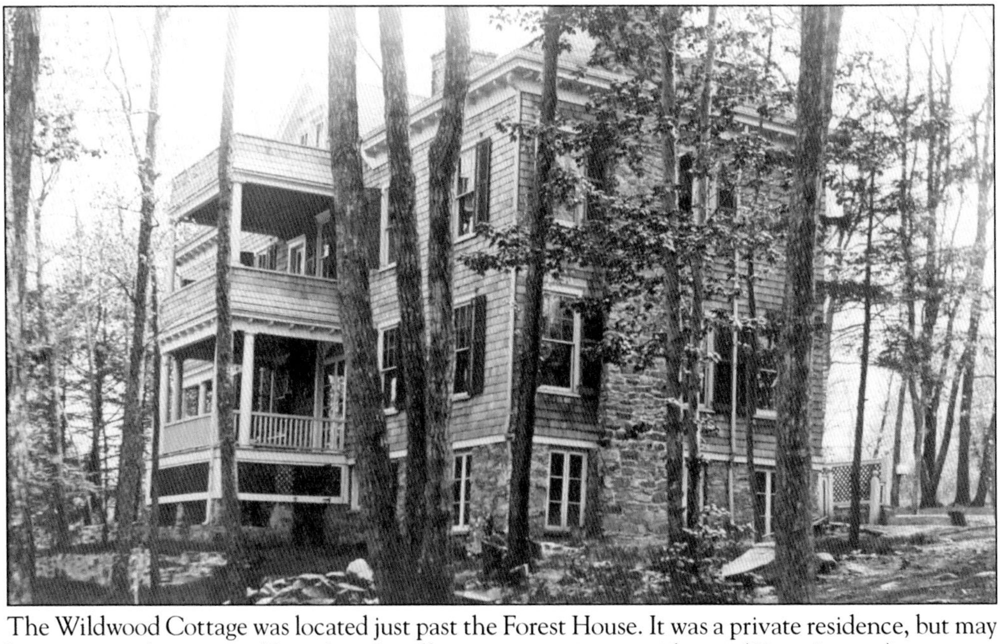

The Wildwood Cottage was located just past the Forest House. It was a private residence, but may have accepted occasional boarders. It still exists as a private residence. (Greg Amato.)

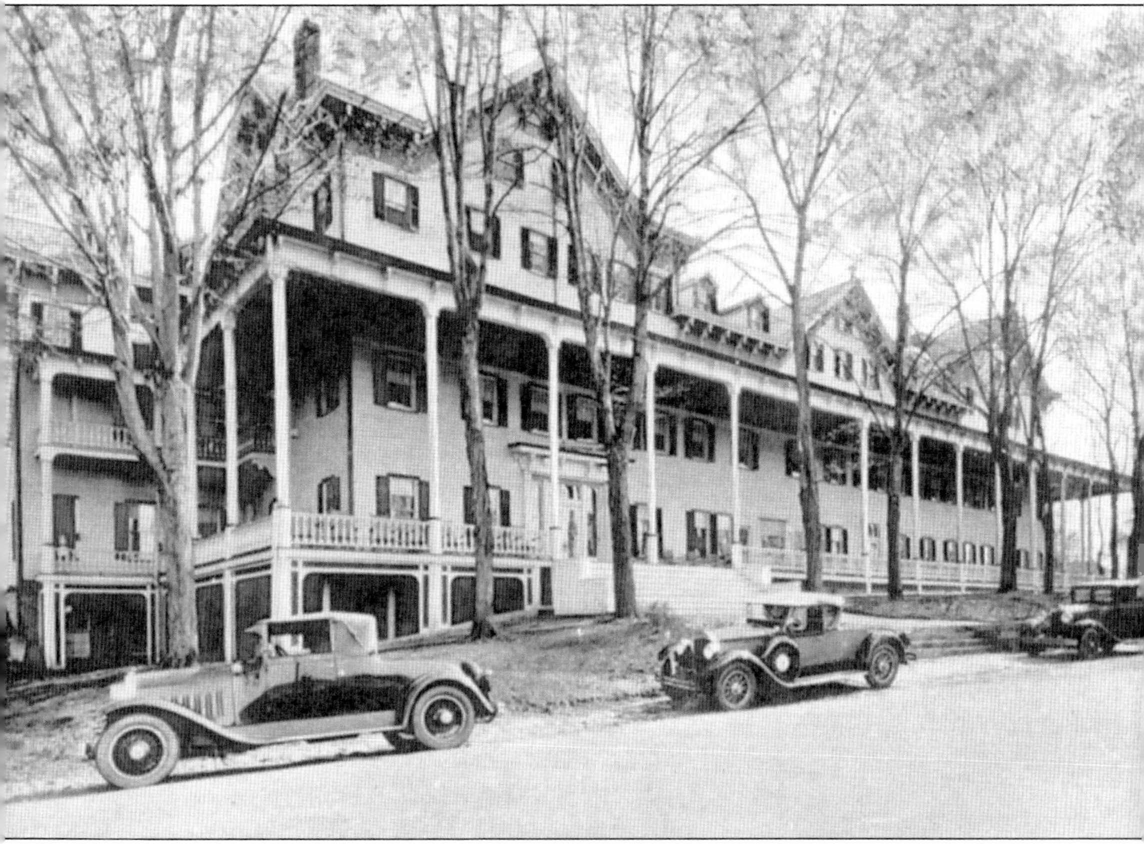

Hotel Mahopac was originally the Thompson House. In 1851, Nathan Thompson, a local hatmaker and shop owner, constructed a boardinghouse on East Lake Boulevard. Over the next 15 years, Thompson expanded the boardinghouse to more than 200 feet in length with 200 rooms. It accommodated 300 guests. In July 1869, the building burned. Thompson, however, was able to rebuild. Emerson Clark acquired the property in 1883, expanding the property to accommodate 400 guests. He also added lakeside docks, a ballroom, bowling alleys, and a billiards room. The hotel was renamed Hotel Mahopac in 1926 when Hans Melgard purchased it. He owned and operated the hotel until 1956. The five-story hotel burned in April 1964. The former location of the hotel is now the site of the White Sail Apartments and Four Brothers' Restaurant. (Karen Melgard Faulkner.)

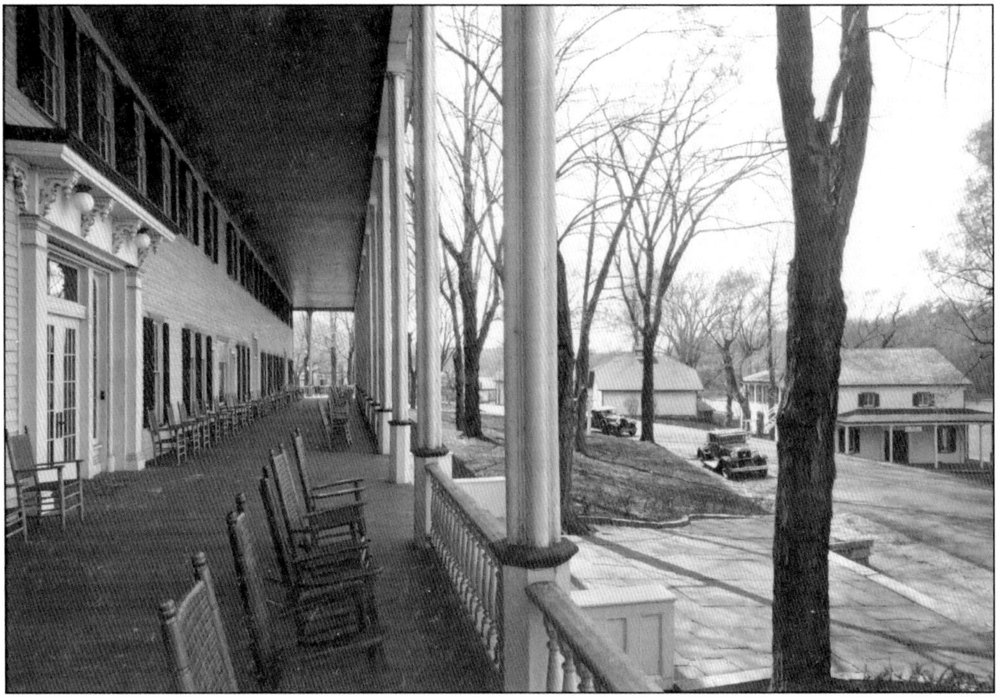

The view of the spectacular wraparound veranda of the Hotel Mahopac dates to the early 20th century. The wooden veranda was over 400 feet long and 22 feet wide. Chairs and tables provided comforts for those using the space. The view shows vehicles along South Lake Boulevard and the hotel's teahouse. Beyond the teahouse is Lake Mahopac. The foreground in the photograph is now the rear part of Four Brothers' Restaurant. (Karen Melgard Faulkner.)

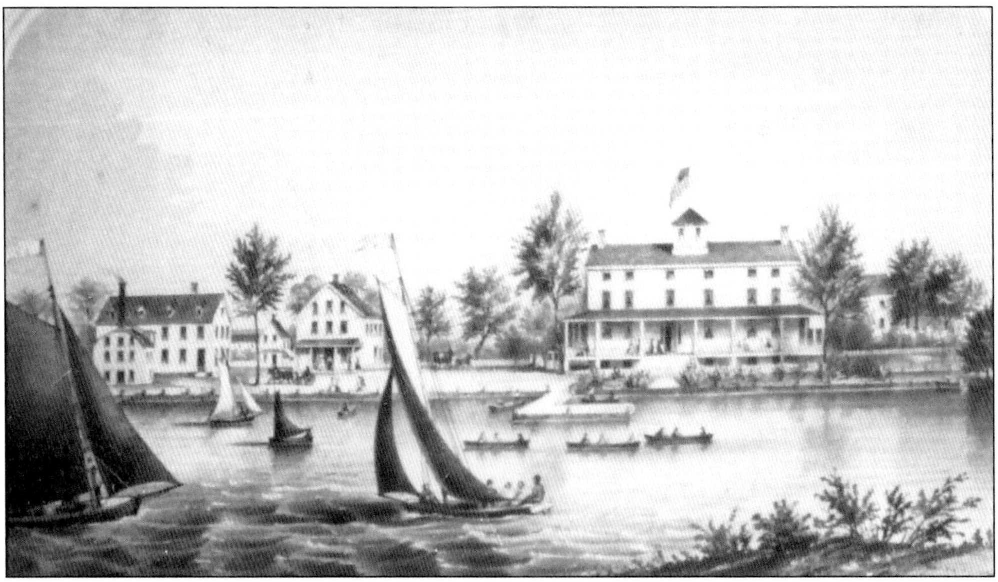

This drawing show's Stephen Monk's Lake Mahopac House, located along East Lake Boulevard prior to its becoming the Gregory House in 1853. The sketch was drawn by G. Hayward of New York City. The hotel commanded an excellent view of Lake Mahopac and the opposite shore. The Lake Mahopac House/Gregory House burned in 1878. (The Town of Carmel Historical Society.)

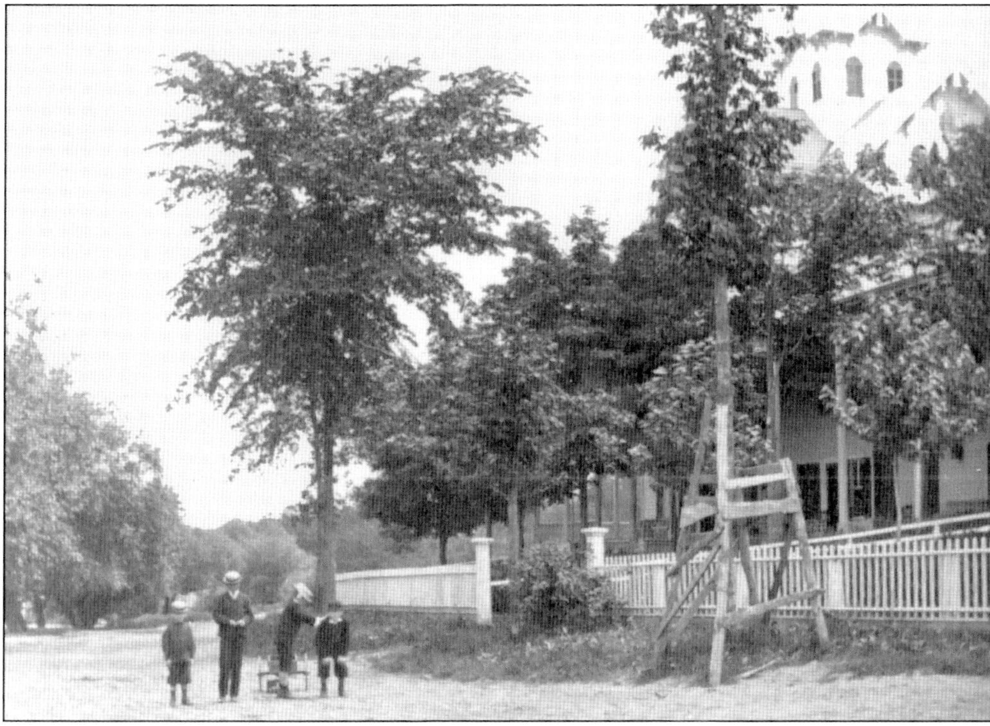

This image shows three boys and possibly a teenage or young adult (typically, only young children wore knickers such as these three boys) on a warm day outside the Thompson House Hotel around 1875. One boy was pulling a cart but now seems intent on doing something to the back of the boy leaning his hands on his knees. (Putnam County Historian's Office.)

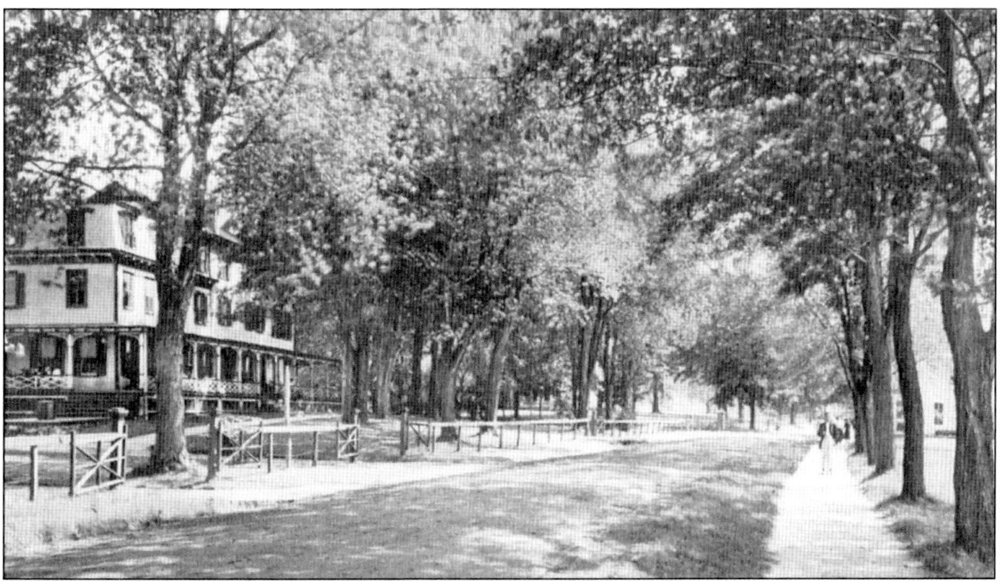

This view is south along East Lake Boulevard during the early 20th century, perhaps early on a Sunday, as people take a stroll along the gravel sidewalks bordering Lake Mahopac to the right. The Carpenter Hotel is seen to the left. (Randy and Carol Tompkins.)

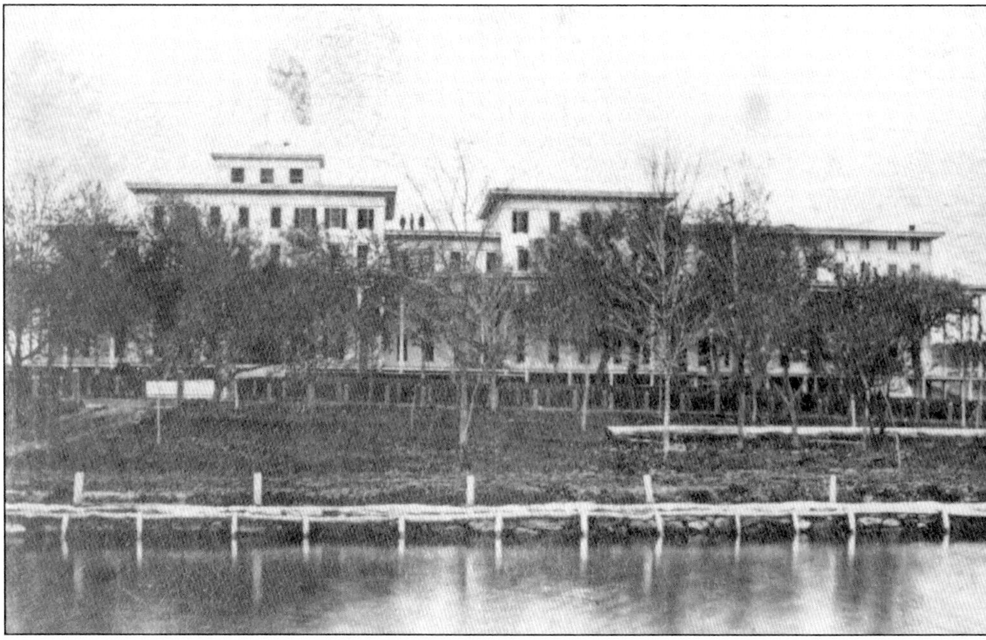

This is the Gregory House around 1875, located along East Lake Boulevard. Three men stand on the roof. Hulda Gregory purchased the hotel from Stephen Monk, conveying the properties to Dr. Lewis Gregory in January 1853. The doctor expanded the hotel and added new facilities. The Gregory Hotel burned on October 2, 1878. The former location of the hotel extended from the existing Knights of Columbus Hall to Croton Falls Road. (The Town of Carmel Historical Society.)

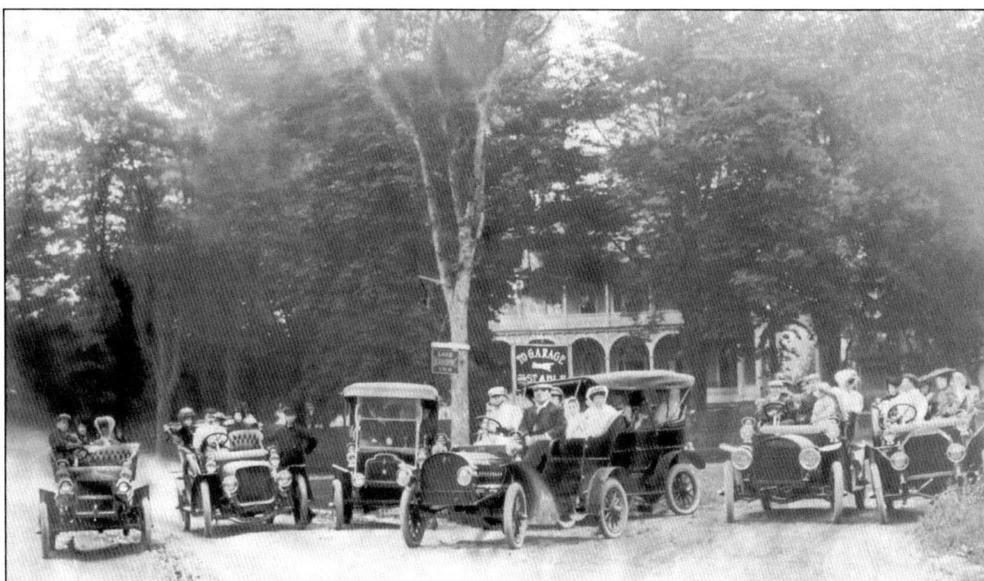

These touring cars are outside of the driveway to the Lake Mahopac Inn. The driveway is to the right while East Lake Boulevard is to the left. (The Town of Carmel Historical Society.)

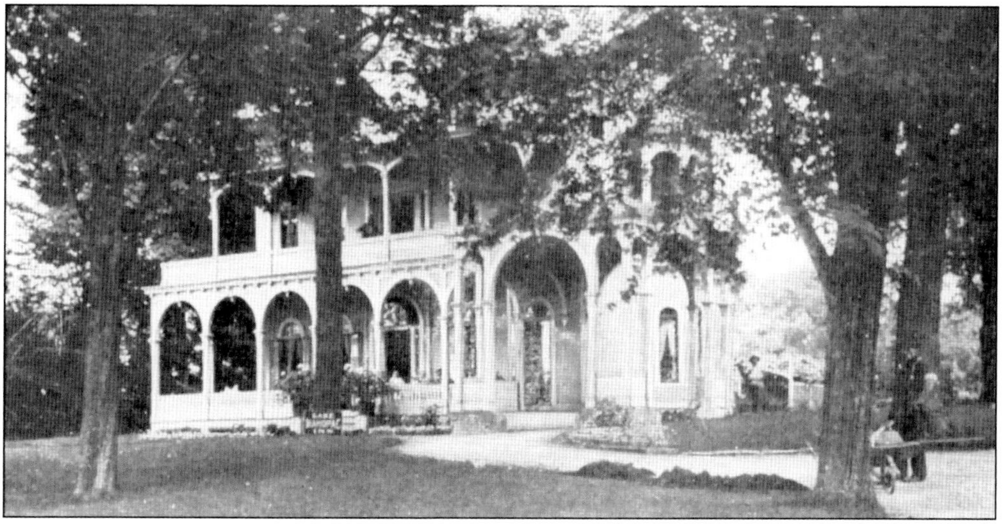

In 1867, Samuel Kaufman bought 100 acres of farmland for $30,000 and built one of the most handsome summer residences at Lake Mahopac at a cost exceeding $150,000. Edson Card purchased the house in 1893. By the early 20th century, the dwelling operated as the Lake Mahopac Inn. It was located at the intersection of East and South Lake Boulevards by what is now CVS Pharmacy. (Mark Fraser.)

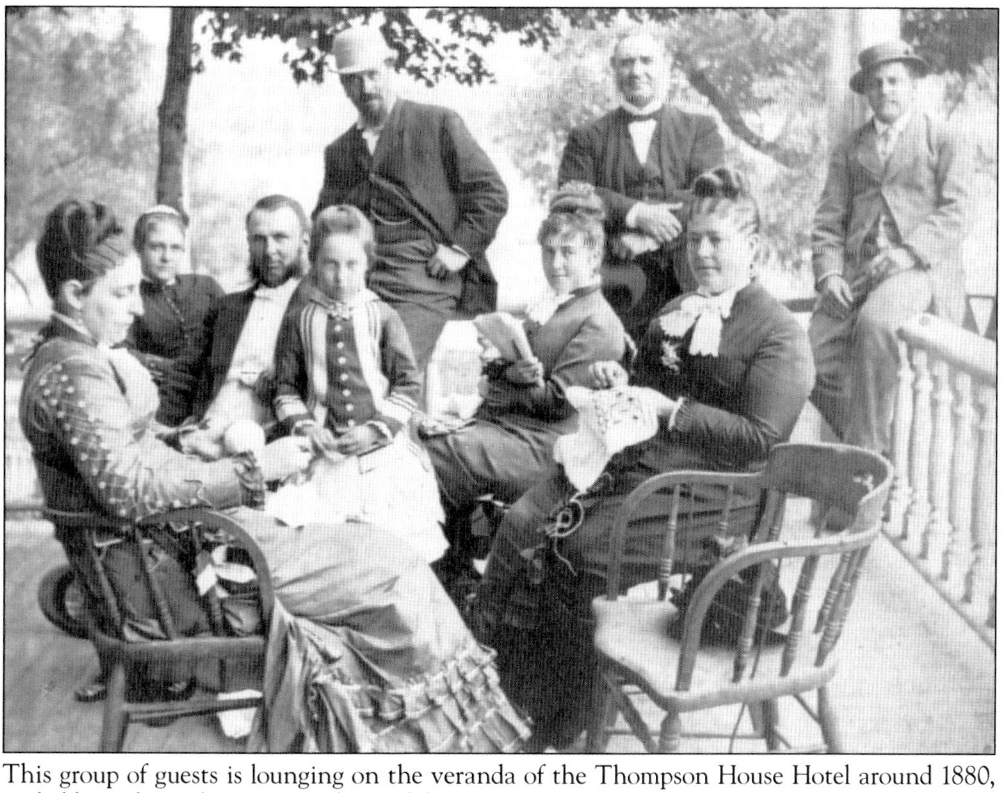

This group of guests is lounging on the veranda of the Thompson House Hotel around 1880, probably in the early summer. Three of the women are doing needlework to pass the time while socializing. The hotel was renamed Hotel Mahopac in 1926. It was located where Four Brothers' Restaurant now stands. (Greg Amato.)

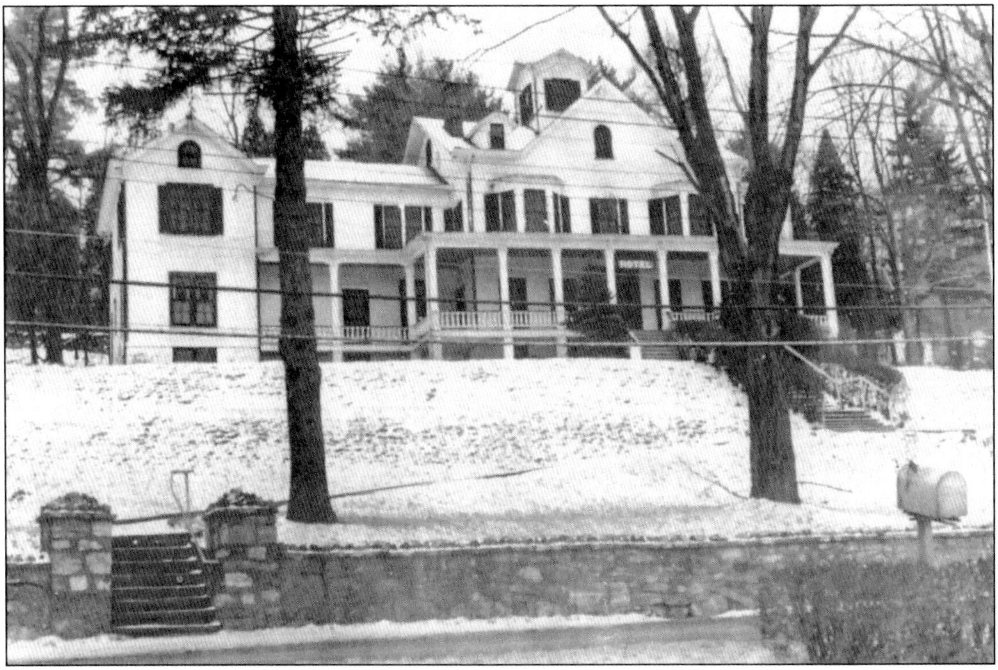

The Ardsleigh House was built in 1912 as the residence of Egisto Fabbri and his family, aristocratic Italians who donated the chapel for Mahopac's Church of the Holy Communion in memory of Egisto's brother Ernesto. The Fabbri family sold their home on the lake to Grady Ardsleigh, who transformed it into the Ardsleigh House Hotel. Smaller than the other lakeside hotels, the Ardsleigh House had 30 rooms and a great lakeside restaurant (now the Terrace Club). It burned down on March 1, 1969. The hotel was located across from the Terrace Club on Route 6N. (Mark Fraser.)

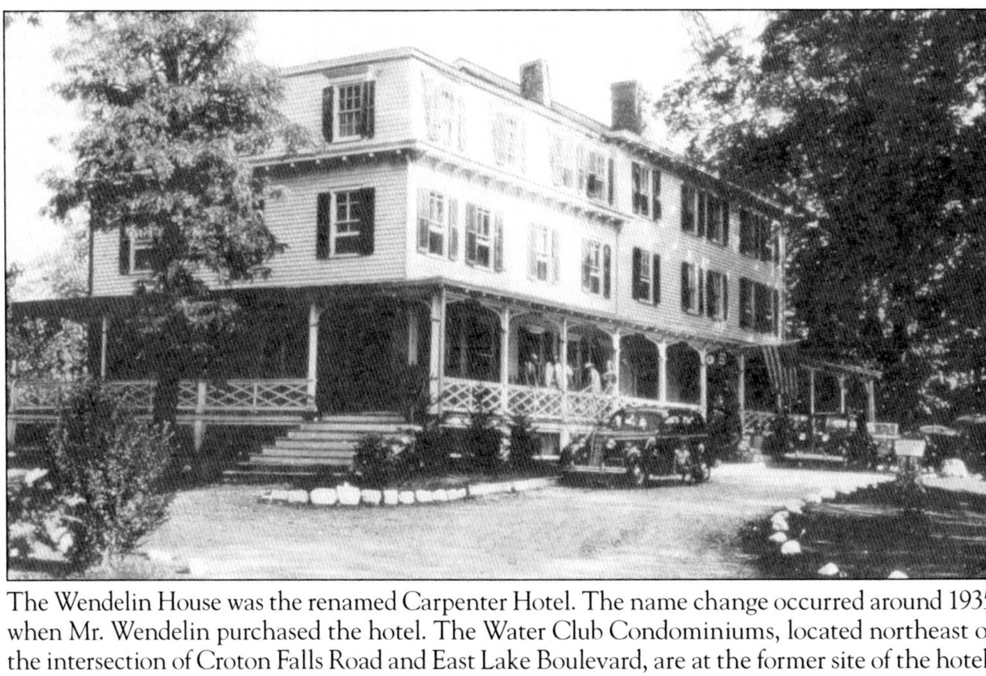

The Wendelin House was the renamed Carpenter Hotel. The name change occurred around 1935 when Mr. Wendelin purchased the hotel. The Water Club Condominiums, located northeast of the intersection of Croton Falls Road and East Lake Boulevard, are at the former site of the hotel. The image shows the house as it appeared in 1944. (The Town of Carmel Historical Society.)

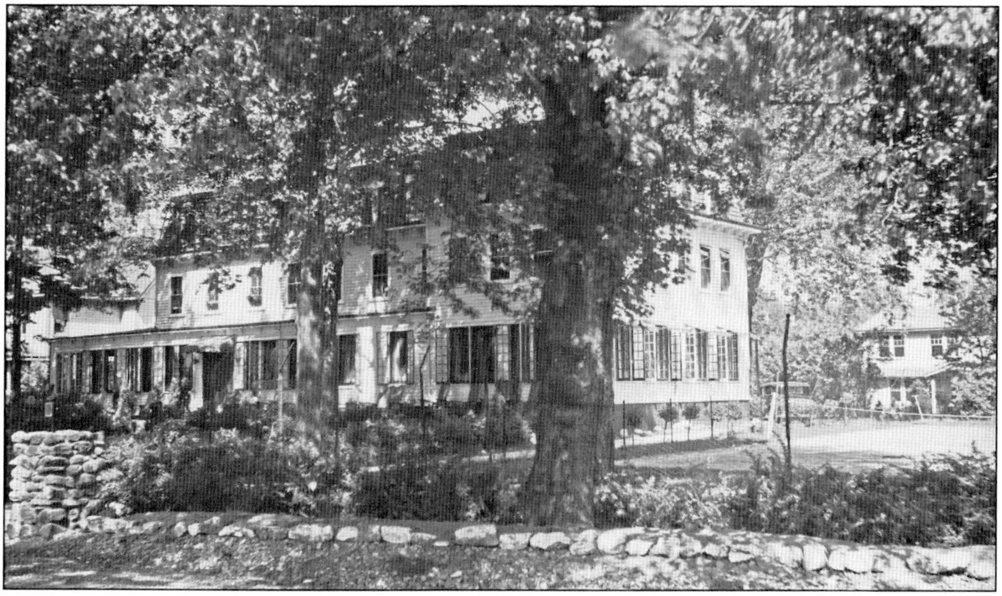

The Viault Cottage was acquired by Lester Baxter who renamed it the Baxter House around 1935. This 1937 image shows the hotel from East Lake Boulevard and an annex in the rear for additional guests. (Muriel Agor Hill, Darlene Hill Lampe, Karen Hill Czysz.)

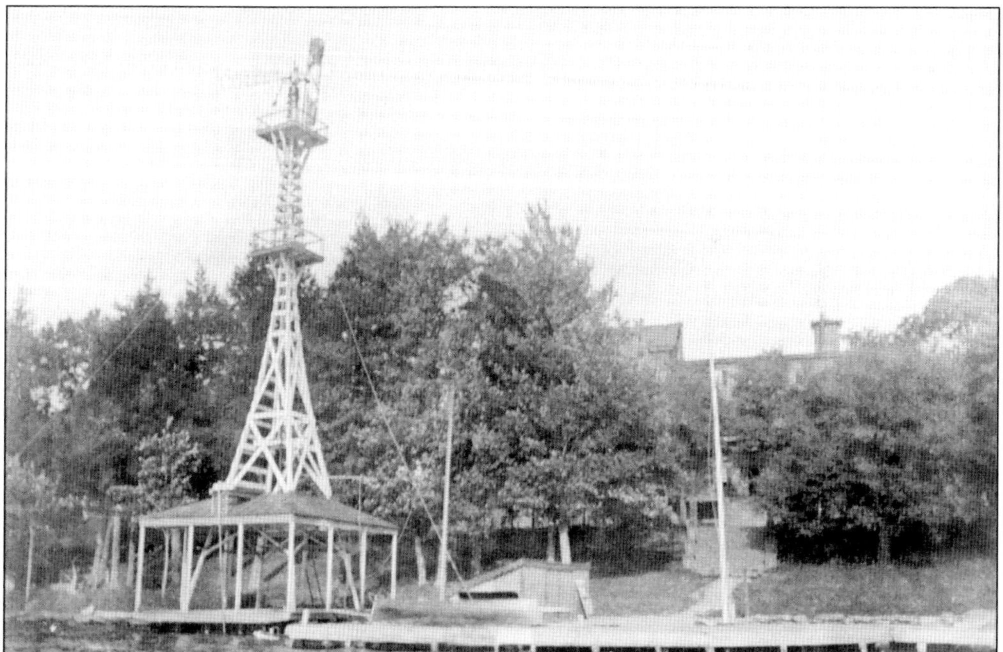

The Cole House was another large hotel located along East Lake Boulevard, just north of the current St. John the Evangelist Parochial School. The 1891 image shows the top of the hotel above the tree line, a windmill within Lake Mahopac near the shoreline, and a lakeside dock. The windmill probably supplied power to pump lake water up the slope to the hotel. East Lake Boulevard is at the top of the flight of steps behind the flagpole. Otis H. Cole owned the Cole House around 1896. (The Putnam County Historical Society.)

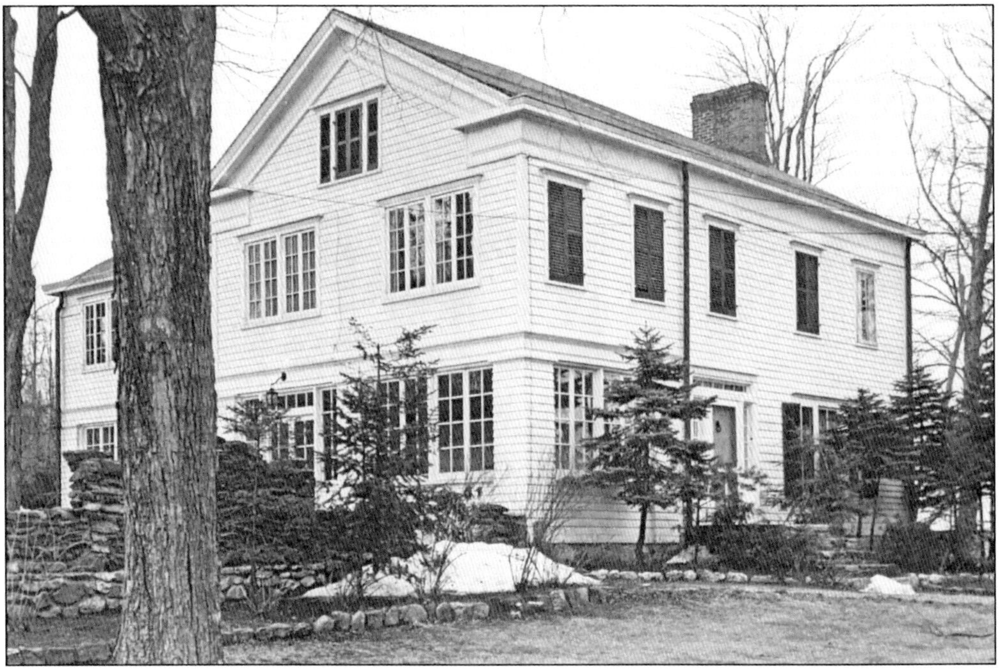

Amy Cole owned the Hidden House boardinghouse on Route 6 in Mahopac. It contained a restaurant named the Princess Inn. She sold Hidden House to the Russian Orthodox Church around 1948 and moved to the Week's Estate, referred to as Innsdale, on the shore of Lake Gleneida in Carmel. Hidden House is now part of the Russian Orthodox church property. (The Town of Carmel Historical Society.)

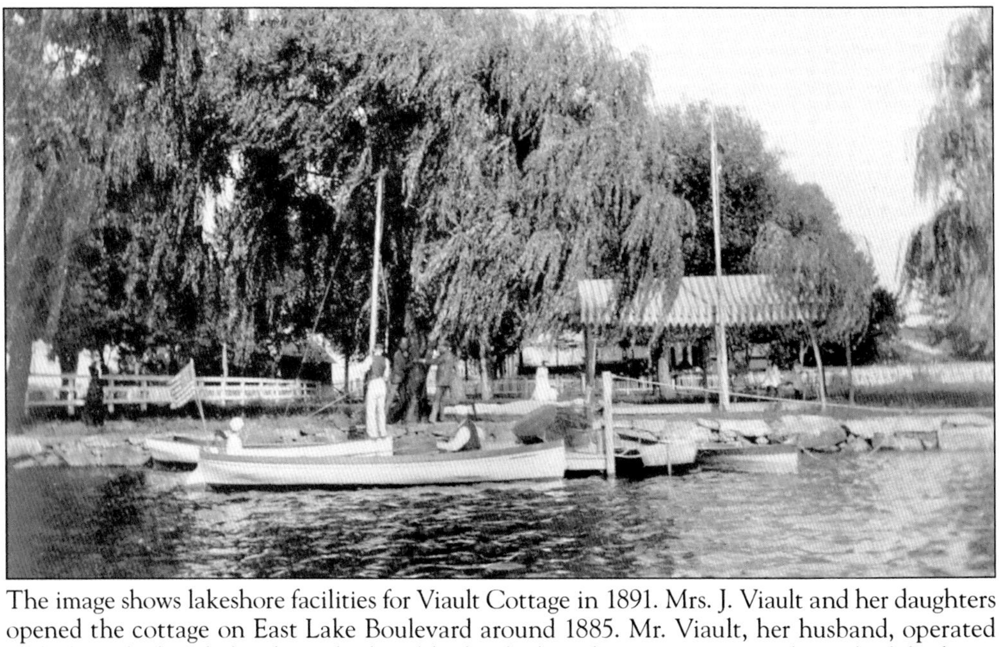

The image shows lakeshore facilities for Viault Cottage in 1891. Mrs. J. Viault and her daughters opened the cottage on East Lake Boulevard around 1885. Mr. Viault, her husband, operated a blacksmith shop behind it. The hotel had a dock and swimming area along the lakeshore. Vegetables were grown behind the house for guests. The cottage later was acquired by Charles Baxter and operated as the Baxter House. (Mark Fraser.)

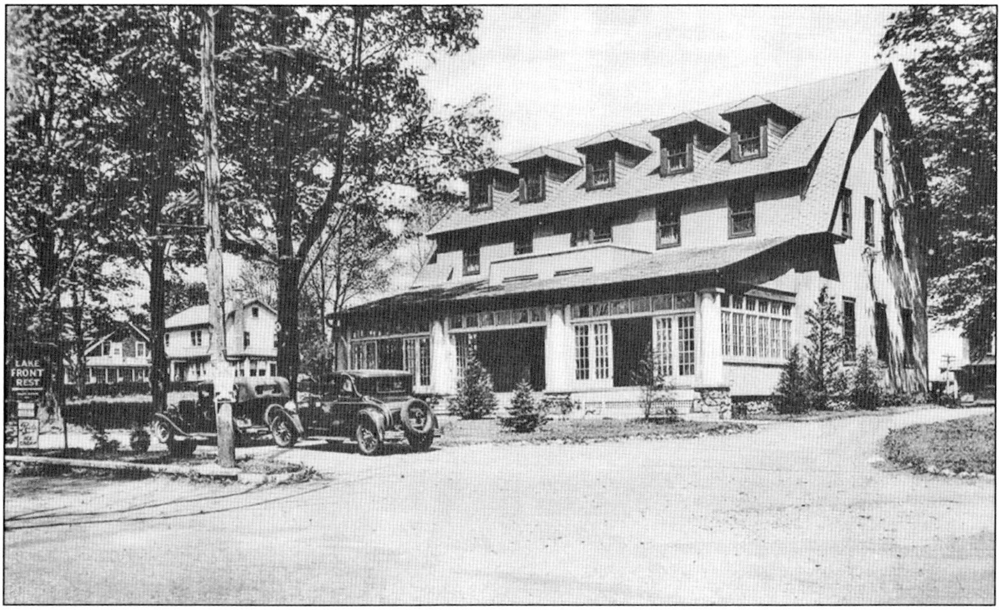

Marx's Lake View House was the boardinghouse of Oscar Marx. It was constructed around 1930 behind his store, located at the intersection of Croton Falls Road and East Lake Boulevard. The boardinghouse had a restaurant and lakefront property. It still exists as an apartment house. (Randy and Carol Tompkins.)

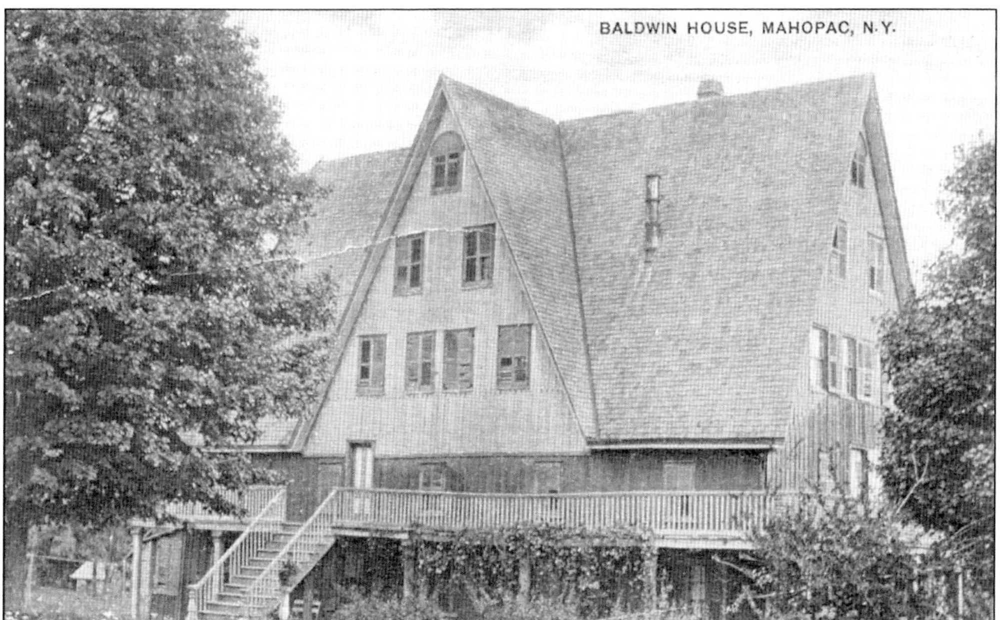

The Baldwin House was located near the current rectory of St. John the Evangelist Church off East Lake Boulevard during the late 19th century. It was owned by Rueben Baldwin and burned sometime before 1900. (Greg Amato.)

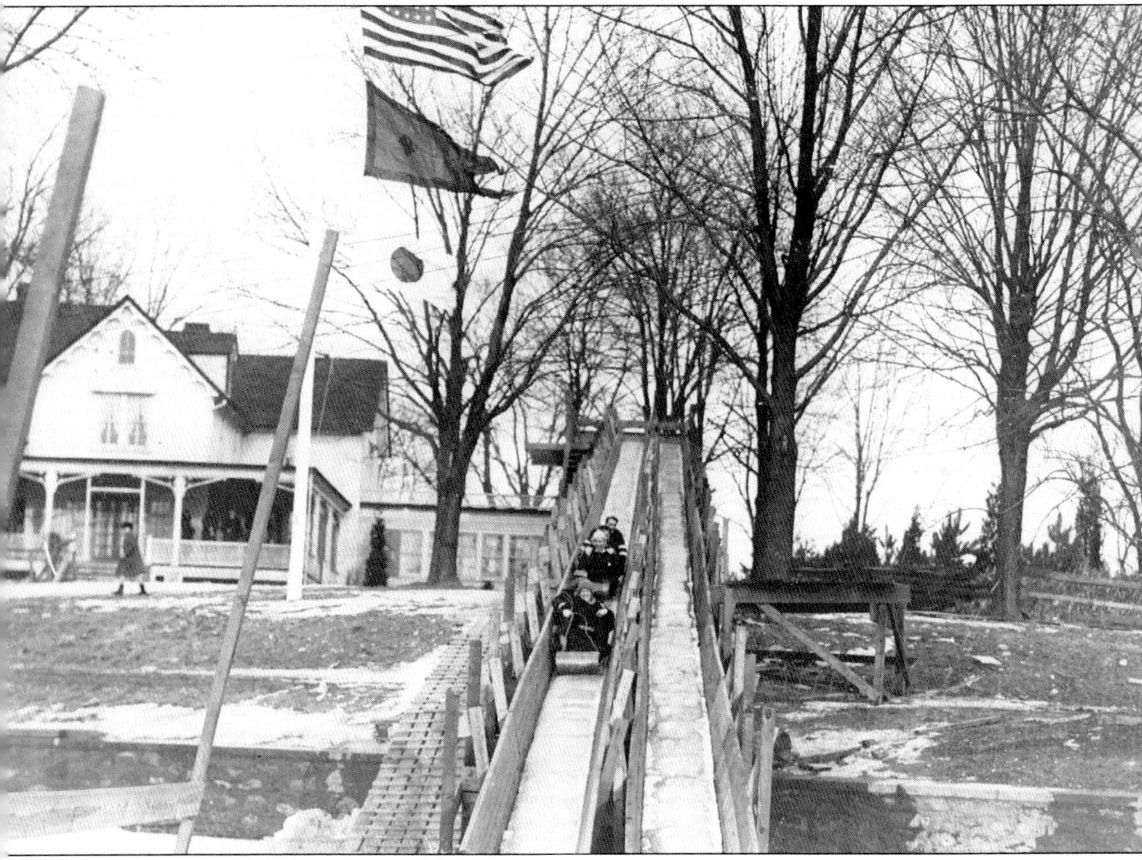

This toboggan run was at the Lake Shore Club on Mahopac Point overlooking Fairy Island Cove in Lake Mahopac. The Lake Shore Club, seen behind the run, was the former Hoguet family residence. Anthony Hoguet acquired the land that was to become Mahopac Point in 1854, which at that time was referred to as Hoguet's Point. His family retained ownership of the tract until 1912, when Henri A.L. Hoguet placed it up for sale. He sold the property as one parcel but maintained the Hoguet's residence, several acres of land surrounding it, and the lakeshore overlooking Fairy Island Cove. (The Town of Carmel Historical Society.)

Eight

Commerce and Services

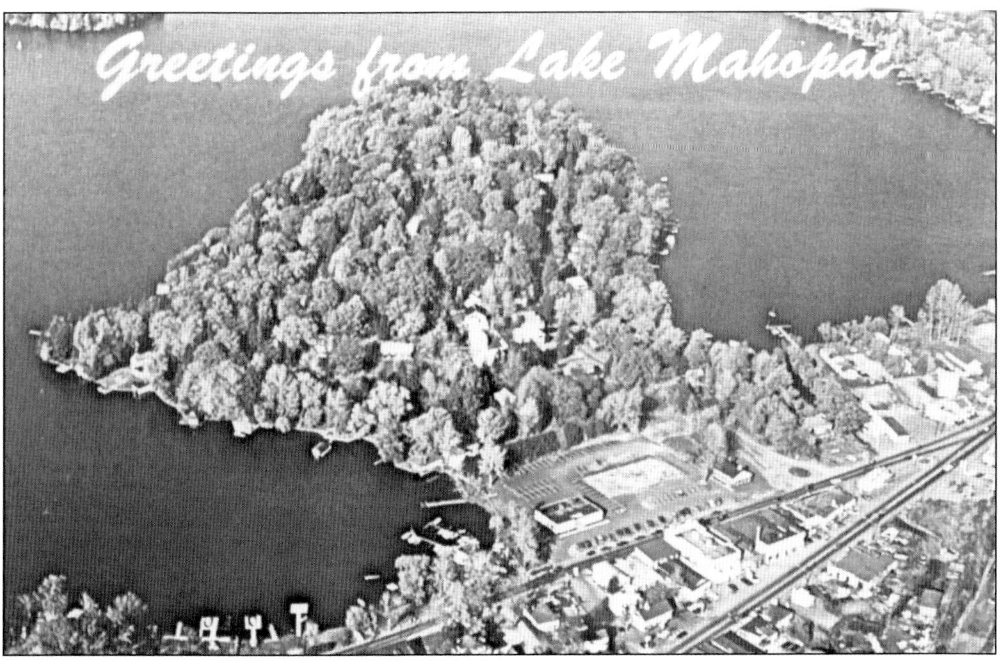

This aerial photograph shows Mahopac Point extending into Lake Mahopac and the Route 6N and Route 6 corridors around 1968. Turtle Creek can be seen entering the lake southeast of Mahopac Point. The large building east of the creek is Mahopac National Bank. Mahopac Point was referred to as Hoguet's Point during the late 19th century. (Greg Amato.)

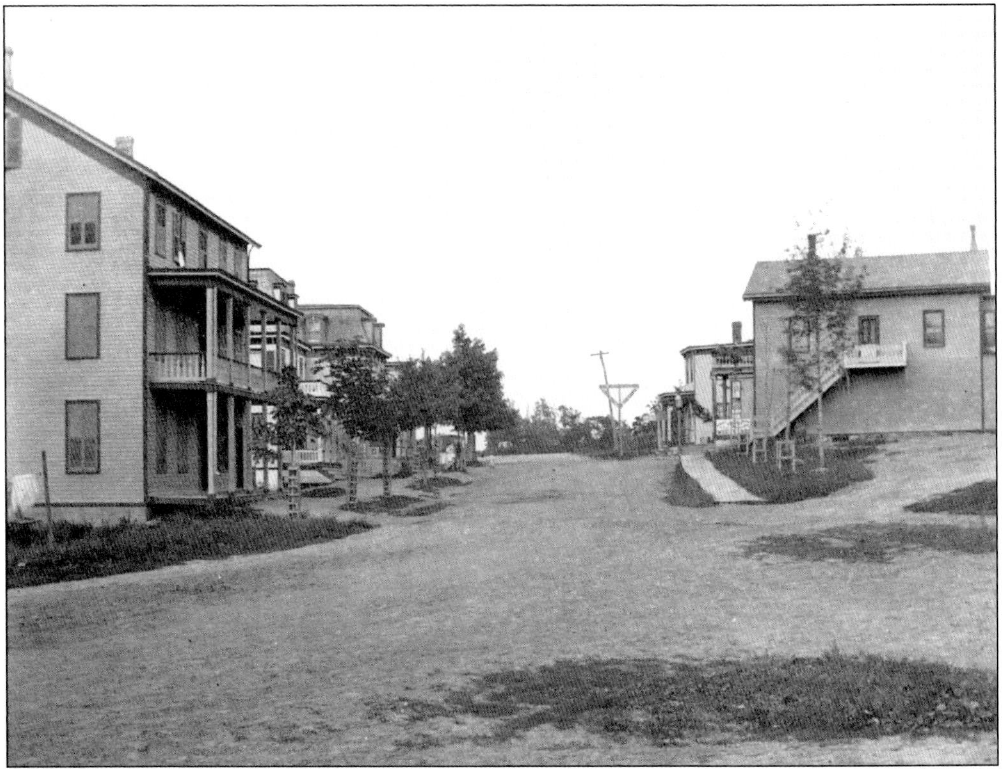

This c. 1885 photograph shows the old Mahopac hamlet prior to building removal to control water pollution. Commercial buildings, boardinghouses, and residences are seen along Croton Falls Road. Its intersection with Mud Pond Road is in the foreground. The Putnam Division Railroad crosses the road by the triangular-shaped railroad sign. The crossing is near the current location of the Putnam County Trailway at Croton Falls Road. (The Town of Carmel Historical Society.)

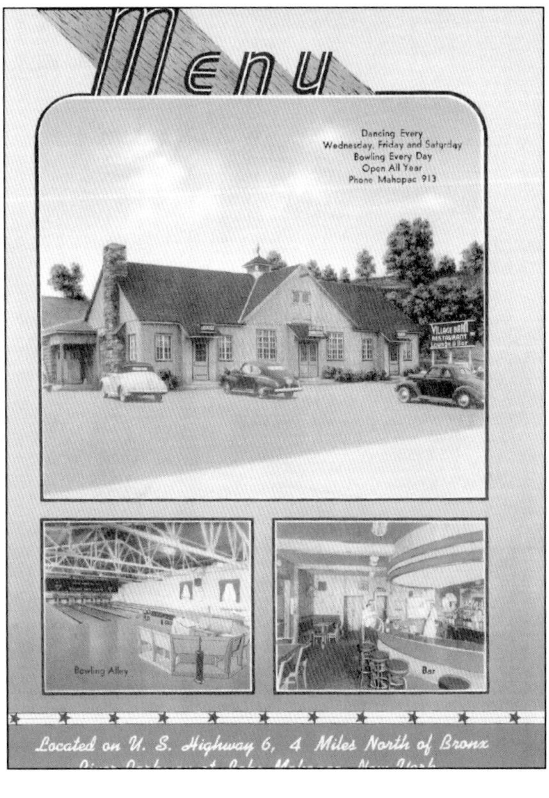

The Village Barn was a restaurant, lounge, and bar located along Route 6 in Mahopac. The menu cover shows the entrance of the restaurant and its interior lounge and bowling alleys as of 1938. The menu indicates its location as four miles north of the Bronx River Parkway rather than the Taconic Parkway, the correct roadway. Note also the simple telephone number. (Aaron Kaas.)

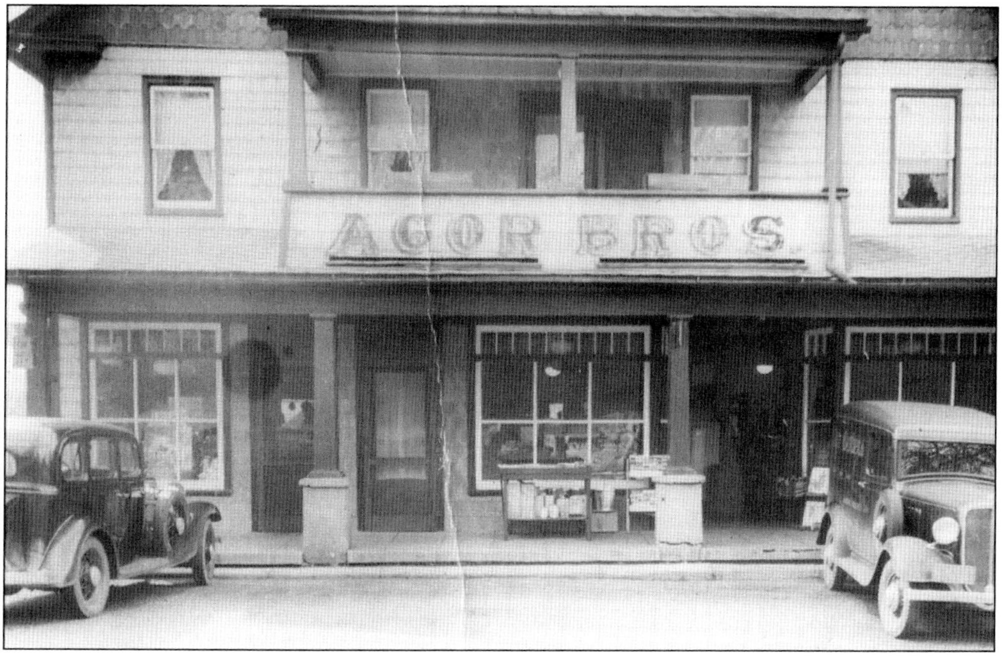

The above photograph shows the Agor Bros. store in Mahopac Falls as it looked around 1930. The building was purchased by the brothers from James Barrett during the mid-1890s and continued to serve the community as a general store until it burned during the fire that devastated a large part of Mahopac Falls on November 7, 1919. The store (below) sold a variety of items such as groceries, newspapers, baked goods, tobacco, and footwear. The store was rebuilt and remained in operation by the Agor family until around 1970 when it closed and became an apartment house. The building is located at the corner of Myrtle Avenue and Brook Road. Shown in the photograph are, from left to right, Chester Tompkins, John Adams, Kelsie Agor, Helen Hietman, Lizzi Barrett, and John Cronk. (Both, Muriel Agor Hill, Darlene Hill Lampe, Karen Hill Czysz.)

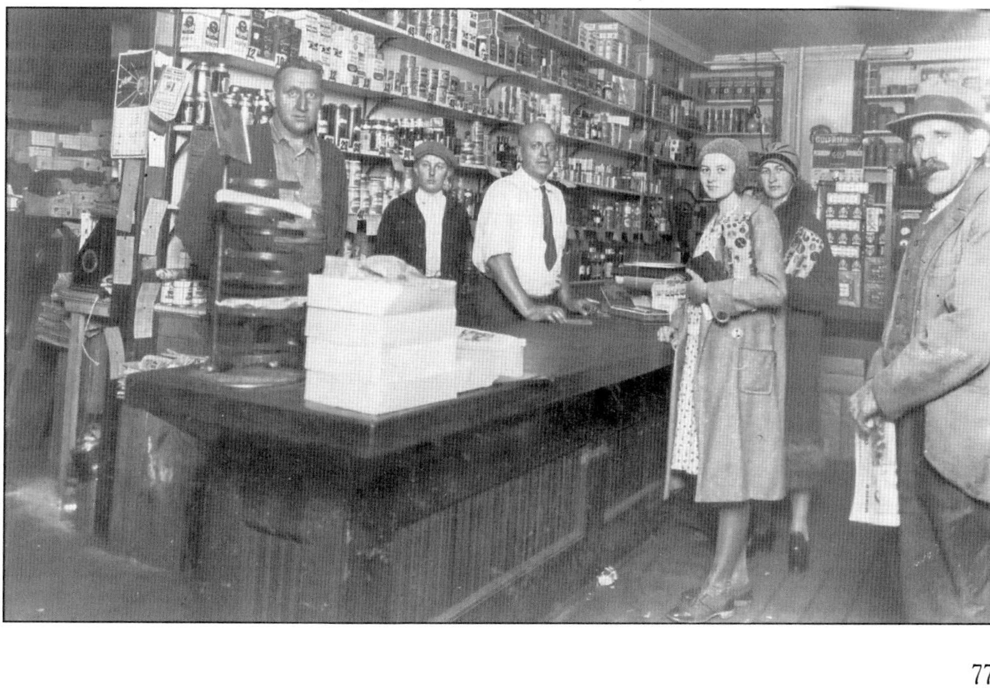

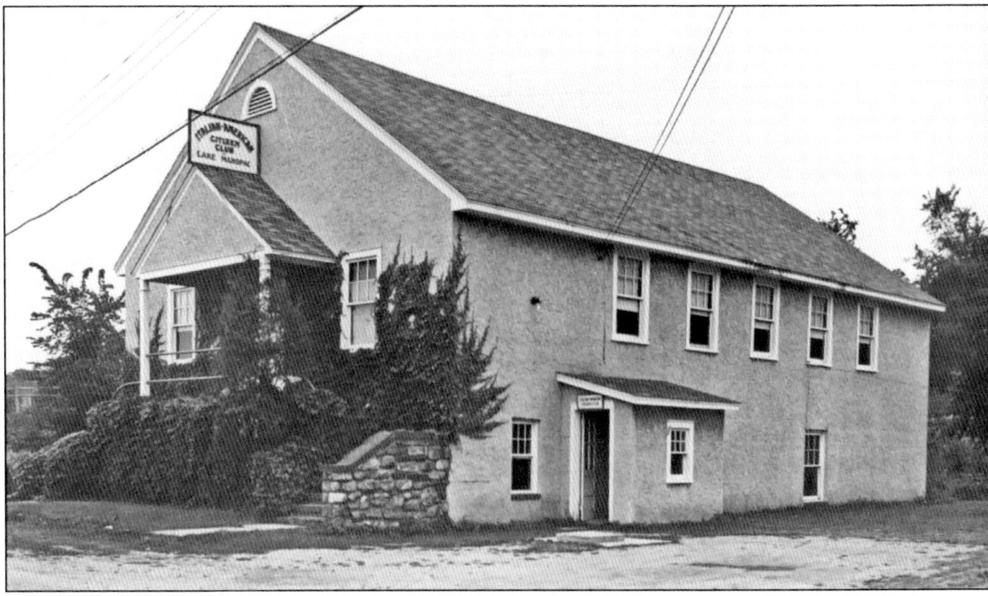

This building is the Italian American Club located at 141 Buckshollow Road in 1934. The president at the time was P. Battista. The building still exists as the home of the Italian American Club of Mahopac. (The Town of Carmel Historical Society.)

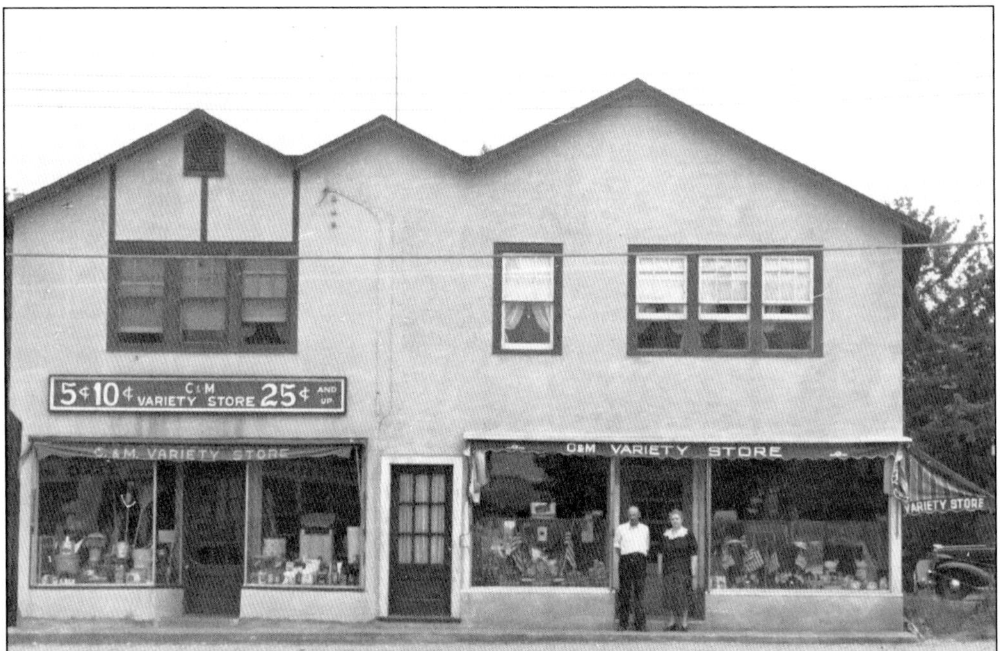

The C&M Variety Store was located at 593 Route 6 near the intersection with Cherry Lane. Prior to around 1960, the Irwin family of Mahopac owned it for years. In the 1960s, John Ceulla owned the store, which was called the Sugar Bowl. It served mainly teenagers, featuring a soda fountain, games, and occasionally live music by local bands. The building is now the home of X-Press Printing and Office Supply owned by the Richard DiCola family. (The Town of Carmel Historical Society.)

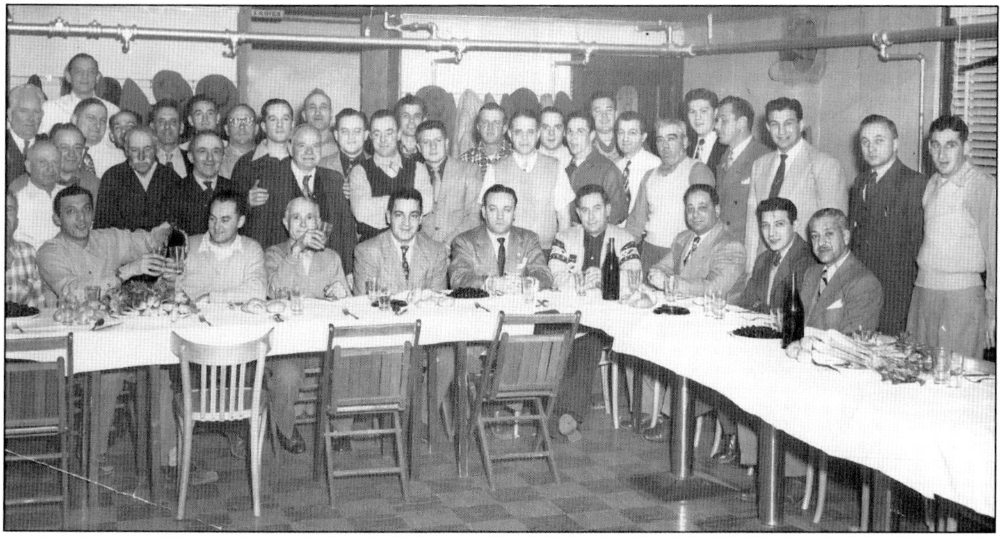

This is a c. 1955 photograph of the Italian American Club of Mahopac at 141 Buckshollow Road during one of its social functions. What appear to be plates of olives, celery, bread, and bottles of wine are present on the table for the enjoyment of all. (Laura Amato.)

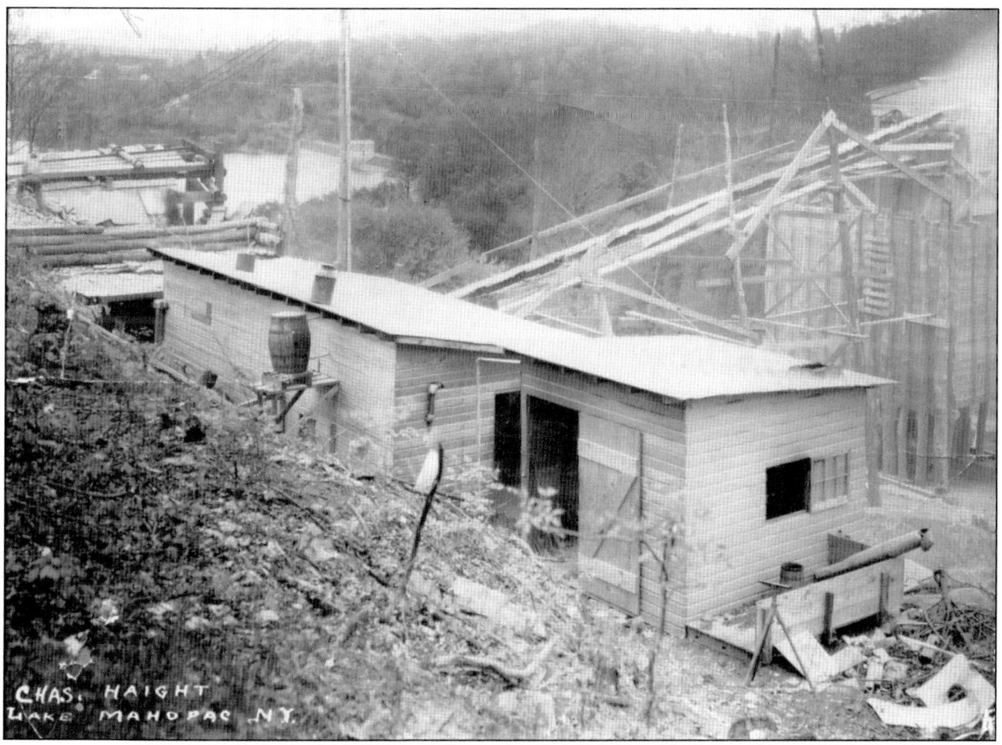

Charles Haight operated this sand and gravel pit along Route 6, near Drewville Road. The West Branch Reservoir, and the earthen dam that forms it, are seen in the upper center. Note the wooden barrel and milk cans, likely for catching rainwater. The dust flying near the structures suggest quarrying operations were underway. The image dates to around 1920. (The Town of Carmel Historical Society.)

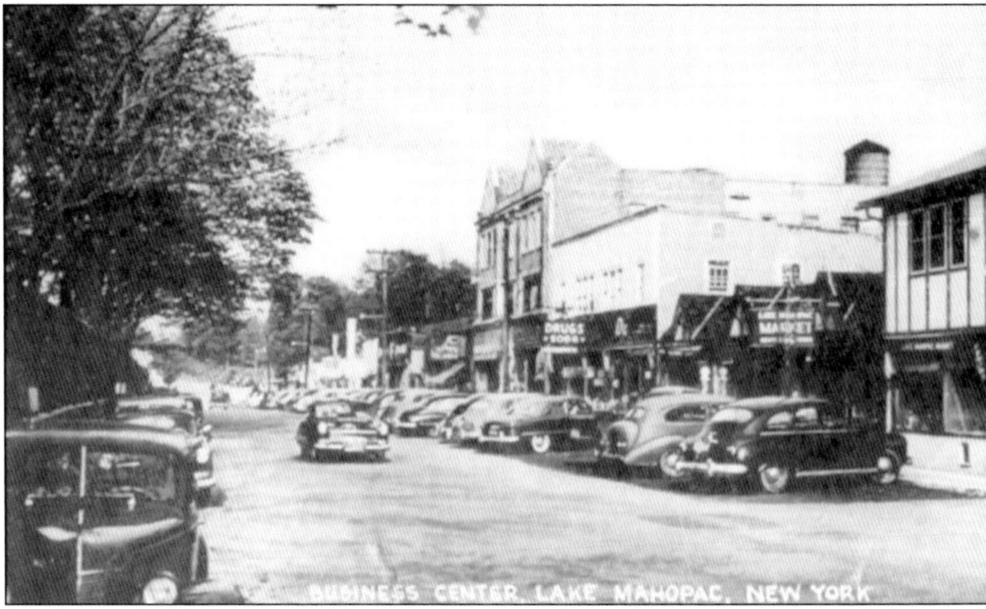

This postcard image shows the main business district along the Route 6N corridor in Mahopac around 1950. (The Town of Carmel Historical Society.)

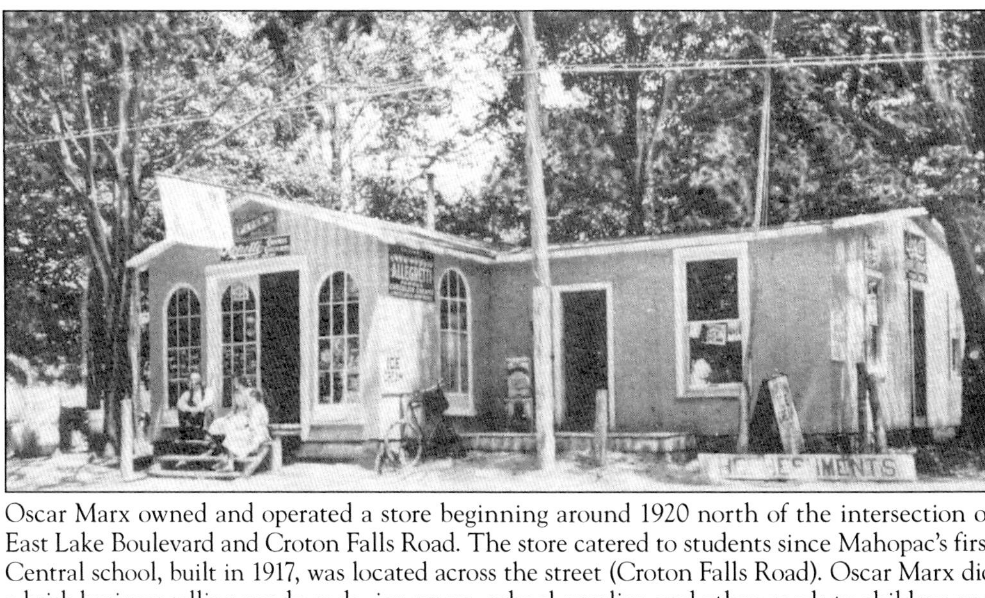

Oscar Marx owned and operated a store beginning around 1920 north of the intersection of East Lake Boulevard and Croton Falls Road. The store catered to students since Mahopac's first Central school, built in 1917, was located across the street (Croton Falls Road). Oscar Marx did a brisk business selling candy, soda, ice cream, school supplies, and other goods to children and their parents. Marx constructed a boardinghouse behind the store around 1930. Soon after, he demolished the store. The building, now an apartment, still exists at the Croton Falls-East Lake Boulevard intersection. (Tony Deluca.)

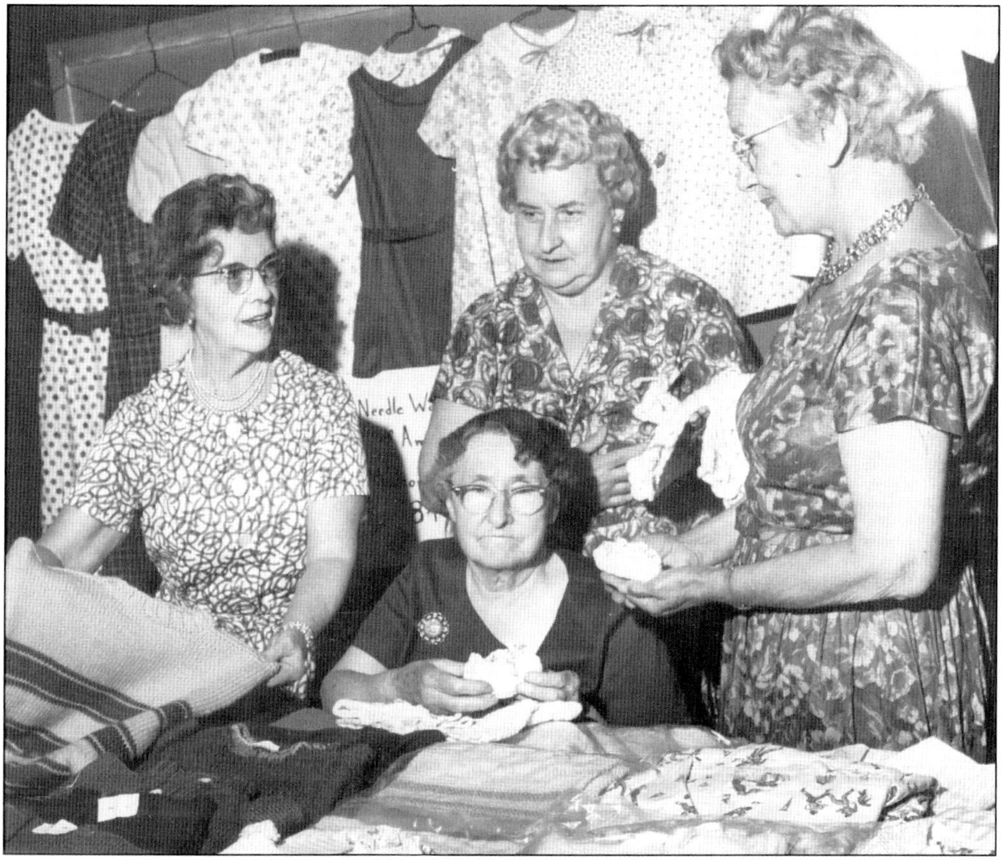

Homemade clothes and are crafts are being arranged for a fund-raiser benefit held at the Mahopac Grange on August 8, 1957. The members shown at one of the craft tables are, from left to right, Marie Merritt, Glenna Lockwood, Mrs. Thomas Roe, and Bea Parker. (Putnam County Historian's Office.)

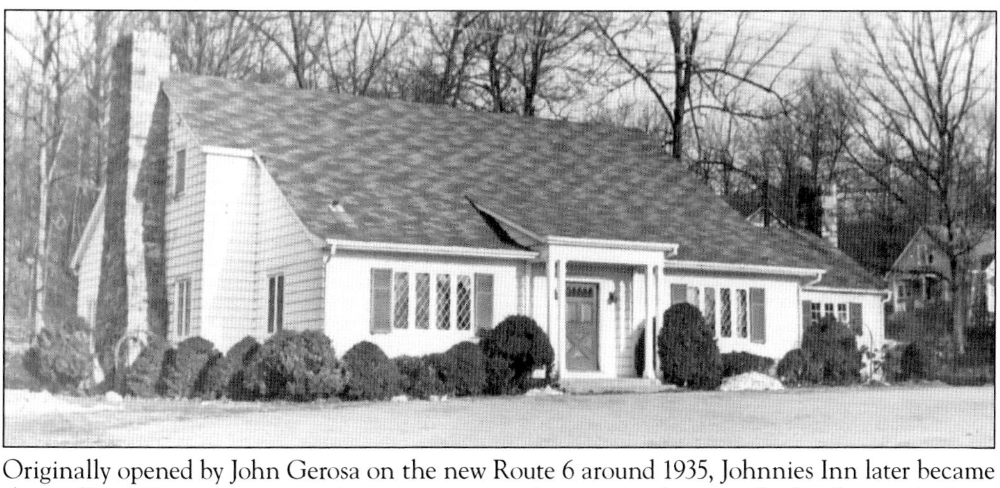

Originally opened by John Gerosa on the new Route 6 around 1935, Johnnies Inn later became the Holland House restaurant. It was a very popular meeting location for local organizations, businesses, and politicians. It had a separate bar and fireplace in the dining room. It is now the location of Cargain Funeral Home. (Greg Amato.)

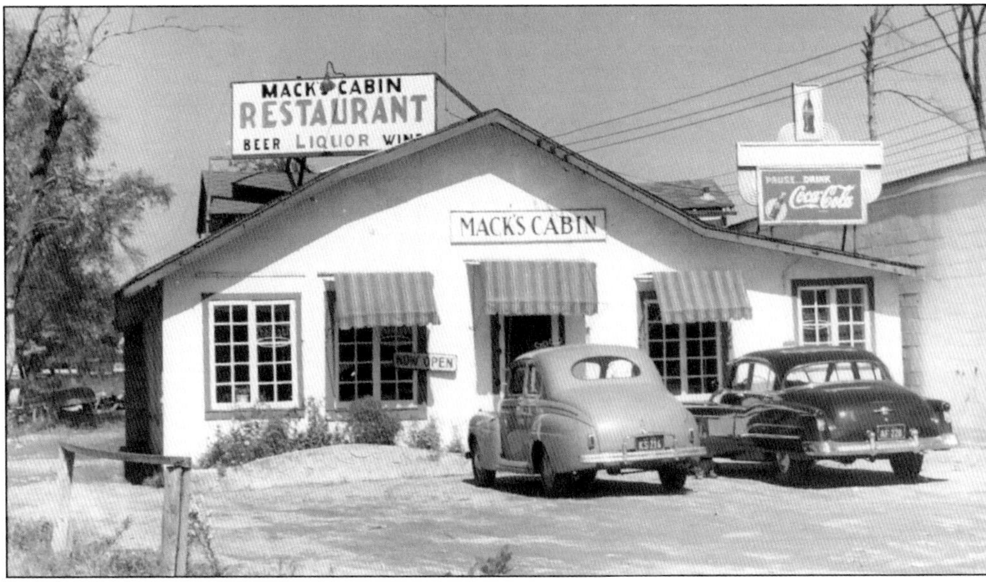

Mack's Cabin Restaurant was located along Route 6N near its intersection with Route 6. The Mahopac National Bank Community Building now occupies the location. The image shows the restaurant as it appeared around 1950 when Max Heitman owned it. Tom Kat Sporting Goods Store constructed a new building at the location in the 1960s. (The Town of Carmel Historical Society.)

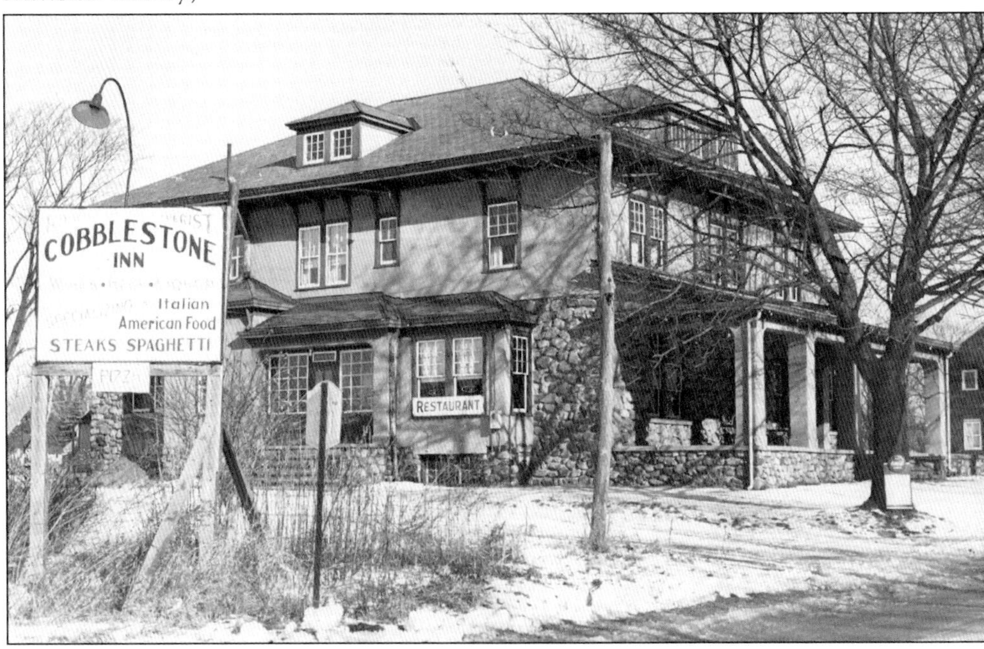

The Cobblestone Inn was located on Route 118 just past the Putnam Division Railroad tracks. The proprietress in 1952, the date of this photograph, was Ann Landau. The former location of the inn is now the Osceola Garage. Many of the restaurant photographs in this book were taken by Sam Hickman, who was on the Alcohol Beverage Control Board of Putnam County, New York. State regulations mandated that photographs be taken of the interior and exterior of all structures holding liquor licenses. (The Town of Carmel Historical Society.)

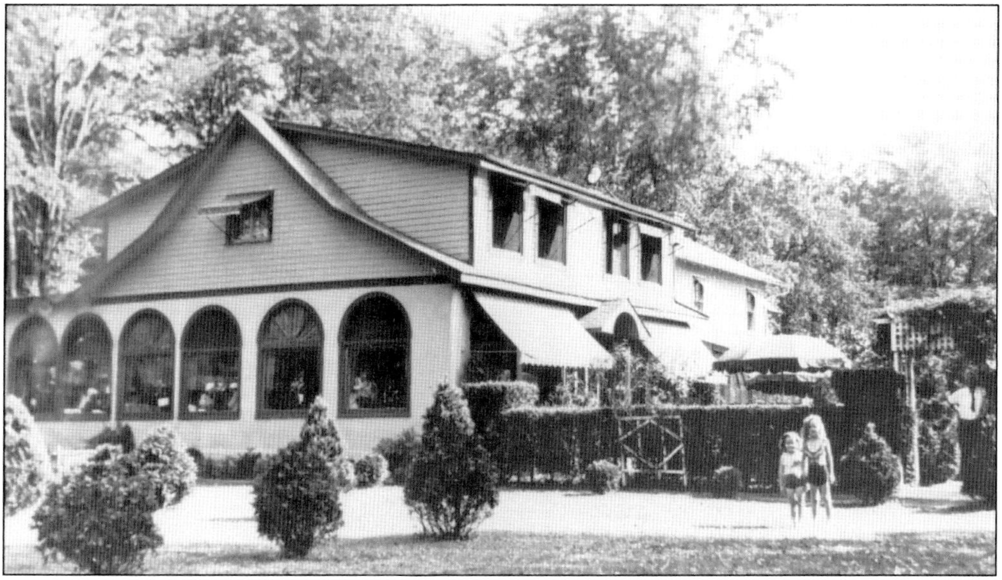

The Willow Tree Tea Shoppe, shown in this 1935 photograph, was owned by Charles D. Baxter. (Muriel Agor Hill, Darlene Hill Lampe, Karen Hill Czsyz.)

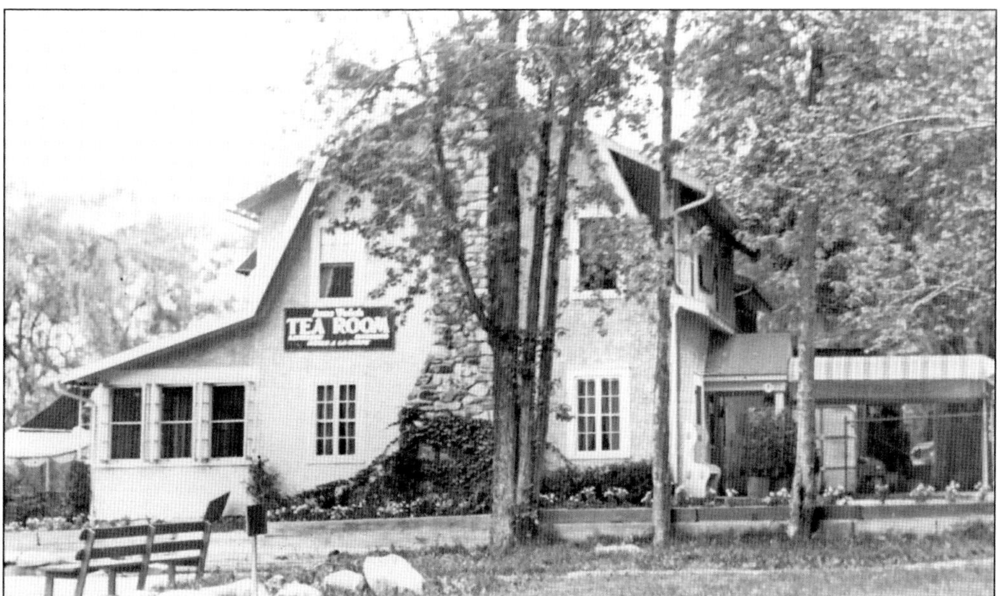

This photograph, taken in 1941, shows Ann Welch's Tea Room on East Lake Boulevard. The building now serves as the Veterans of Foreign Wars Hall. (The Town of Carmel Historical Society.)

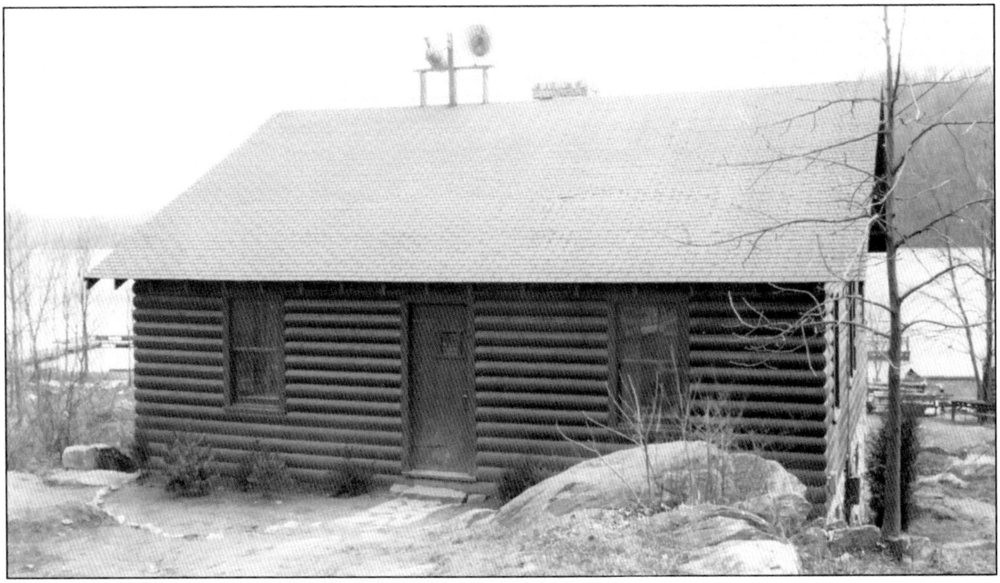

Long Pond Inn was a rustic-style restaurant located on Long Pond Road near Lake Sycamore. Boating, swimming, outdoor dancing, and other activities occurred there seasonally. The loud speakers on the top of the building brought music to all. This image shows the restaurant as it appeared in 1938 when Marjorie Hadfield operated the establishment. The building still exists in a very modified form but has been closed for a number of years. (The Town of Carmel Historical Society.)

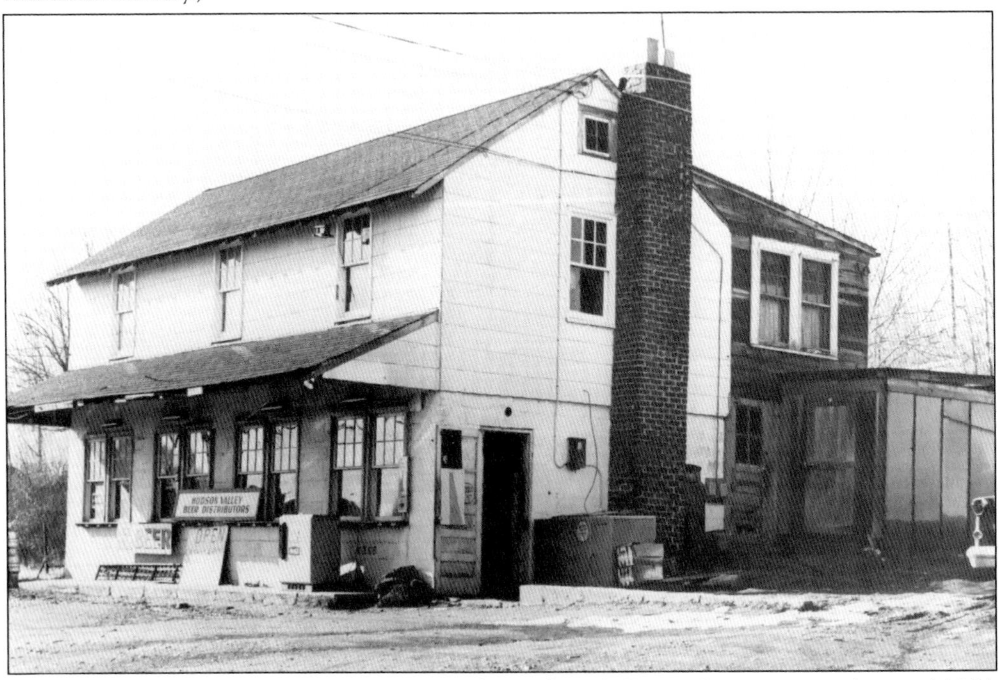

This is the Hudson Valley Beverage Company located at 250 Route 6, as it appeared around 1964. At that time, James Cardillo purchased the business from a Mr. Bloom. He delivered beverages to homes in Putnam and Westchester Counties. The company remains in business along Route 6. (Al and Karen Cardillo Lindeman.)

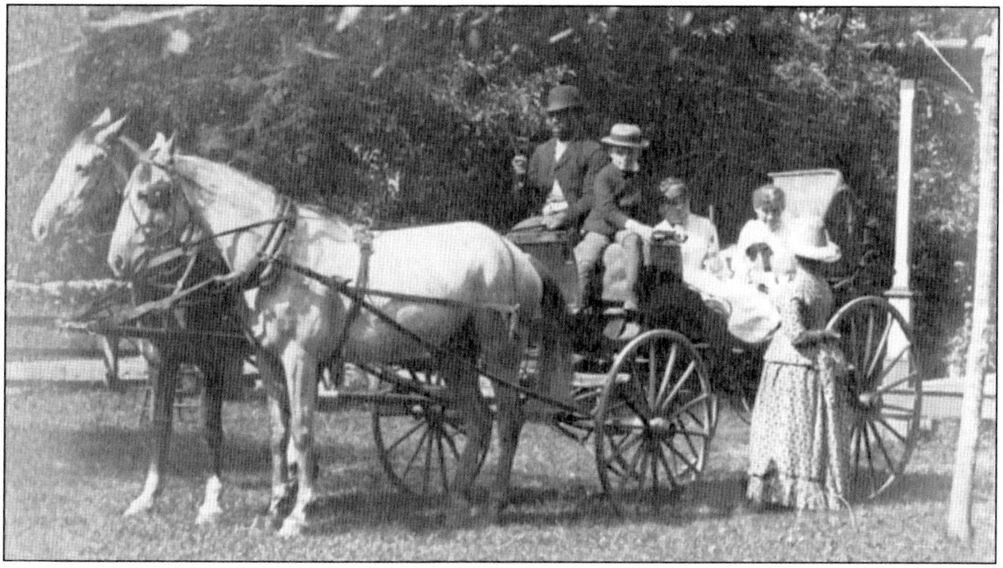

The description written on the back of the original of this 1885 photograph states that it shows a family (a mother and her three children) leaving a carriage at Mahopac hamlet to play a game of pins, probably referring to bowling. The family members were guests at Bailey Cottage, part of the Dean House Hotel, which provided the transportation. (The Town of Carmel Historical Society.)

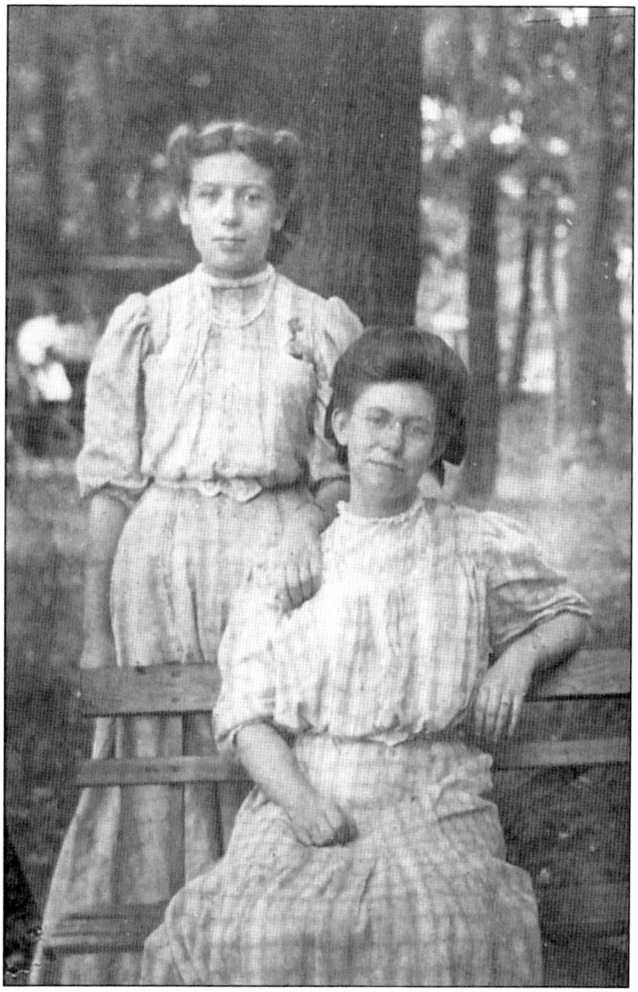

The young lady standing in this c. 1912 image is Minnie Elizabeth Shear. Her sister Freda M. Shear is seated. Both lived at their parents Locust Hill Farm, along Shear Hill Road. Minnie remained at the farm after marrying Howard Smith. She was a farm wife but also had a career as a professional organist and music teacher. Her music career began at the Union Valley Methodist Episcopal Chapel and the Lake Mahopac United Methodist Church. (Richard Smith.)

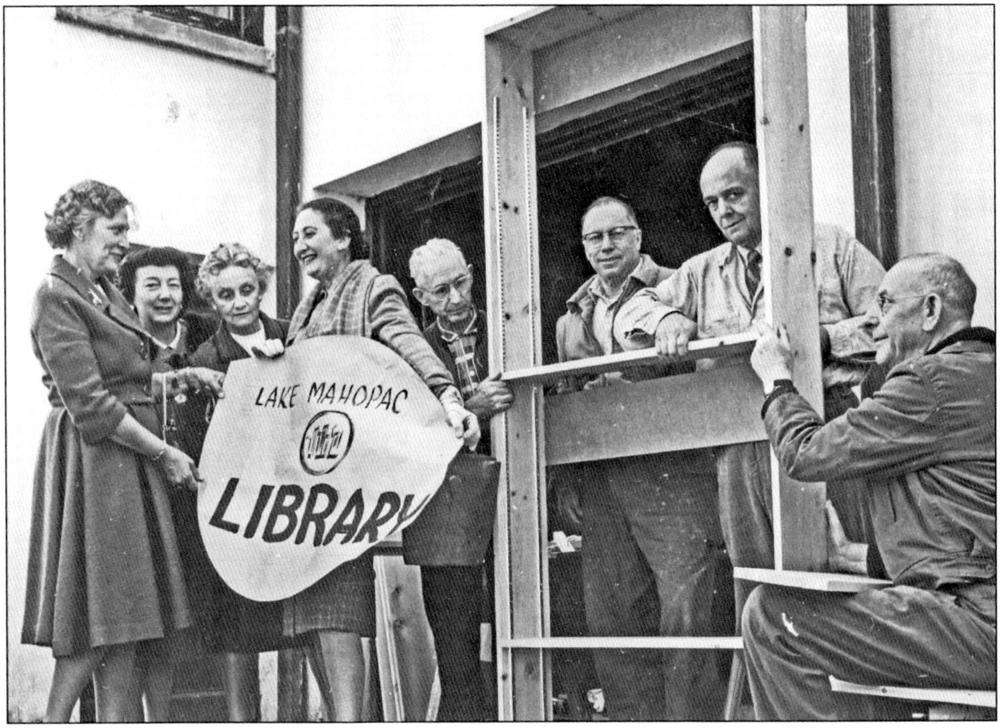

This photograph was taken on April 4, 1962, at the new Mahopac Public Library. Pictured are, from left to right, Ottille Truebe, Mrs. Walter Burghardt, Ruth Dain, Belle Levine, Thomas Roe, Louis Horowitz, Waldo Erickson, and Manny Schleinn. The women are looking over a library sign while the men examine a bookshelf being constructed for the library's use. (Putnam County Historian's Office.)

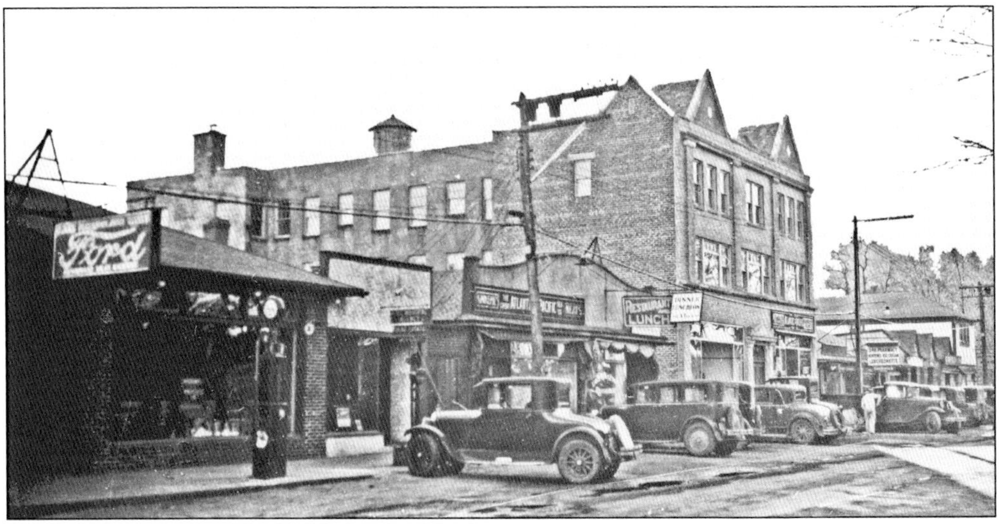

This image shows downtown Mahopac along South Lake Boulevard (Route 6N) around 1925. Raymond Hill's Garage and Ford dealership are on the left, while two Great Atlantic and Pacific (A&P) stores, separated by a restaurant, are to the right. All are part of a multistory brick building that was demolished in 1941 and subsequently rebuilt. The D&H Pharmacy, started by Edward Dwyer and Carl Hazard, is to the far right in a single-story structure. (Ted Dwyer.)

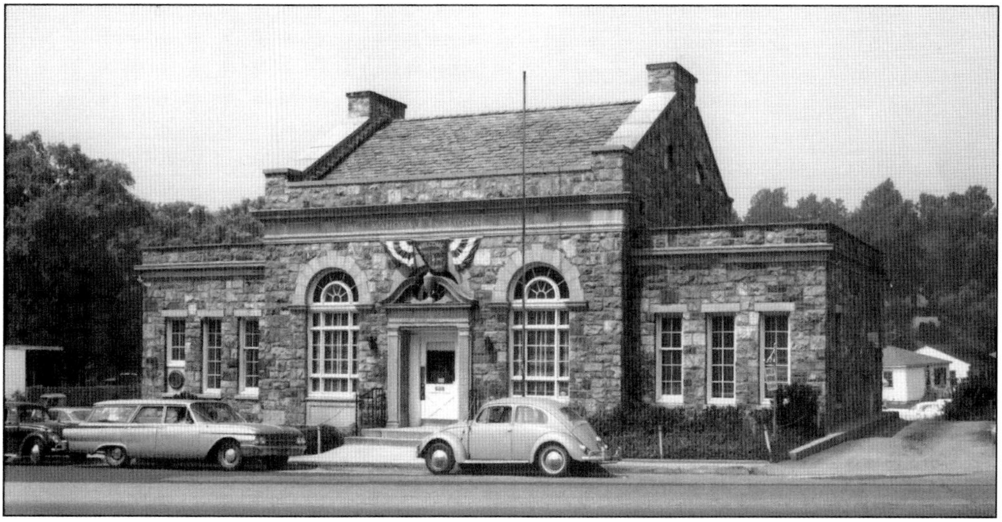

Mahopac National Bank opened in a small one-story building on South Lake Boulevard, just east of Cherry Lane in Mahopac in 1927 with $35,000 in resources. The original board of directors consisted of Edward S. Agor (president), William H. Spain, Willis H. Ryder, Emerson Clark, and William H. Agor. Clark and Spain served as later presidents. The bank proved to be a success. The current bank, a Mahopac landmark, shown in this photograph was constructed from 1929 to 1930 with $500,000 in resources. As with other banks, the Mahopac National Bank was permitted to issue its own currency printed by the US Printing Office and signed by the officers of the bank until the practice was outlawed by the federal government in 1934. (Mark Fraser.)

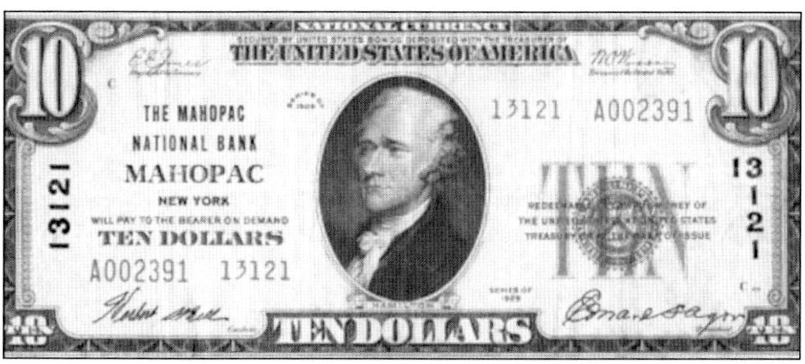

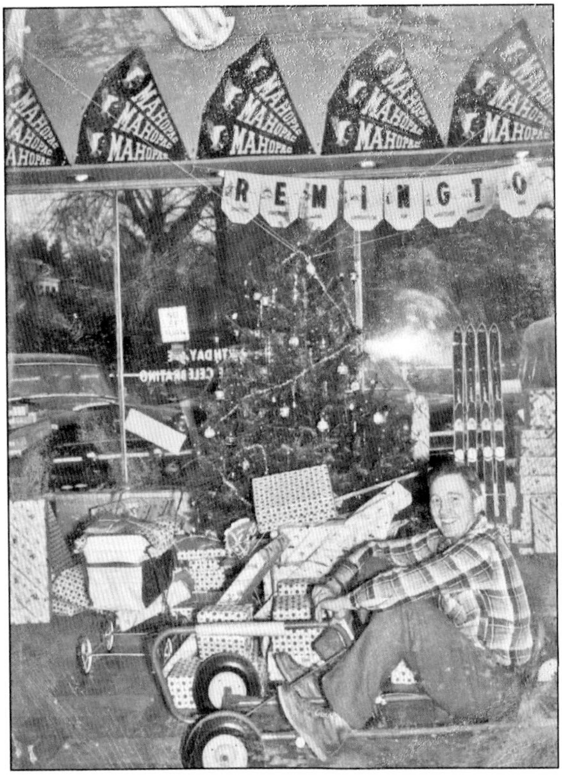

This 1957 image shows the owner of Tom Kat Sporting Goods Store DeLong "Bud" Kellogg during the Christmas season. Bud's first name, DeLong, derived from the patriarch of his family, Julius DeLong. Tom Kat was started by Kellogg and his brother-in-law Joseph MacFarlane in 1948 and was a Mahopac landmark for many years. The store relocated a number of times over the years. (Jeff Kellogg.)

This aerial image shows the intersection of Route 6 and Clark Place in the early 1950s. The Dain Supply Company is shown at the bottom of the photograph. The Brooklyn Coffee House is now located where the Mobile Gas Station is situated. Note the railroad tracks crossing Route 6. (The Town of Carmel Historical Society.)

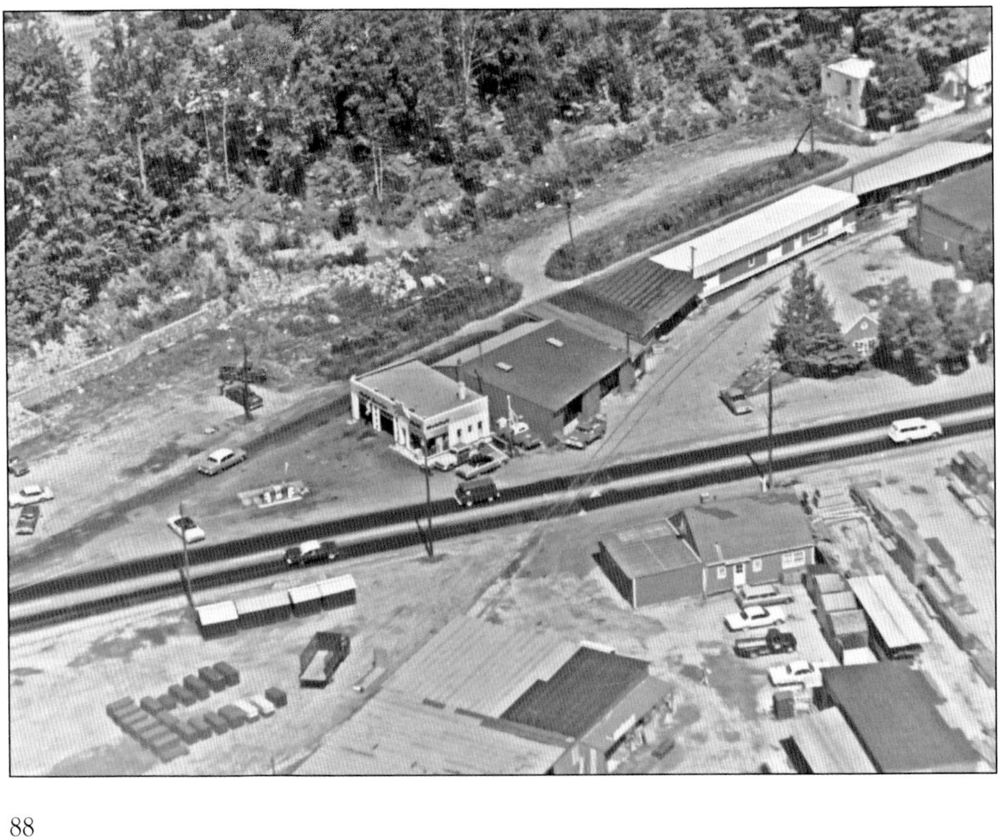

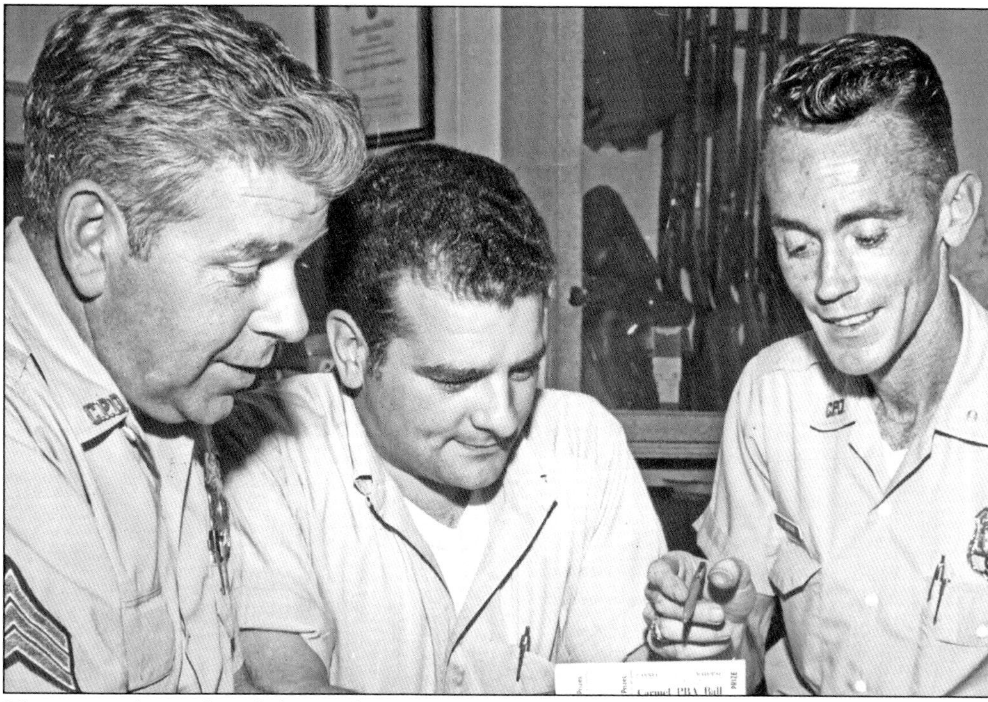

This image shows, from left to right, Sgt. Charles Leonard, patrolmen Greg Amato, and Alfred Iasoni (the Police Benevolent Association president, vice president, and secretary) discussing the upcoming October 1968 PBA Ball to be held at the Putnam Country Club. Tickets were $7.50 per couple and there were light refreshments and a band. The yearly ball was a major social event and always had a full house. (Putnam County Historian's Office.)

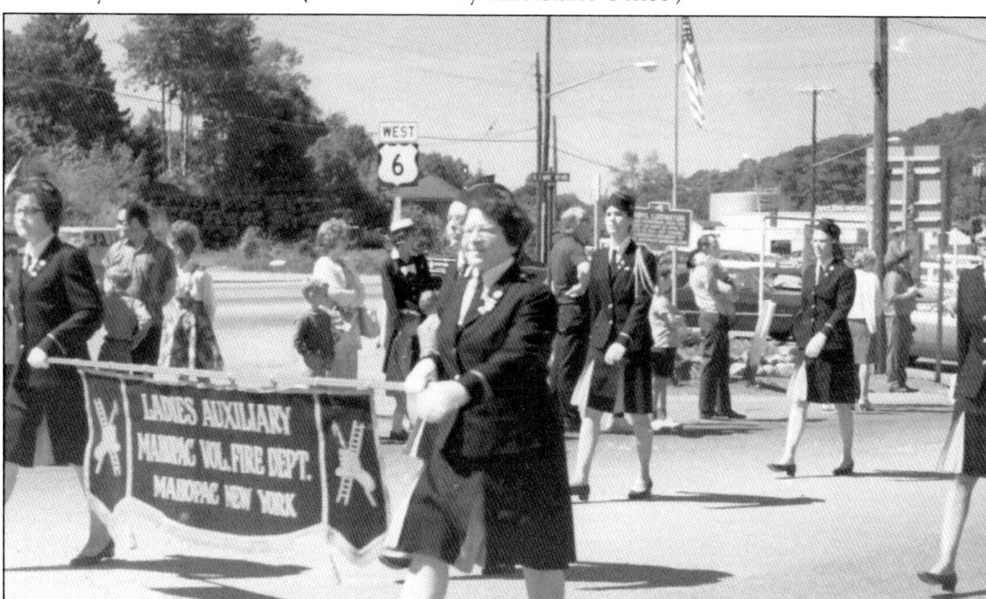

Ladies auxiliary members marching in the Mahopac Volunteer Fire Department parade in 1970 are nearing the intersection of Routes 6N and 6. In the foreground is May Amato, the ladies auxiliary president, holding the organization banner. (Laura Amato.)

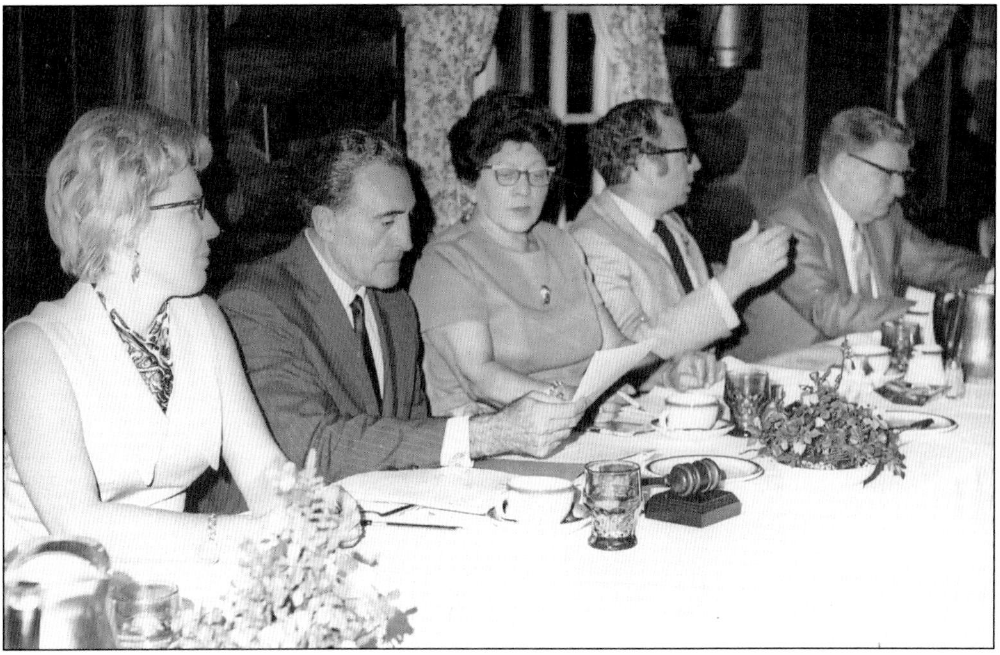

The people shown are members of the board of the Chamber of Commerce of the Mahopacs, Inc., in session in November 1972. A main topic is the planning of the Christmas street lighting project. It was the first major Christmas lighting project carried out by the community. Pictured are, from left to right, Regina Morini, George Bergamini, May Amato, Jack Nussbaum, and David Dampman. (Laura Amato.)

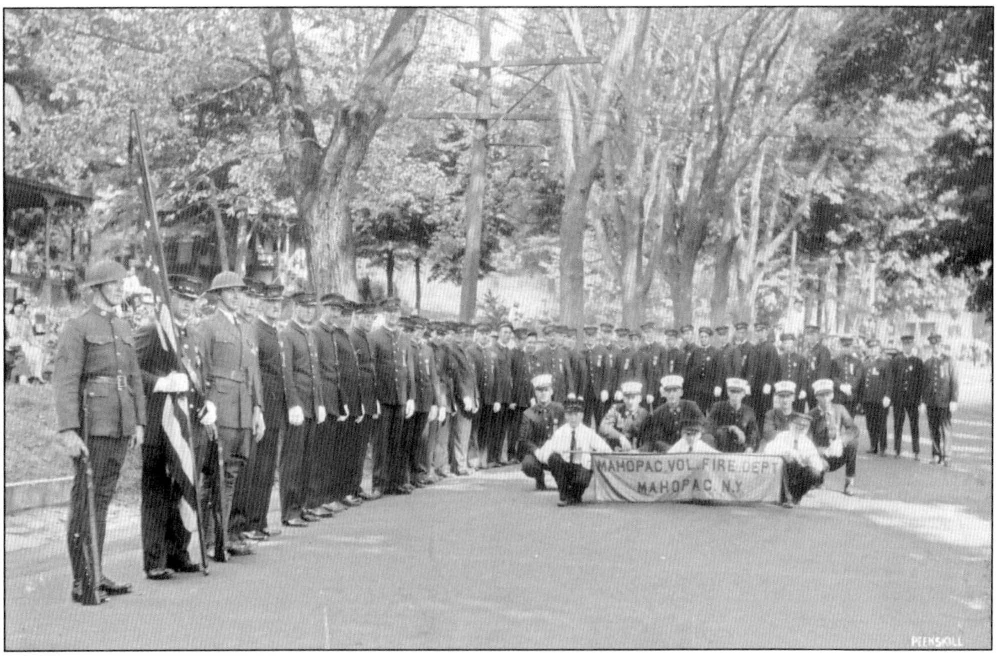

This image shows 52 Mahopac firemen at attention in the Peekskill Anniversary Parade in August 1930. They won the award for best appearance in the parade. (Mahopac Volunteer Fire Department.)

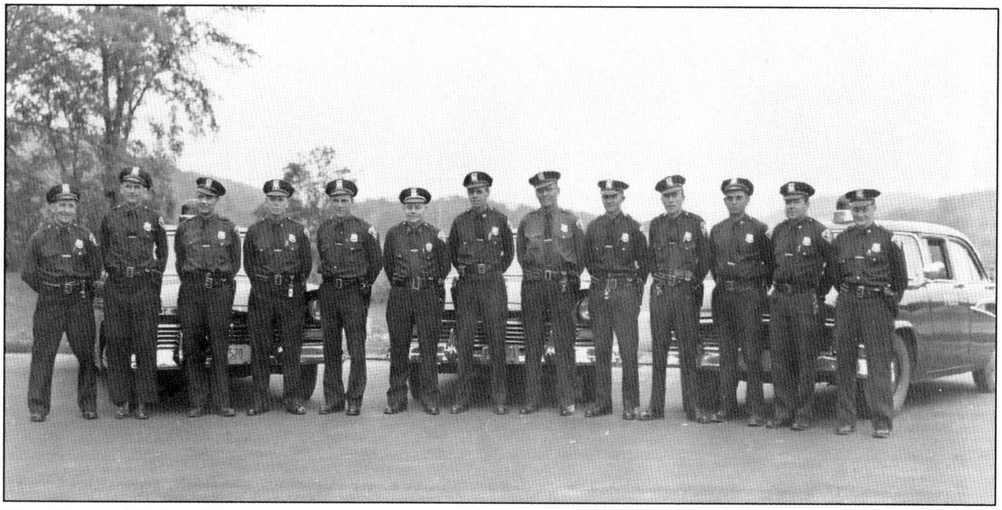

The Carmel Police Department was organized in 1940. Prior to its organization, patrolmen were known as constables. This c. 1956 photograph shows the department's officers as of that year. Pictured are, from left to right, Adelbert "Snooky" Adams, Morgan Seymour, Louis Butironi, Louie Ward, unidentified, Frank Bailey, Howard Hartwell, Louis Wright, Wesley Belfi, John Sanders, Stanley Hart, unidentified, and Herbert "Chipper" Adams. (The Town of Carmel Historical Society.)

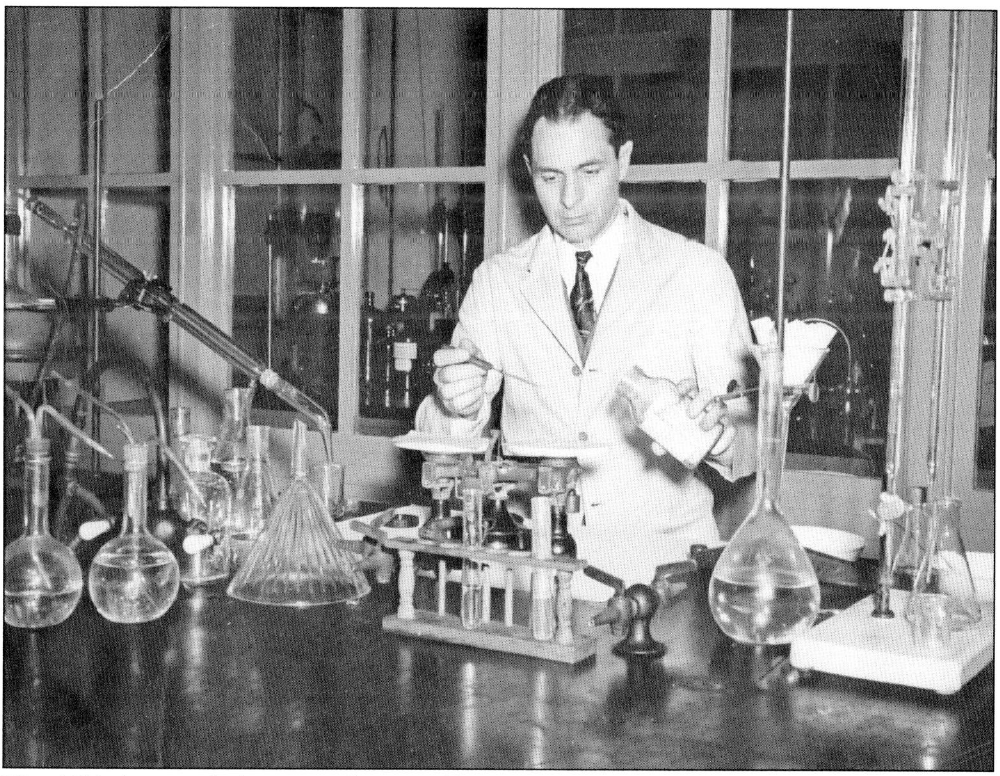

This 1954 photograph shows patrolman Wallace C. Barrett, the first Putnam County police officer to attend the FBI training academy. Barrett later became Carmel police chief around 1948–1953 and Carmel town justice in 1965 for one term. (Ellen Barrett Lupinacci.)

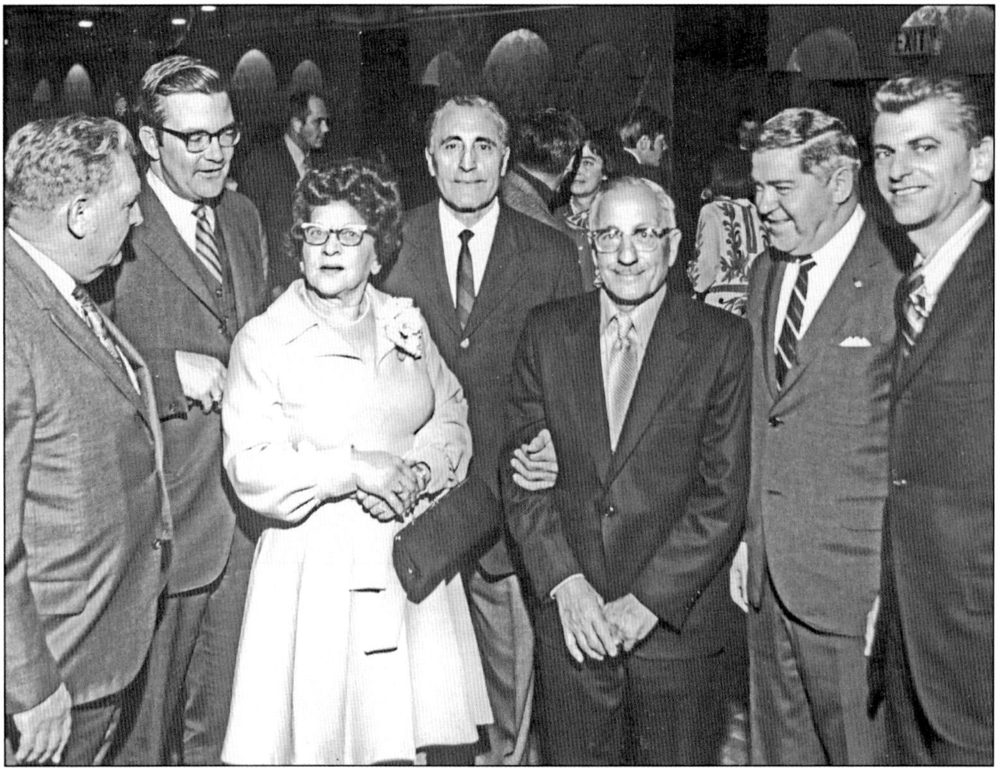

The event shown is the Mahopac Chamber of Commerce annual dance held at Lombardi's Restaurant on Route 6 on November 26, 1970. Pictured are, from left to right, David Dampman, Joseph Costello, May Amato, George Bergamini, Tom Camarco, Al Foshay, and Lionel Schwartz. (Putnam County Historian's Office.)

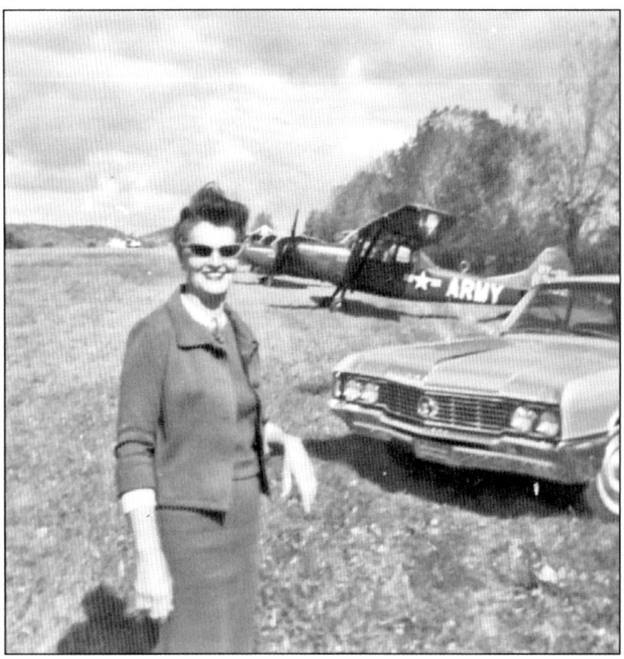

This image shows Ruth Crane Agor at the Mahopac Airport on the Agor Farm off Hill Street around 1964. The aircraft behind her is a US Army Cessna L-19/O-1 Bird Dog Observation Aircraft. The airport contained a 1,800-foot-long grass landing strip. Its appearance did not change much over the years. The airport closed around 2001. It served small private, commercial, and military planes but only during daylight hours. Dusk landings sometimes required the single runway to be illuminated with small lights. The former airport is now a soccer field. (John Agor.)

Nine

The Railroad

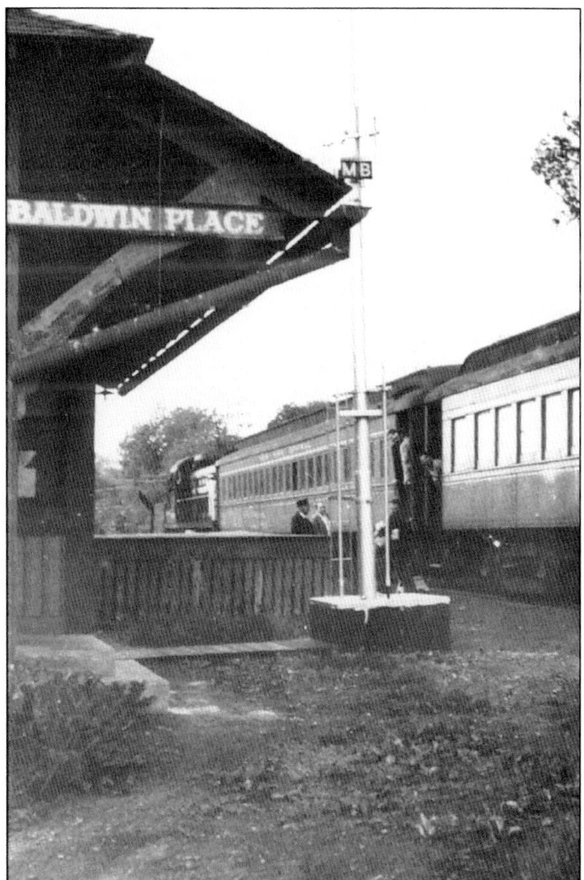

This popular photograph was taken at the Baldwin Place Station on the last day of regular passenger service on the Putnam Division on May 29, 1958. Farewell messages to "The Old Put" can be faintly seen written on the side of the first coach. (The Town of Carmel Historical Society.)

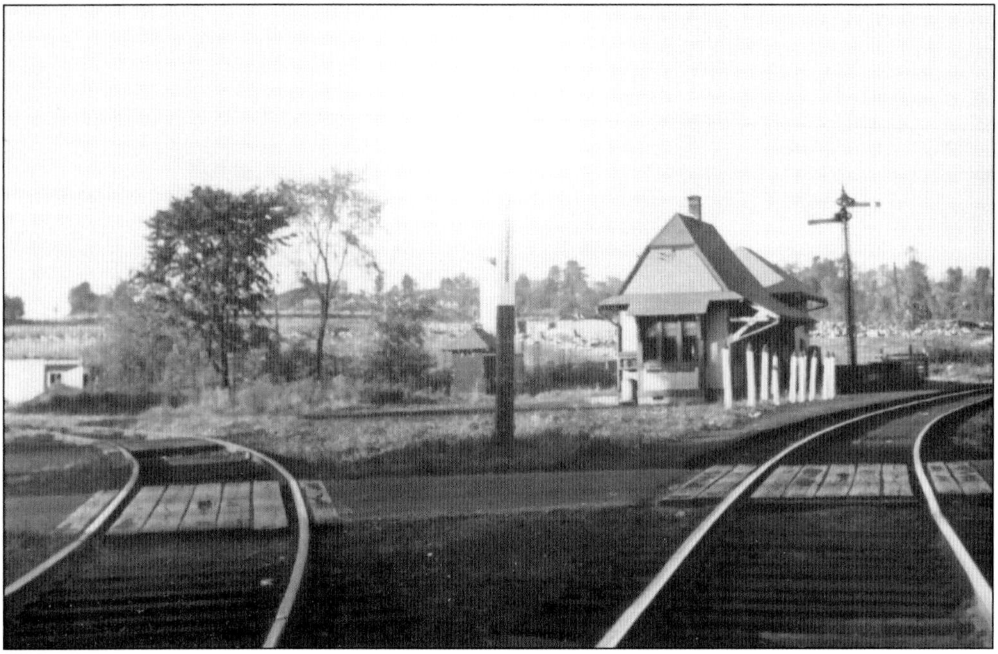

Just over the county line from Westchester into Putnam County was the Baldwin Place Station of New York Central's Putnam Division Railroad. The station, shown at right, sits on the main line of The Old Put, as it was commonly referred to. Originally constructed as the New York City and Northern Railroad in 1880, it was taken over by the "Central" in 1894. The track to the left is the four-mile Mahopac Falls Railroad. (The Town of Carmel Historical Society.)

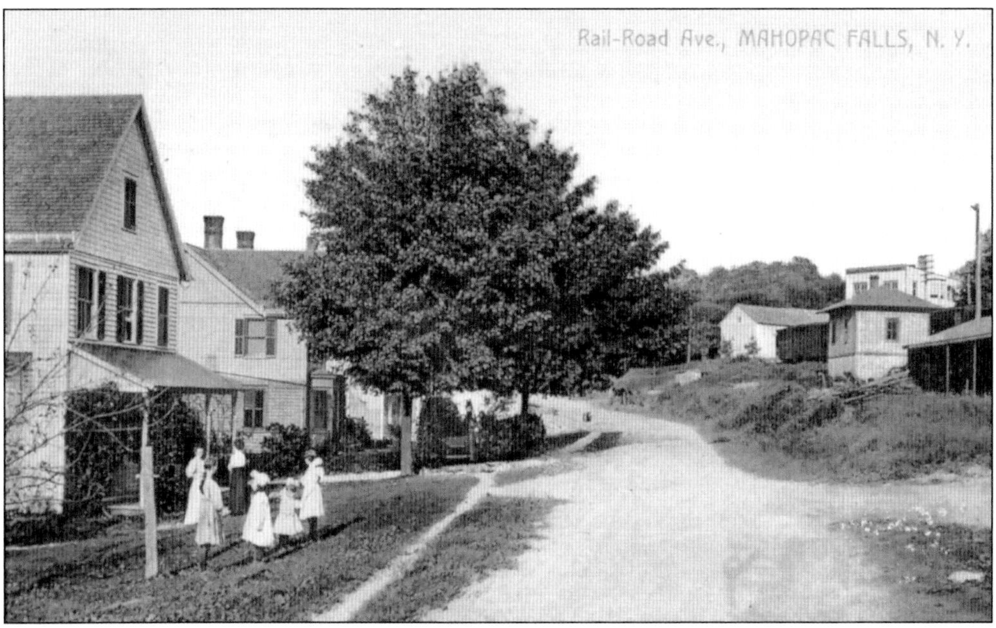

This postcard scene is of Railroad Avenue (present-day Potter Road) looking north toward the intersection with Myrtle Avenue in Mahopac Falls. The Mahopac Falls Station and freight shed can be seen on the bluff at right. Part of a boxcar is visible by the station. (Greg Amato.)

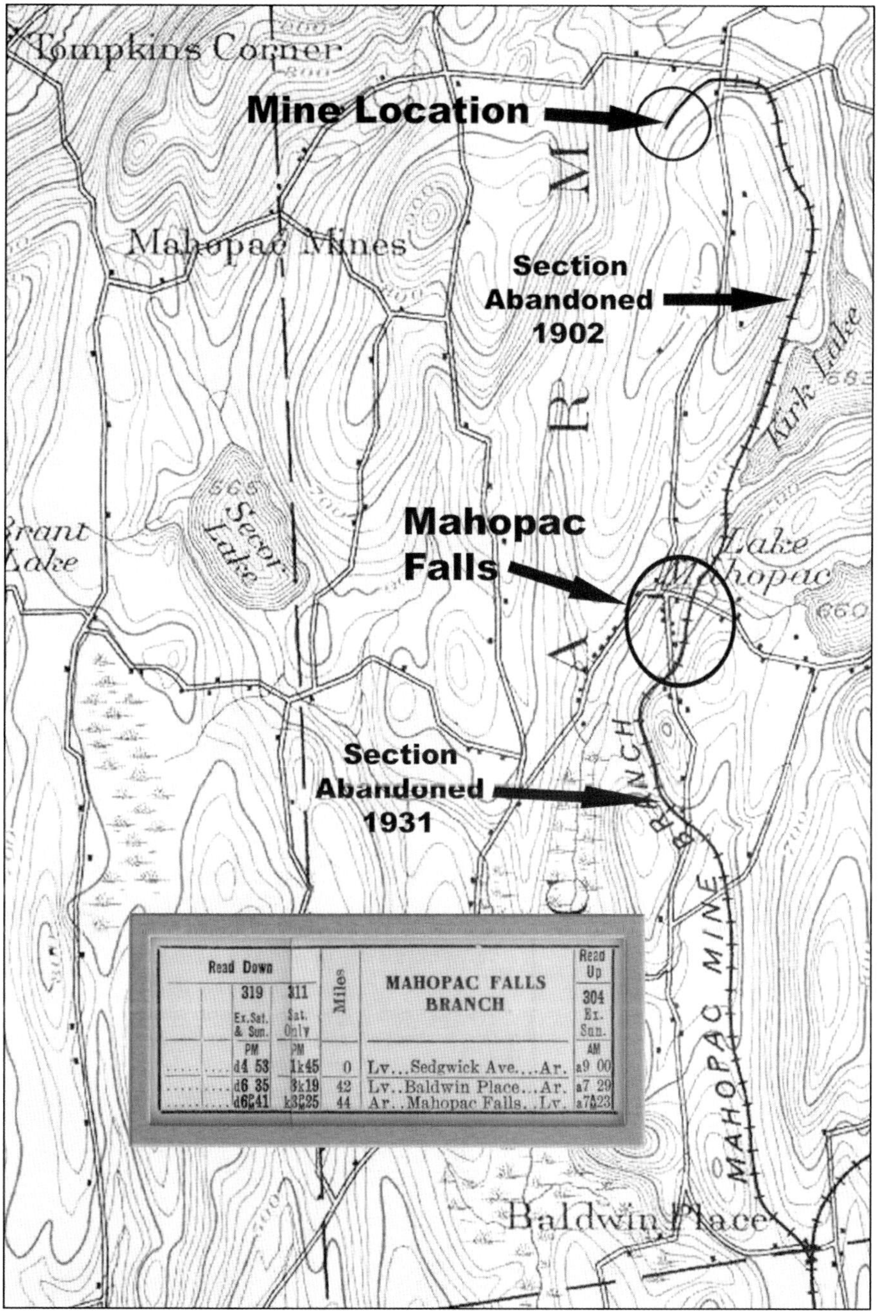

Read Down				Miles	MAHOPAC FALLS BRANCH	Read Up
		319 Ex.Sat. & Sun.	311 Sat. Only			304 Ex. Sun.
		PM	PM			AM
.....	....	d4 53	1k45	0	Lv...Sedgwick Ave....Ar.	a9 00
.....	....	d6 35	3k19	42	Lv..Baldwin Place...Ar.	a7 29
.....	....	d6 41	k3 25	44	Ar..Mahopac Falls..Lv.	a7 23

The Mahopac Falls Railroad was constructed in 1884, connecting Baldwin Place to Mahopac Mines, a distance of 4.05 miles. It was used primarily to transport iron ore from the mine. There were passenger stations at Mahopac Falls and Mahopac Mines as well as a turntable just east of the mine. Apples, milk, and other farm products also were moved out by rail while coal was brought in. A cave-in occurred at the mine in 1891. The community around the mine dwindled after the collapse, resulting in the last two miles of the line being abandoned in 1902. Service to Mahopac Falls continued until 1931. The base map is part of the US Geological Survey 1892. Also shown is part of the Mahopac Falls Branch timetable of September 30, 1928. (Brian Vangor.)

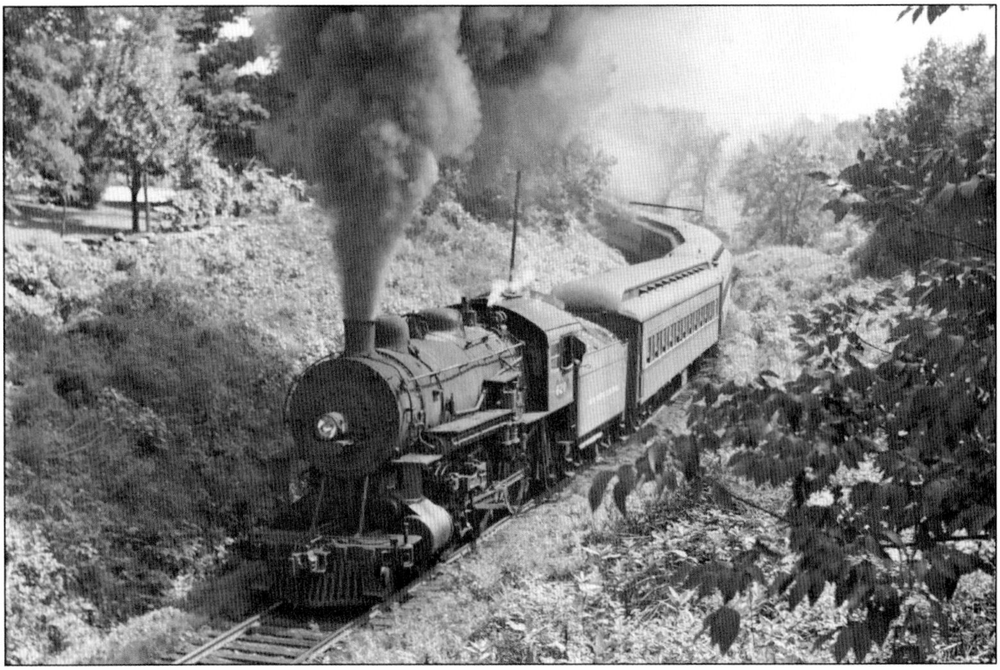

The Mahopac Branch of the Harlem Division Railroad was a 7.22-mile line, which connected Goldens Bridge to Mahopac. Also called the Goldens Bridge Branch, it was placed in service on July 4, 1871, and originally provided a way for New York City passengers to reach the summer resorts situated on Lake Mahopac. Here, 10-wheeler No. 820 pulls its string of passenger coaches along the uphill grade just prior to passing under Union Valley Road. (The Town of Carmel Historical Society.)

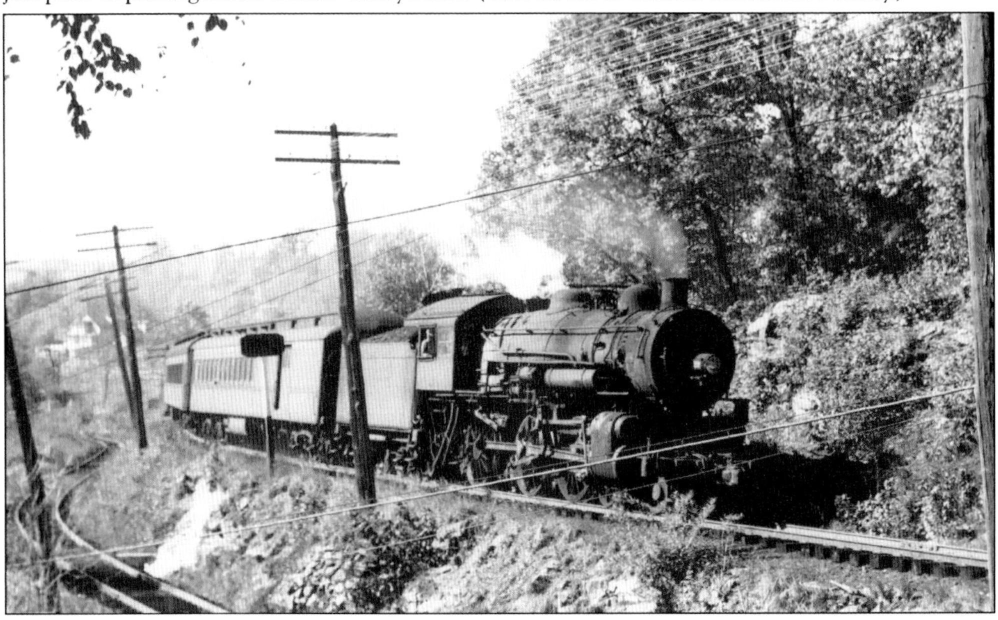

Here, a 10-wheeler on the main line of the Putnam Division rolls toward Mahopac. The track below is the branch from Goldens Bridge, slowly rising to the elevation of the Put. The scene is on Buckshollow Road, just west of the merger of the two lines at Harlem Crossing (officially, crossing "XC" in New York Central terminology). (The Town of Carmel Historical Society.)

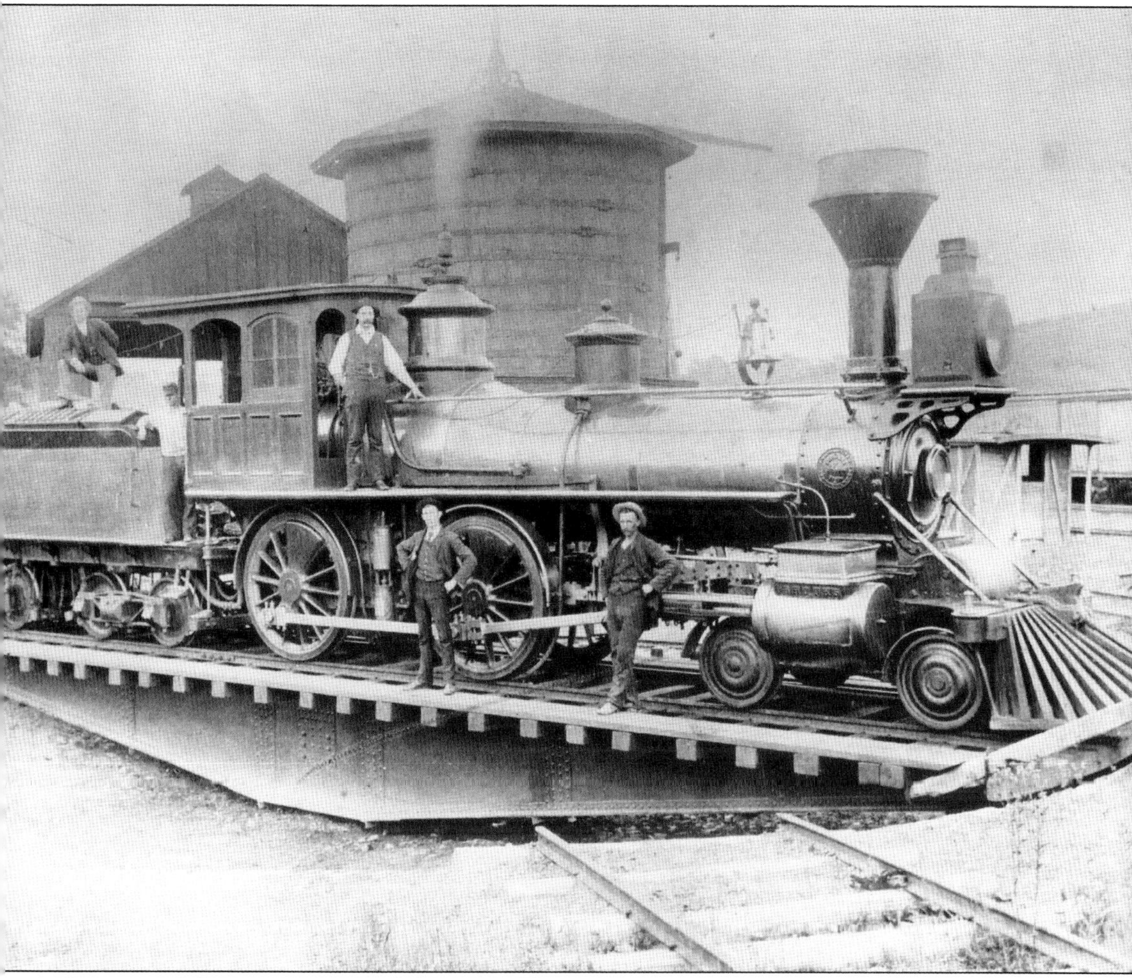

This turn-of-the-century view of the turntable in Brewster shows a Brooks 4-4-0–type steam locomotive preparing for its trip south through Mahopac to New York City. The turntable served many functions. (The Town of Carmel Historical Society.)

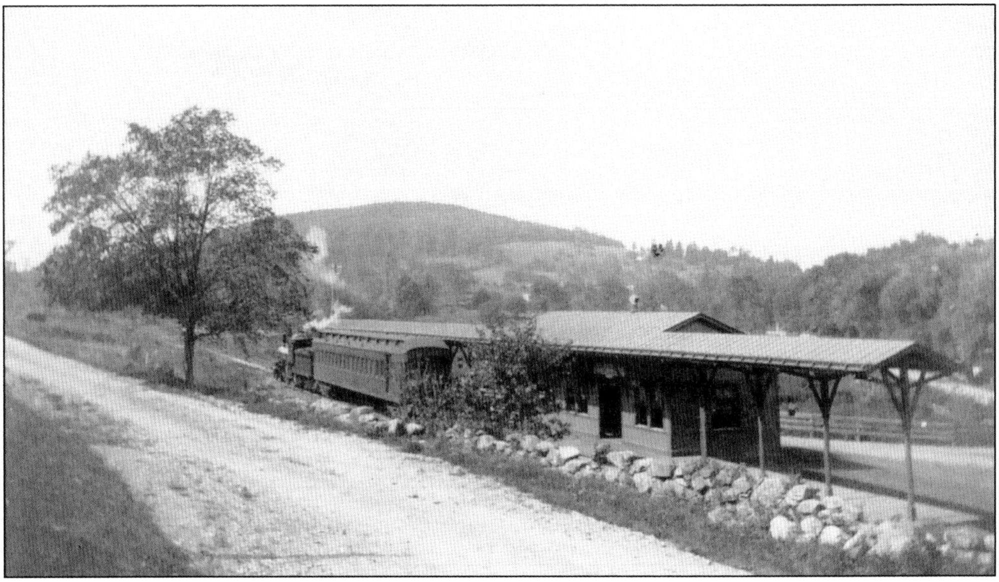

These photographs show similar scenes approximately 15 years apart. The above photograph dates to 1891 and shows the New York Central Railroad's Goldens Bridge Branch Depot at Mahopac. The railroad was extended to Mahopac in 1871 with this first station constructed in 1880. The rail line terminated at the depot. The station was located at the intersection of Thompson's Run and Buckshollow Road near what are now the Spain Agency Building and the Sunoco Gas Station. The road to the right is now Route 6N. The bottom image dates to 1914 and shows the area slightly to the east of the above image and what is now the Routes 6 and 6N intersection. Route 6 had not yet been constructed. The station was moved closer to Buckshollow Road around 1934 due to construction of Route 6. (Both, the Putnam County Historian's Office.)

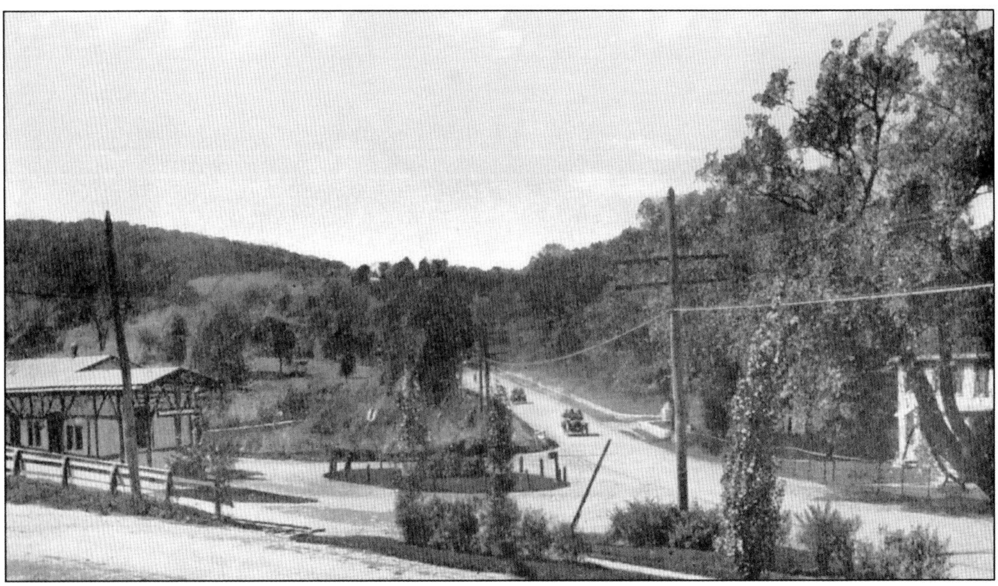

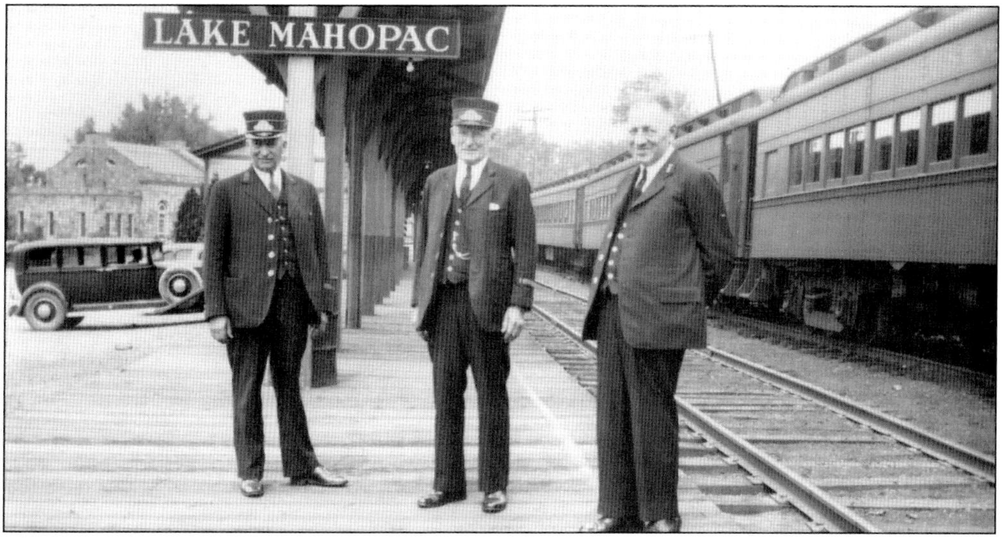

The view shows the Harlem Division's Goldens Bridge depot. Three conductors pose for the photographer. The Mahopac National Bank building can be seen behind the 1930 Packard sedan. (The Putnam County Historian's Office.)

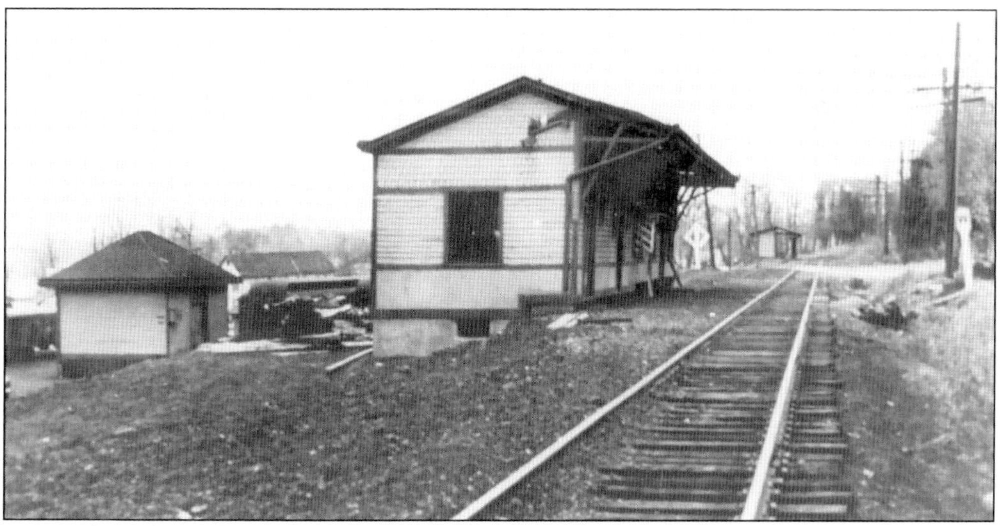

Here is the Lake Mahopac Station on the Putnam Division main line. The freight house below and to the left was on the stub end of the Harlem Division's Goldens Bridge Branch. What is now Buckshollow Road crosses the tracks to the middle right of the image. The Mahopac Hotel can be seen in the distance, straight down the track. This station (now the American Legion Hall) and the freight house (now the Freight House Café) still stand today. (Denis Castelli.)

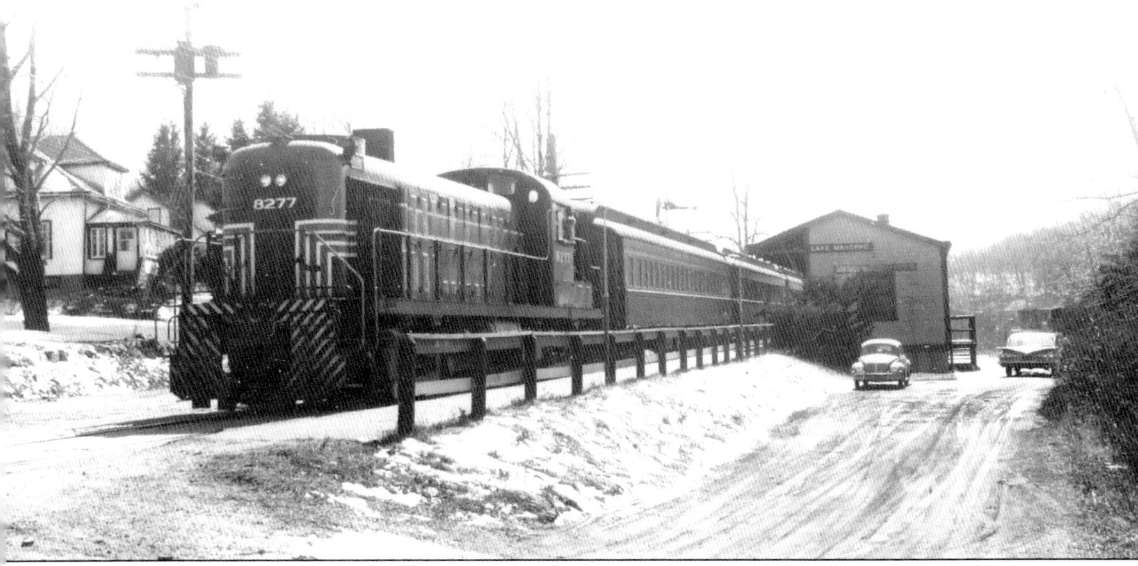

A New York Central RS3 diesel locomotive is stopped at the Lake Mahopac Station in February 1959. This is a Harlem Division train that has crossed over to the main line of the Putnam Division on its way to Brewster. Passenger service had ended on the Put the previous May. This service from Goldens Bridge would end in April. After another decade of local freight service in Mahopac, the final rails were removed in 1969. (The Town of Carmel Historical Society.)

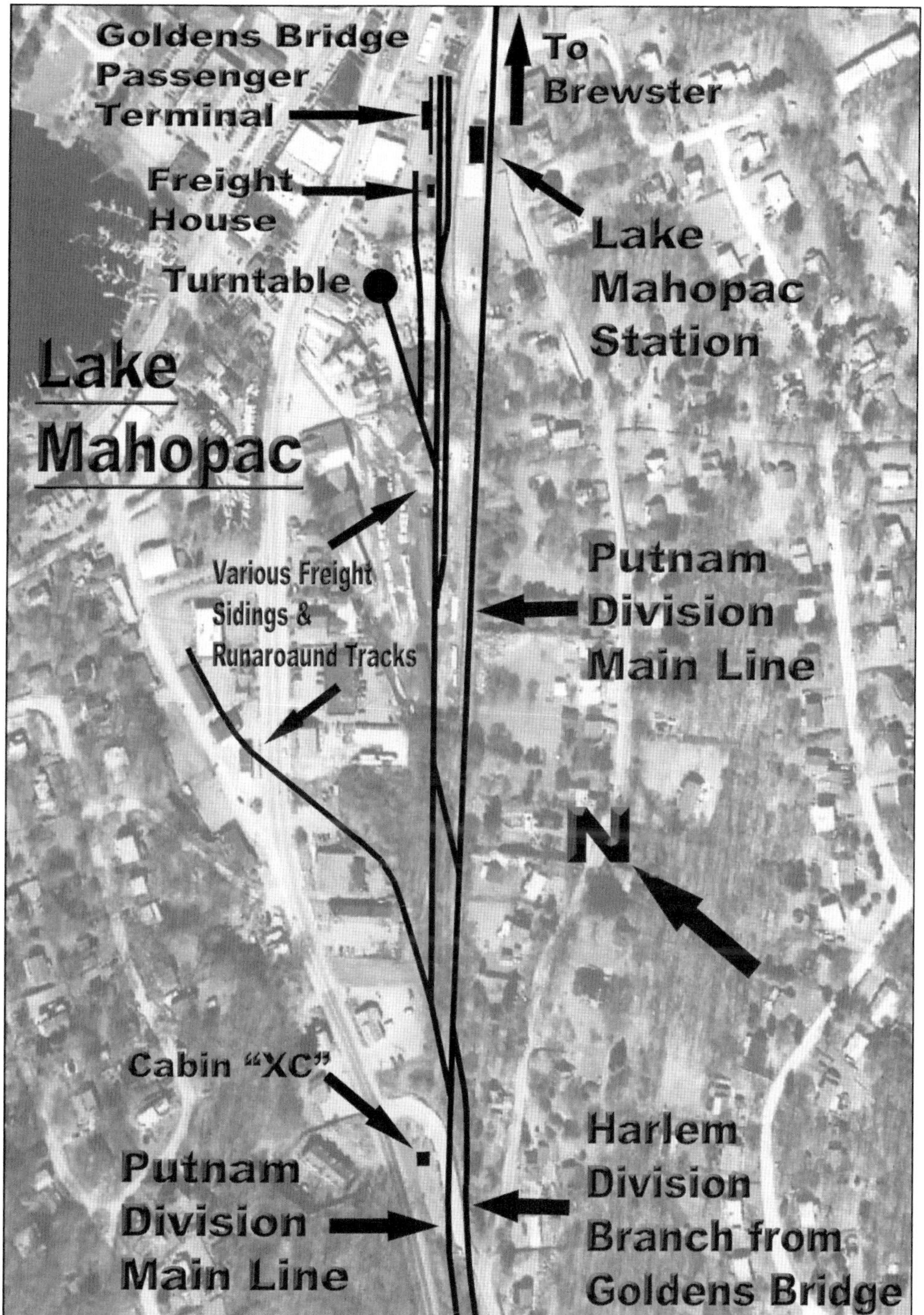

The track configuration in Mahopac was complex and underwent many changes, especially after 1940. This map is representative of several decades. The Putnam Division and Harlem Division met at Harlem Crossing (officially, crossing "XC"). Here, a man stationed in tiny Cabin "XC" operated the switches. The Put continued to its Lake Mahopac Station and on to Brewster. The Harlem branch terminated at its depot just north and below the level of the Put. (Brian Vangor.)

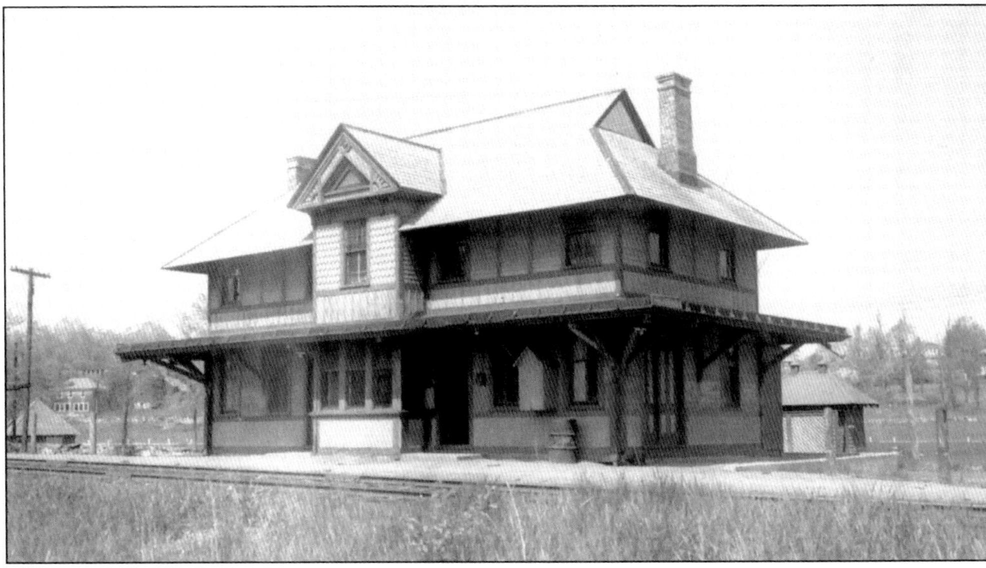

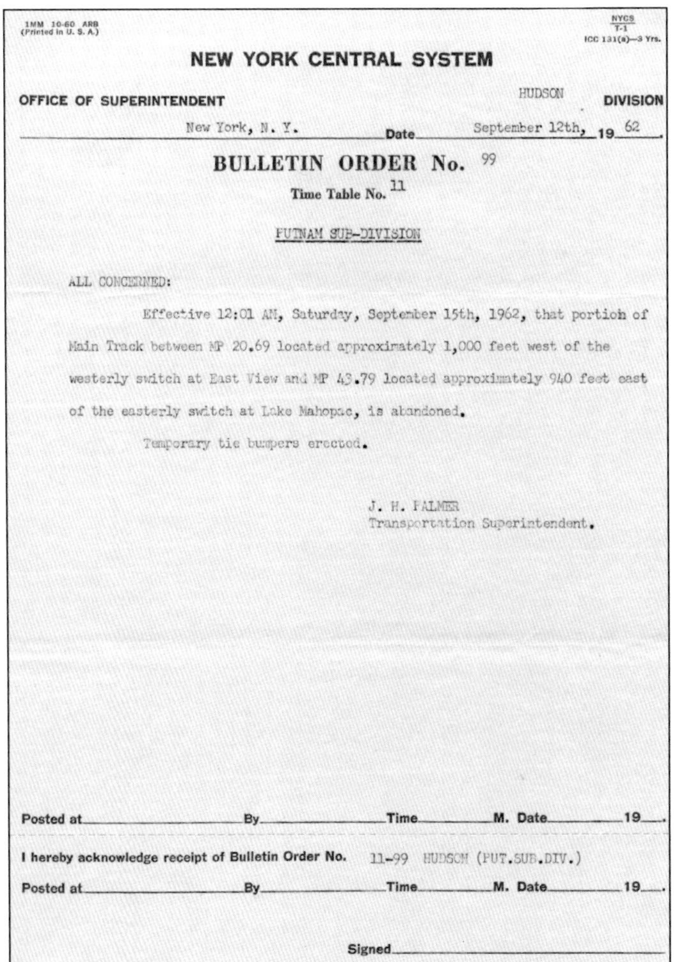

1MM 10-60 ARB
(Printed in U. S. A.)

NYCS
T-1
ICC 131(a)—3 Yrs.

NEW YORK CENTRAL SYSTEM

OFFICE OF SUPERINTENDENT HUDSON **DIVISION**

New York, N. Y. **Date** September 12th, **19** 62.

BULLETIN ORDER No. 99

Time Table No. 11

PUTNAM SUB-DIVISION

ALL CONCERNED:

Effective 12:01 AM, Saturday, September 15th, 1962, that portion of Main Track between MP 20.69 located approximately 1,000 feet west of the westerly switch at East View and MP 43.79 located approximately 940 feet east of the easterly switch at Lake Mahopac, is abandoned.

Temporary tie bumpers erected.

J. H. PALMER
Transportation Superintendent.

Posted at______ **By**______ **Time**______ **M. Date**______ **19**___.

I hereby acknowledge receipt of Bulletin Order No. 11-99 HUDSON (PUT.SUB.DIV.)

Posted at______ **By**______ **Time**______ **M. Date**______ **19**___.

Signed______

The image shows the Mahopac Station of the Putnam Division Railroad as it appeared around 1920. Built by the New York and Northern Railroad in the 1880s, it was the largest station in the area. Its approximate location was across Croton Falls Road from today's Carmel Town Hall. In the early 20th century, the Mahopac Fire Department rented rooms on the second floor as its first headquarters. (Greg Amato.)

This New York Central abandonment notice cut the middle out of the Putnam Division, leaving two truncated ends of the railroad. Afterward, trains could only reach Mahopac from Put Junction in Brewster. In 1969, the line was farther cut back to Carmel, ending almost 100 years of rail service in Mahopac. (The Town of Carmel Historical Society.)

Ten

The Land and its Residents

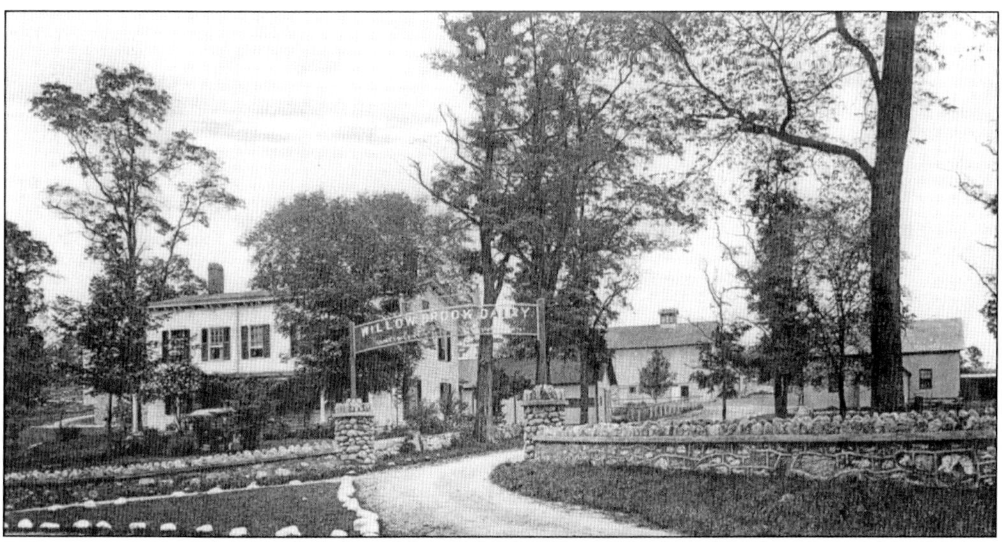

The Willow Brook Dairy Farm was located at Route 6 and Baldwin Road. It was a large operation supplying dairy products region wide. This photograph shows the farm as it appeared around 1914. The Borden Milk Company acquired the farm in 1930. It later became Mahopac Farms. The early-19th-century house is gone, but the barn, outbuildings, and stone pillars seen in the photograph remain. (The Town of Carmel Historical Society.)

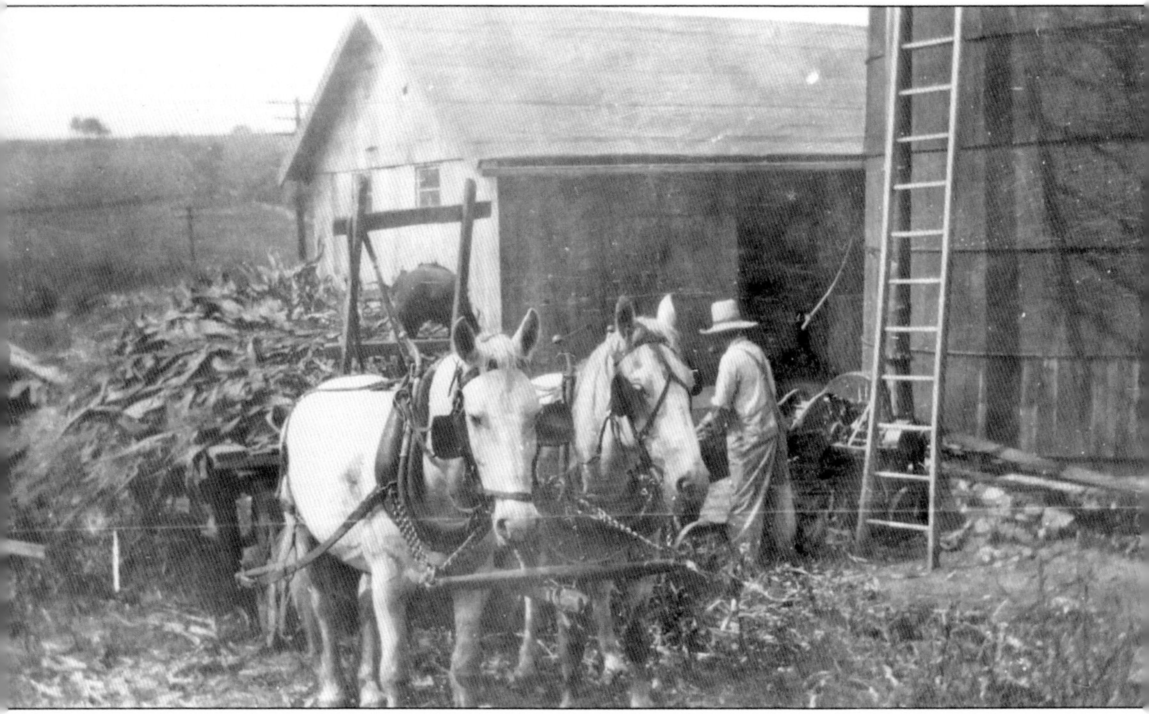

This c. 1920 image shows Howard Smith unloading corn from a wagon to a hired hand for storage in the nearby silo. Smith farmed Locust Hill Farm located along Shear Hill Road. Howard Smith and his wife, Minnie Shear Smith, owned the farm. Minnie took in boarders at their early-19th-century farmhouse, which still exists. Visitors from New York City would travel to the area by railroad to spend time on the farm. The farm was a working farm with about 21 milk cows. Milk was placed on a road platform along Shear Hill Road for collection and sent to the Van Cortland Dairies where it was sold as Grade A milk. (Richard Smith.)

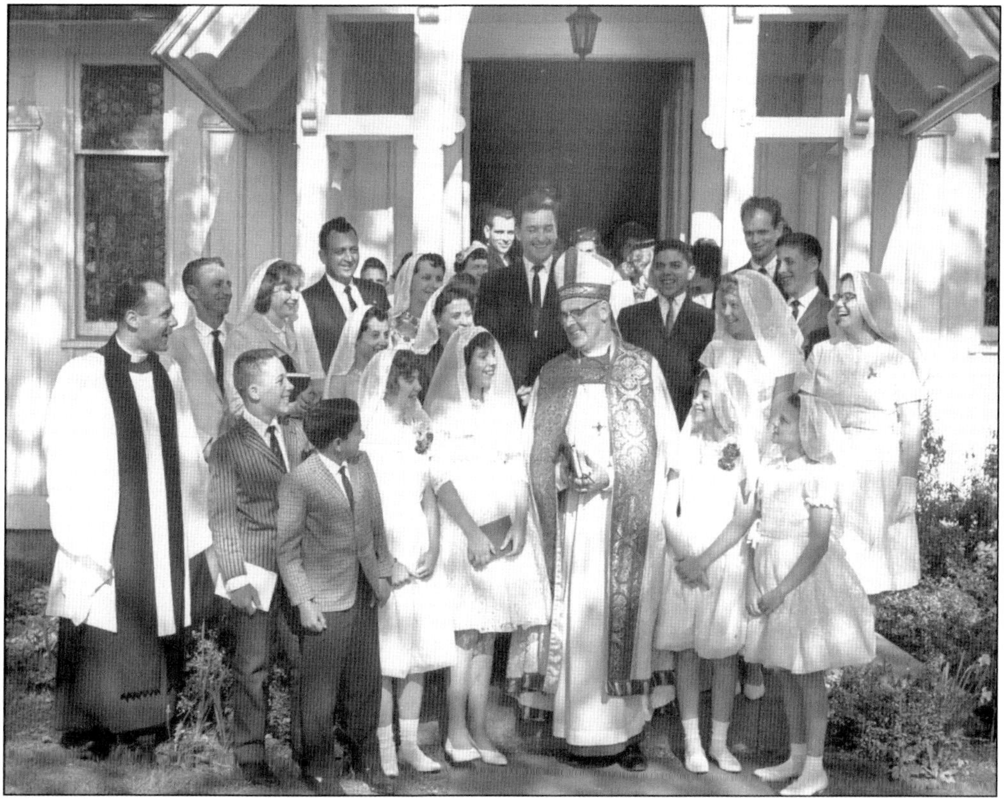

This image shows smiling children and adults after the Confirmation service held at the Church of the Holy Communion on May 16, 1963. At the time, the church was located on East Lake Boulevard. (Putnam County Historian's Office.)

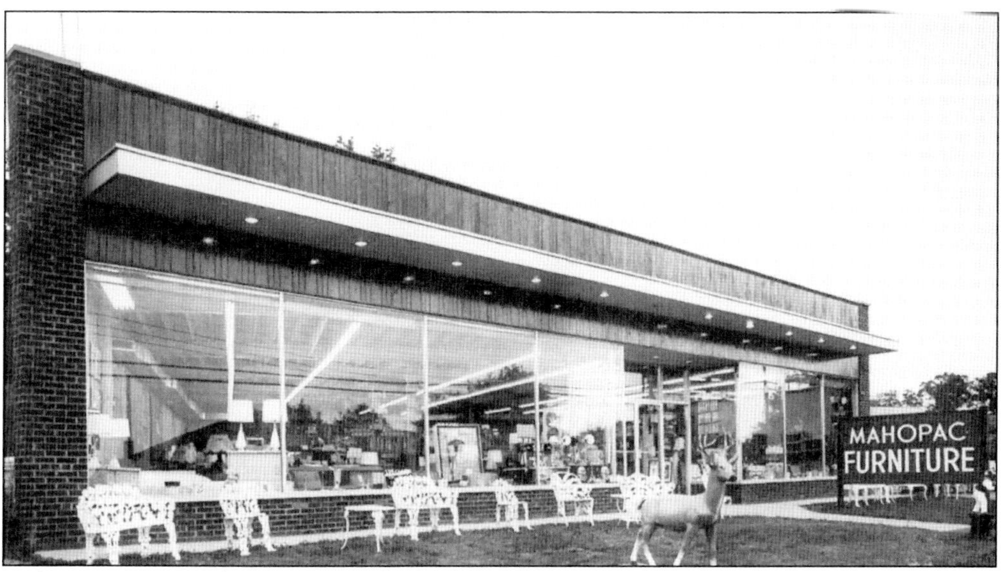

Mahopac Furniture Shop was located along Route 6. The photograph was taken on June 15, 1956, a few months after the store opened. (Terry Gusmano Gandolfo.)

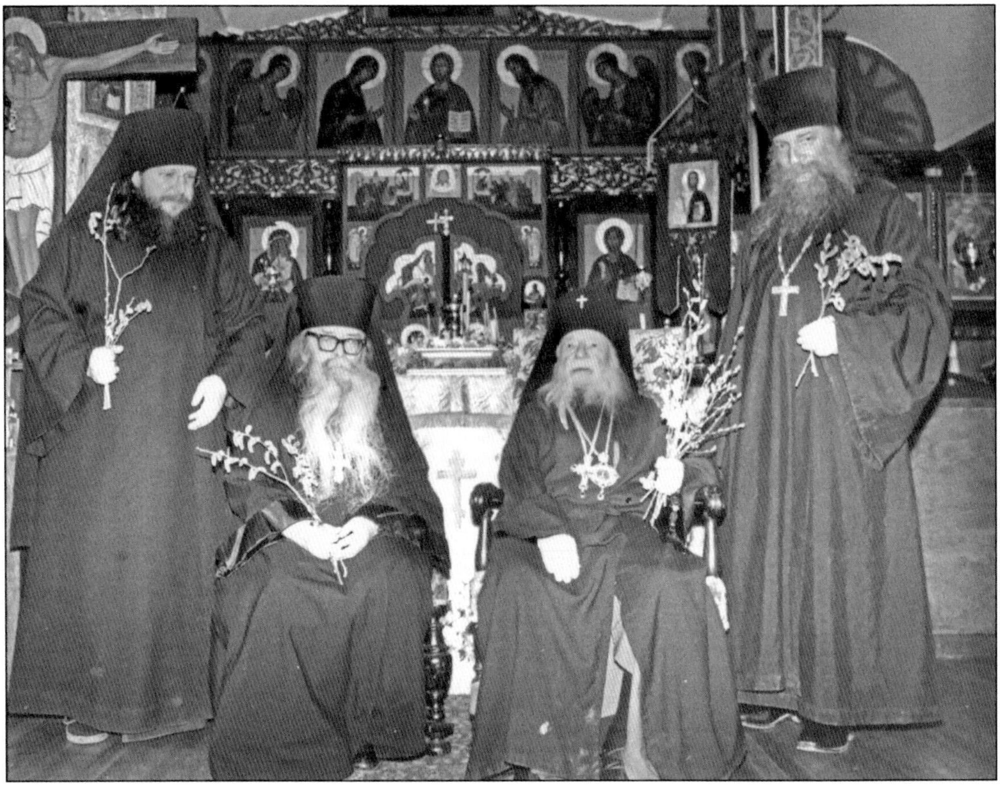

Our Lady of Kursk Russian Orthodox Church was established in 1950 when Prince Sergei Sergeyevich Beloselsky-Belozersky, in anticipation of the arrival from Europe of the Kursk-Root Icon of the Mother of God, purchased Amy Cole's Hidden House restaurant in Mahopac for the church. The church still exists along Route 6. This April 16, 1987, view of the altar shows, from left to right, Monk Gariel, Archimandrite Theophan, Archbishop Seraphim, and Arch Priest Konstantin. (Putnam County Historian's Office.)

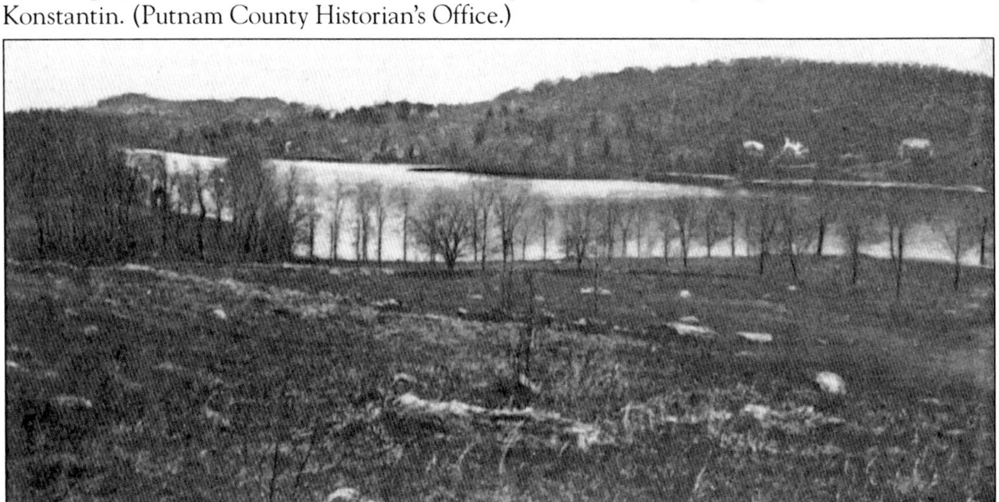

This view, taken around 1920, looks across Lake Mahopac to South Lake Boulevard from the Bungalow Colony. The colony was later renamed Mahopac Hills to make it more respectable. (Mark Fraser.)

The young lady in the Red Cross uniform is Dorothy Rowley Brady. She is standing on the front steps of the DeLong residence (later the Westcott home) on July 4 around 1920. The house was located where St. John the Evangelist Church now stands. (Susan Brady Mauldin.)

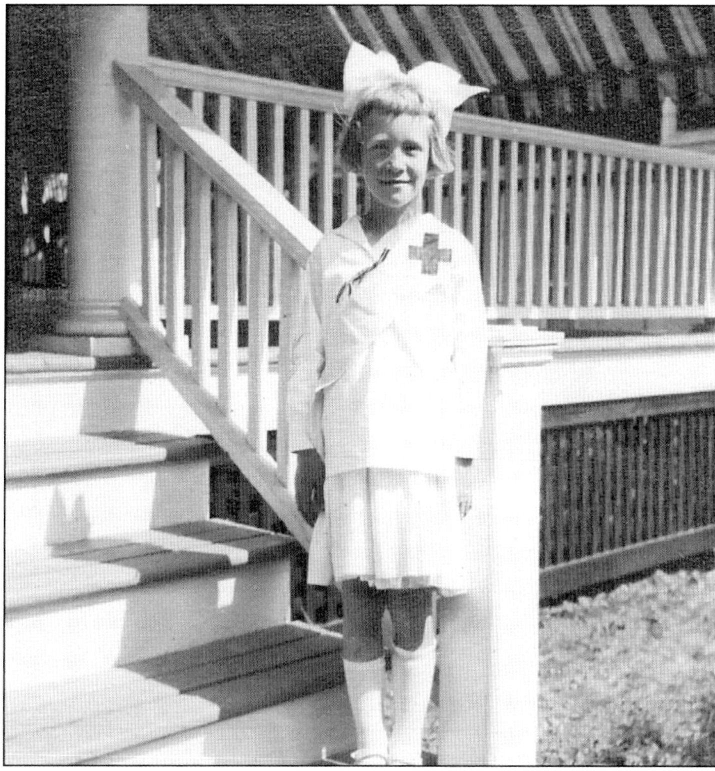

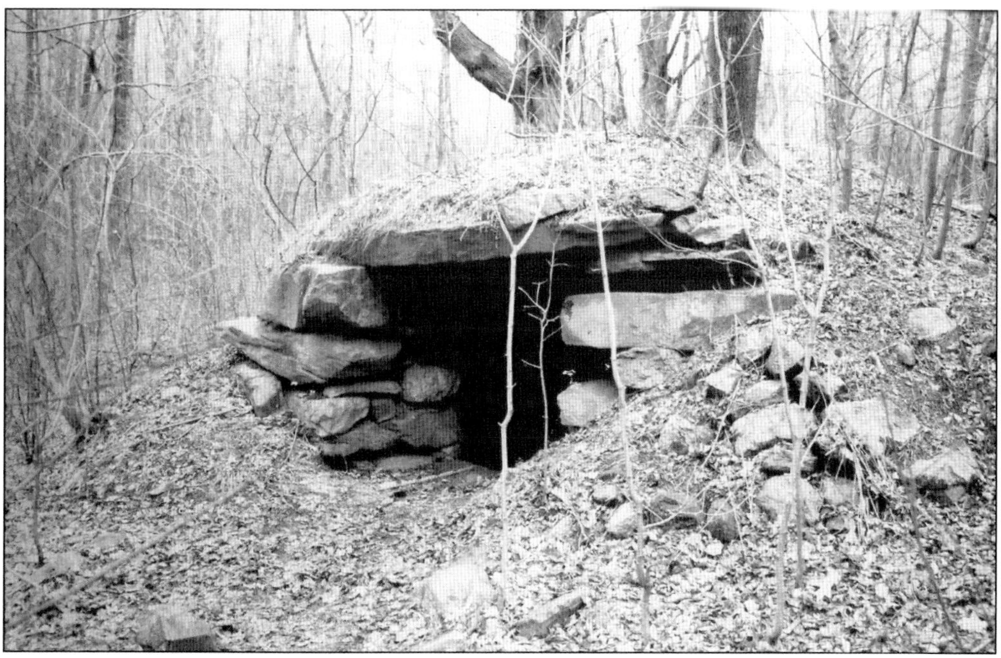

Stone structures, commonly called stone chambers, are found in many parts of Mahopac and in Putnam County generally. They primarily date from the late 18th to early 20th century. All were associated with agriculture, primarily dairy farming. The example seen here is located on the now closed portion of Lockwood Lane, near Lockwood Lake. (Eugene J. Boesch.)

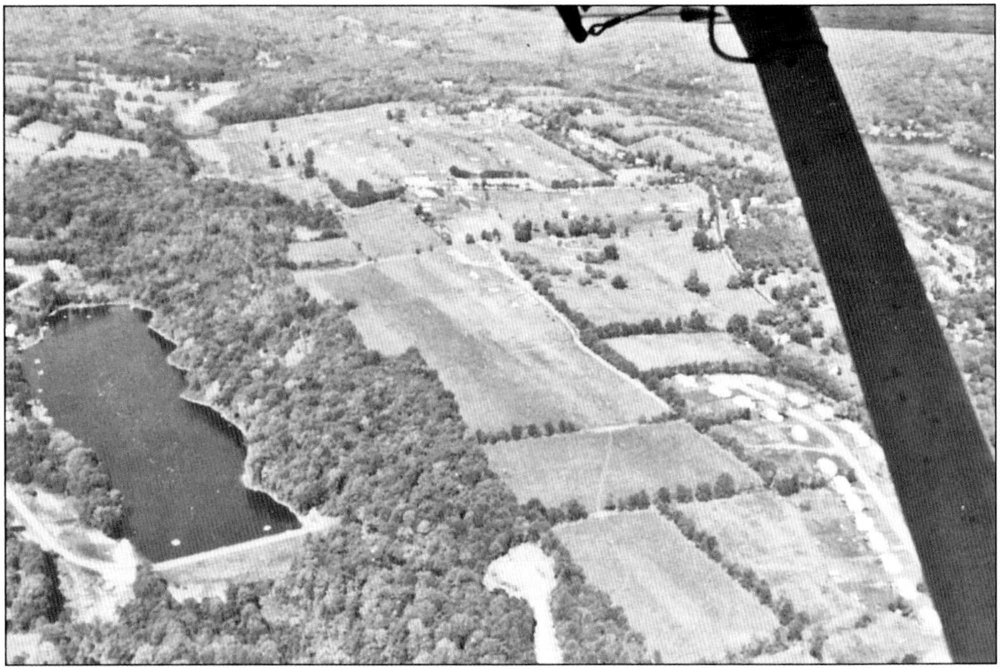

The aerial photograph looks north and shows Agor Farm and the surrounding land around 1955. To the left is Lake McGregor. In the center is Mahopac Airport. Note planes parked near the access road and landing strip. The early-19th-century Hill-Agor Farmhouse, a National Register of Historic Places property, is near the trees northeast of the airfield. Putnam National Golf Club, with sand traps, is located north of Agor Farm. (John Agor.)

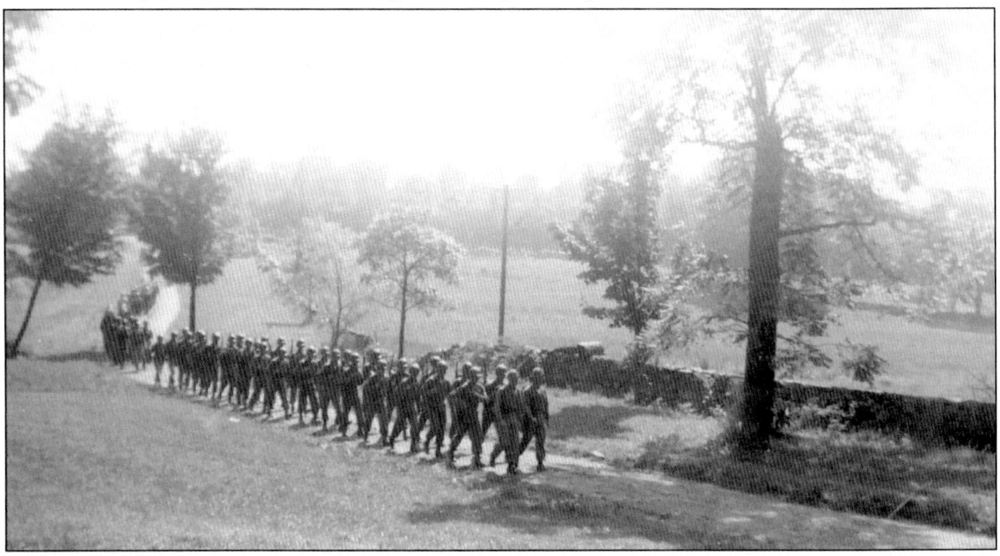

West Point cadets are seen marching up the entranceway of the Agor Farm from Hill Street in this image that was taken in 1952. The cadets bivouacked for a few weeks each summer during the 1950s on the farm. Military jeeps, trucks, and other equipment accompanied them. Tents were set up on the farm for sleeping and to feed the troops in the vicinity of what is now Scott Drive. The cadets practiced maneuvers and underwent other training throughout the property. (John Agor.)

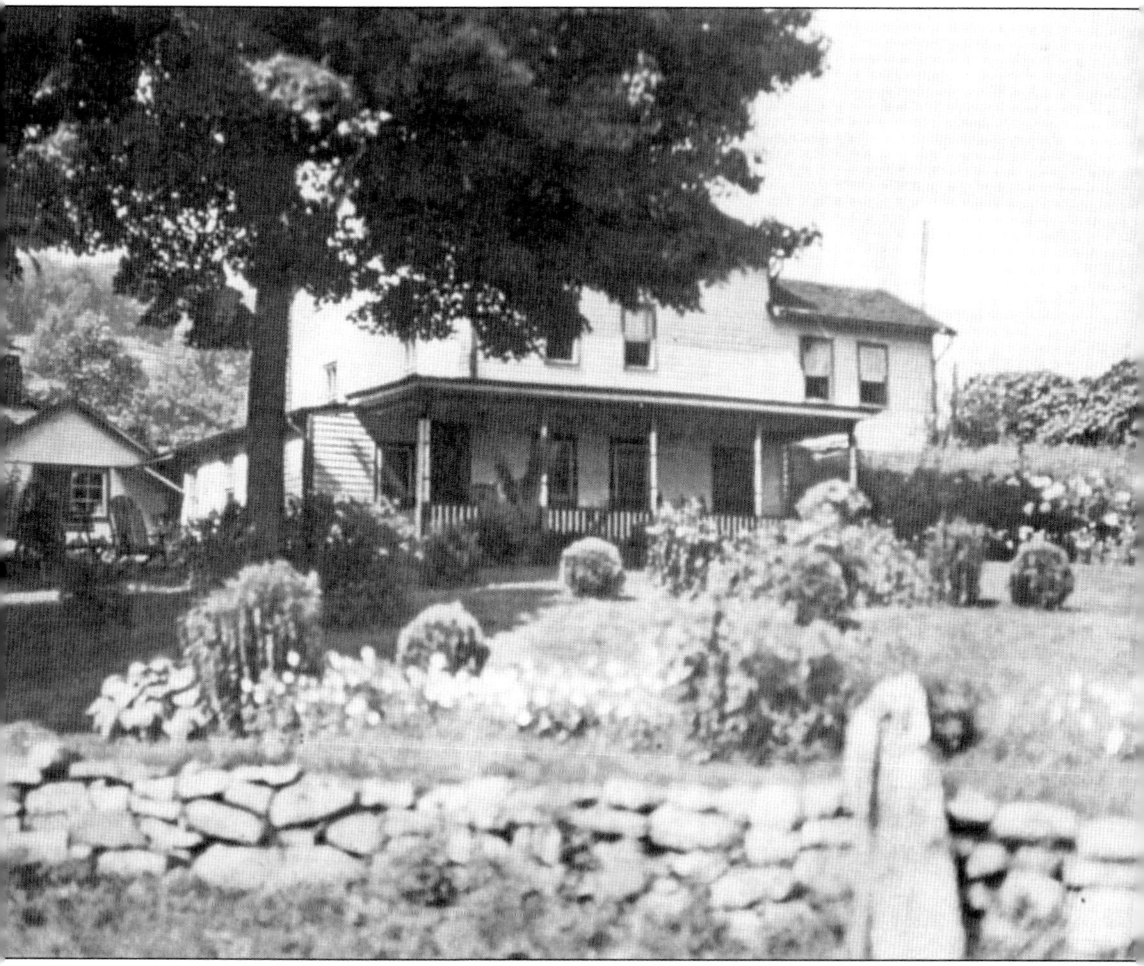

This image shows the mid-19th-century residence and part of the farm of William Heitman located along Mexico Lane near Barrett Hill Road in 1938. (Putnam County Historian's Office.)

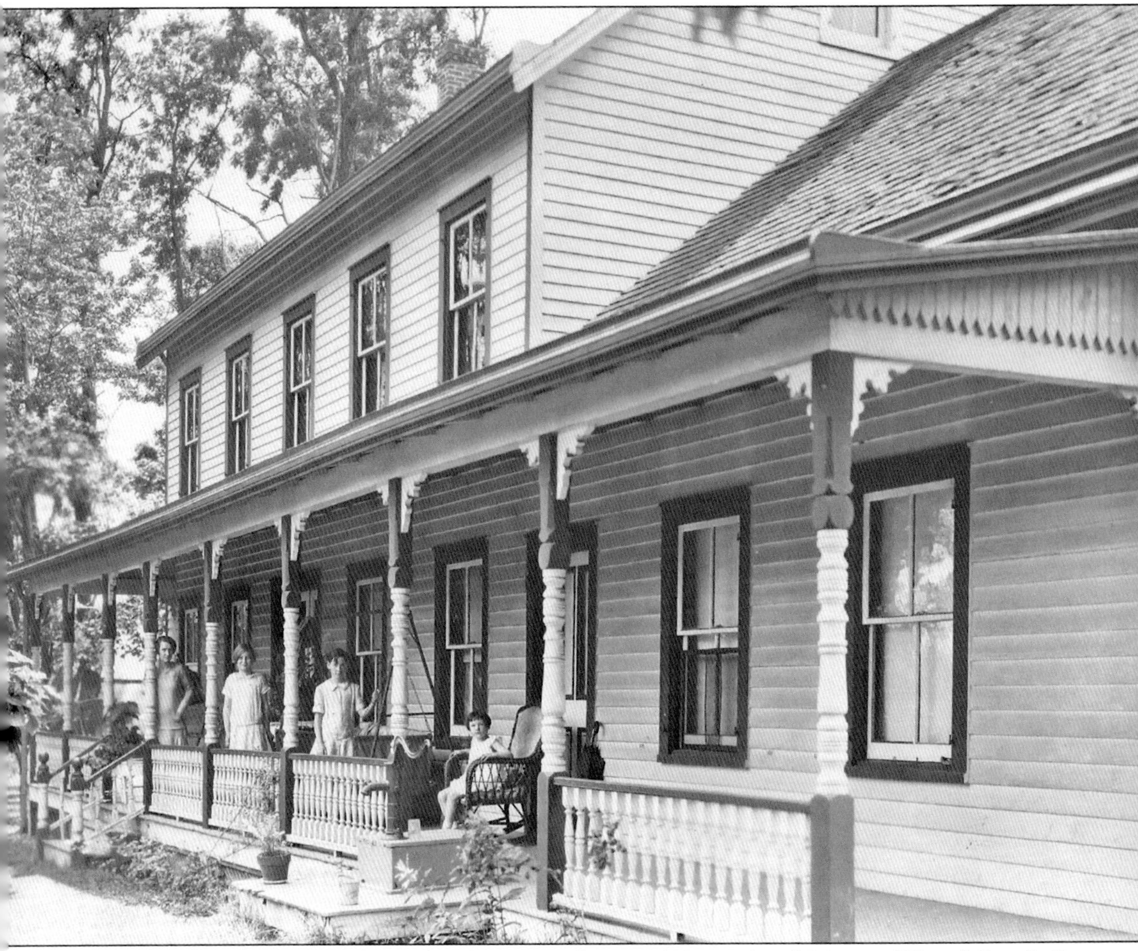

This photograph shows the mid-19th-century home of Howard and Minnie (Shear) Smith. It is the residence for Locust Hill Farm, which Minnie also operated as a boardinghouse. The image shows the house around 1925. The little girls are boarders. Very often, the same families would travel by train to Croton Falls and stay for vacations year after year. The woman towards the end of the porch is Shirley Gilmore, a singer from New York City. She came often and became a close friend of Minnie Smith. (Richard Smith.)

Daniel R. Shear (right) was born on February 16, 1822, and died on June 22, 1892. A farmer, he owned Locust Hill Farm on Shear Hill Road, named after the family. Daniel married Martha Anderson on December 31, 1851. They had three children: Simon, Coleman, and Susan. Daniel's father was Martin Shear and was born in 1781. Martin also was a farmer and is buried in the old Lake Mahopac Methodist- Episcopal Church Cemetery on Lake Mahopac (behind the parochial school for St. John the Evangelist Church). His wife was, Latitia Baldwin, and was born in 1791. She also is buried in that cemetery. (Both, Richard Smith.)

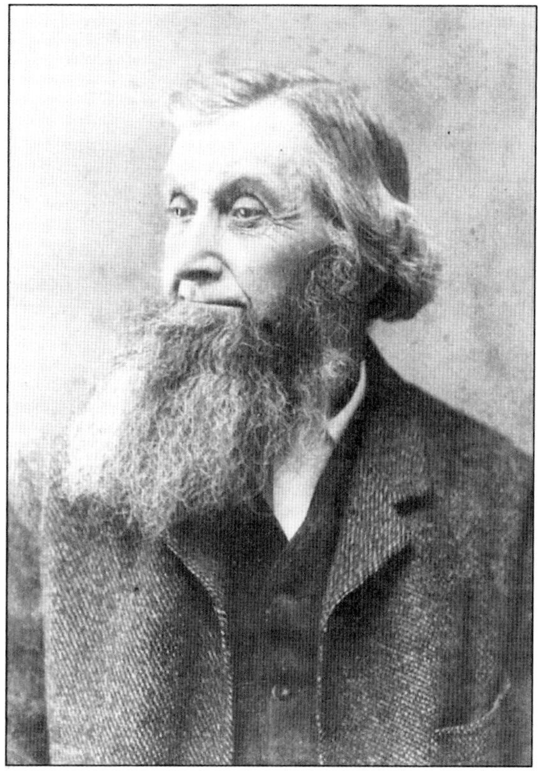

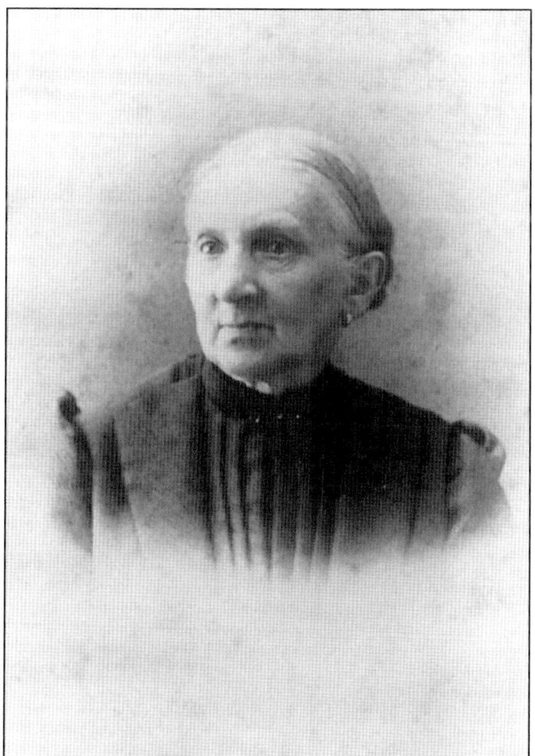

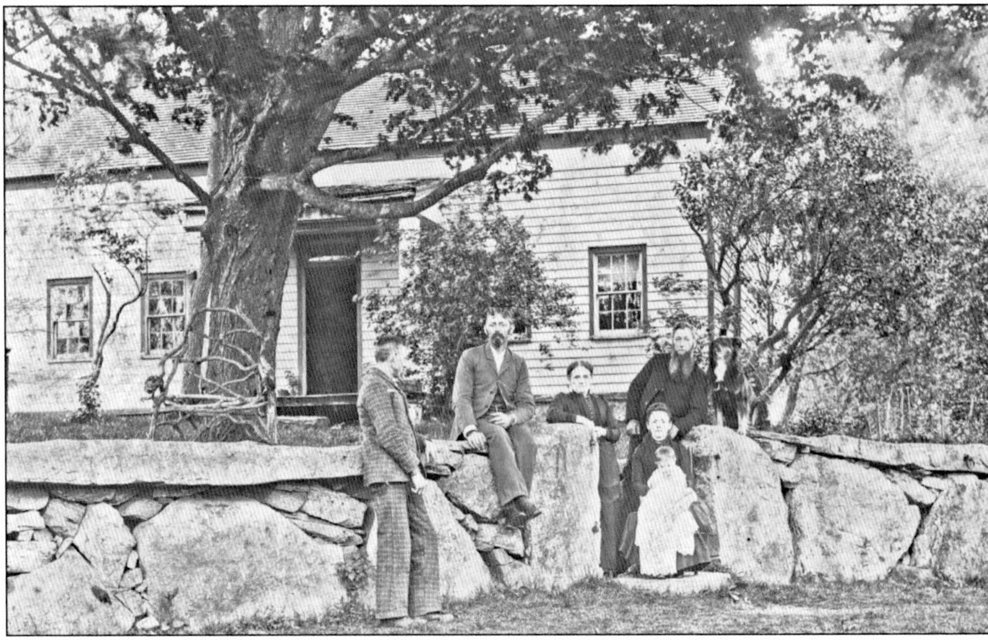

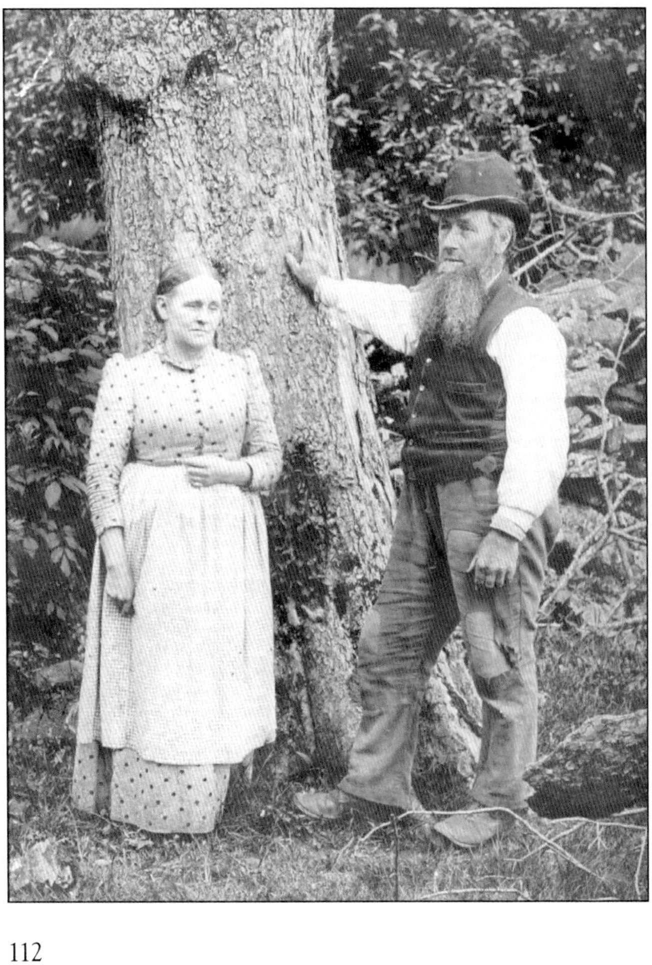

This 1895 photograph shows the Harrison Hill family and farmhouse located at Mahopac Mines. Harrison Hill was a farmer. He is the man with the long salt and pepper beard standing behind his daughter and grandchild. His wife is standing to his right. All in the photograph have on their dress clothes suggesting the day may be Sunday or a holiday. (Putnam County Historian's Office.)

This photograph shows Harrison Hill (still with his salt and pepper beard) and his wife in their everyday clothes around 1910, fifteen years after the 1895 photograph that was previously shown. Note the patches and rips in Hill's pants, as well as his worn hands indicating that he and his wife were a hardworking farm couple. (Putnam County Historian's Office.)

The photograph shows Julius DeLong, born in Brooklyn in 1855, and his wife, Sara Hillary, at their home on East Lake Boulevard around 1925. Julius was most noted for discovering that treated cattle hairs were fire-resistant and when added to asbestos, made good and safe insulation for a house. His company was named Keystone and the product was marketed through the Johns-Manville Company. (Susan Brady Mauldin.)

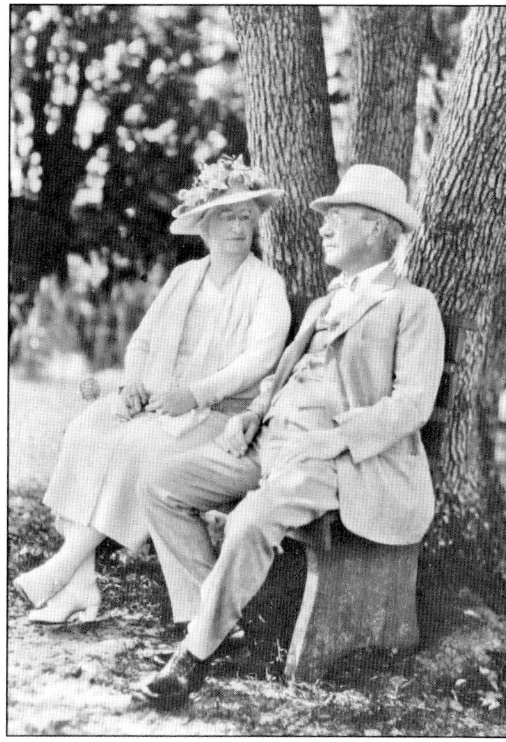

Graymanse is the hand-hewn granite mansion located along North Lake Boulevard. It was constructed in 1856 by William Tilden, who had purchased 24 acres along the north shore of Lake Mahopac. The home was a replica of the well-known mansion Graystone-on-the-Hudson in Yonkers. Graymanse has been extensively altered over the years, but it is still one of the most elegant residences on Lake Mahopac. (The Town of Carmel Historical Society.)

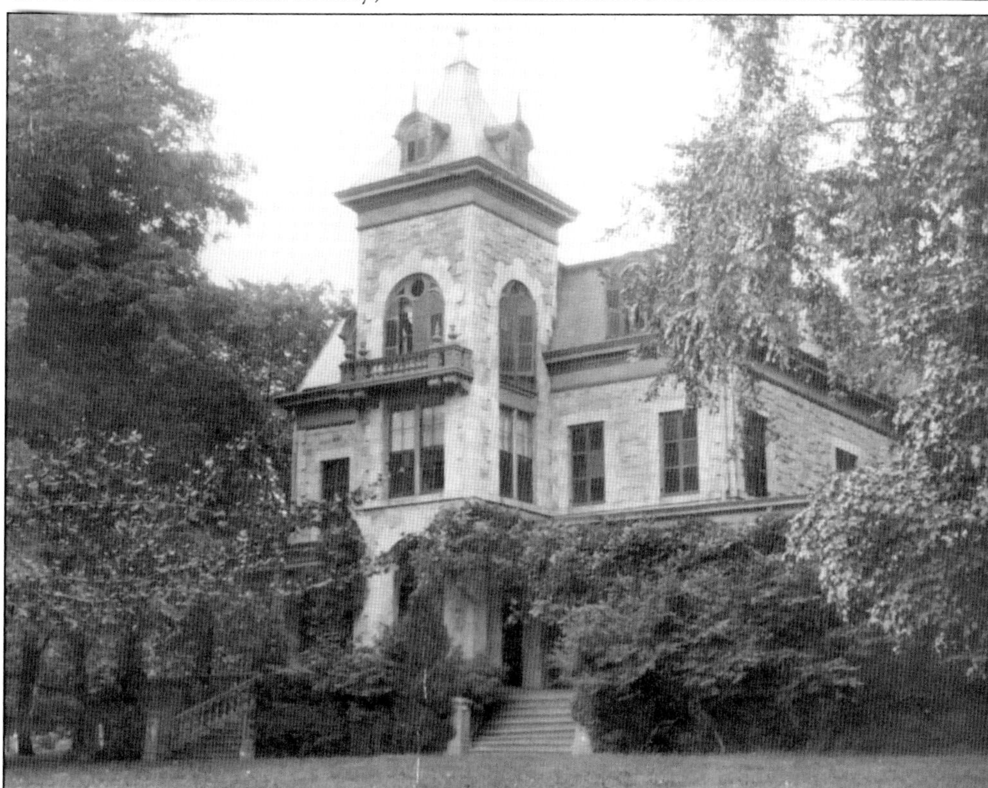

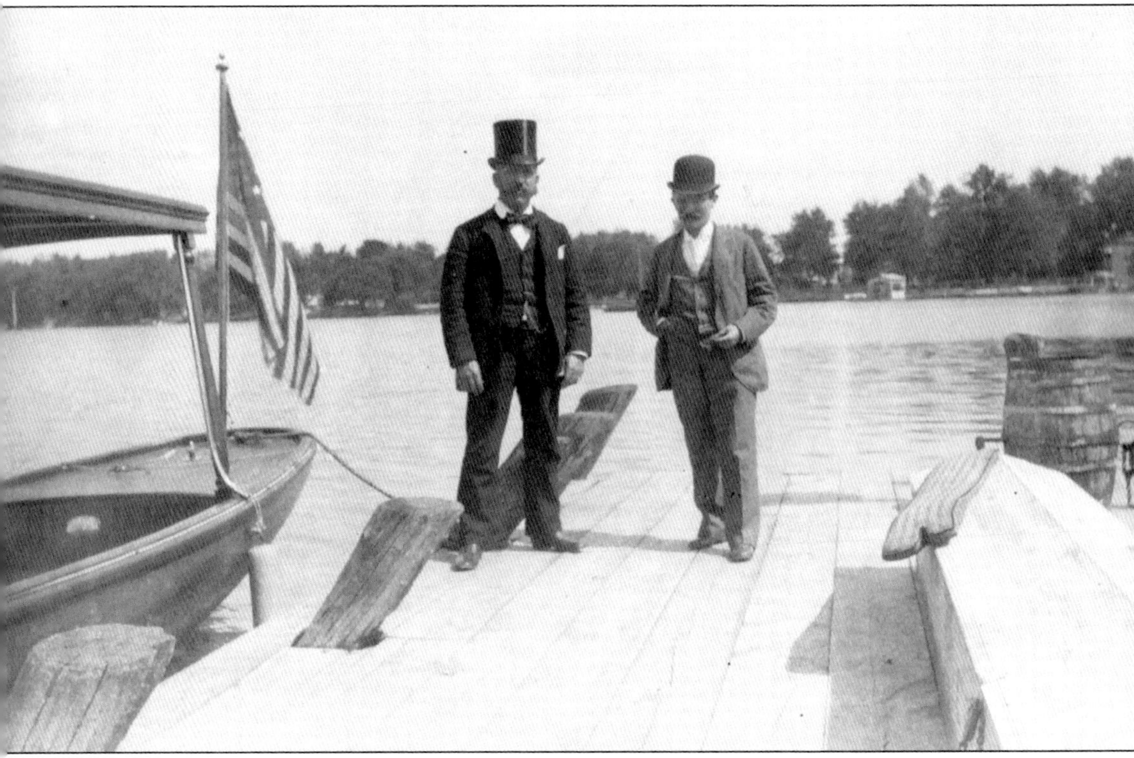

This photograph shows William Senior, a local undertaker, and Fred Randall on a Fairy Island dock at Lake Mahopac in September 1891. Senior, in particular, looks well-dressed, perhaps indicating he visited Fairy Island on business. The house of Anthony Hoguet is seen directly across the lake. William Senior's father also was an undertaker of some renown. He was born in London, England, in 1816, immigrating with his parents to America. He became the most prominent undertaker in New York City and had charge of the burial of Henry Clay and many other distinguished men. Senior Hill is named after him. (Putnam County Historian's Office.)

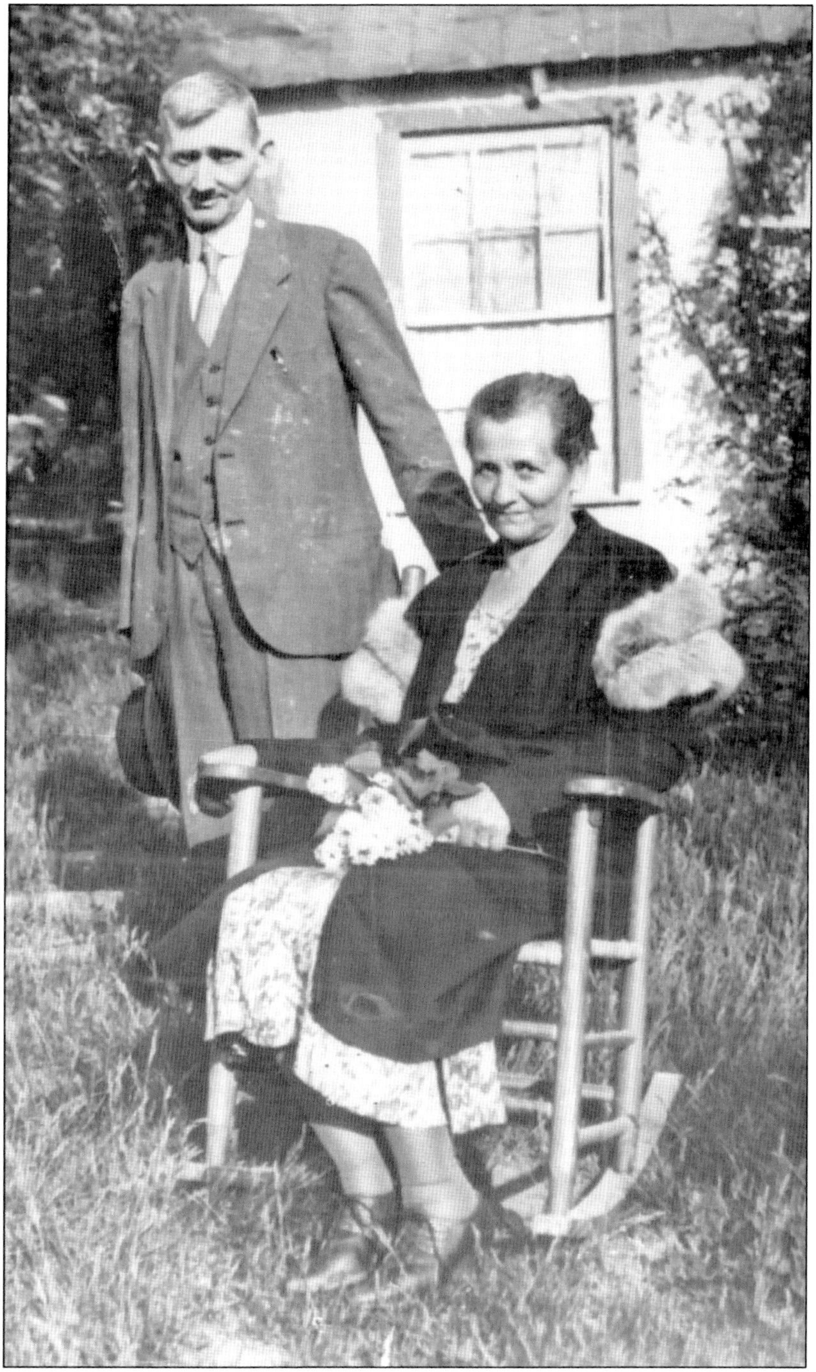

Samuel and Lena Amsterdam, who wed in 1900, are shown in this photograph outside of their 18th-century dwelling along Long Pond Road around 1940. The home and associated buildings served as a boardinghouse from around 1902 to 1942. The house remains in the family to this day. Samuel would pick up boarders at the Mahopac Mines Railroad Depot about a mile away, first by horse and wagon and later by automobile, and transport them to his establishment. Samuel in his youth attended the Mahopac Mines School. (Karen and Gerry Levitis.)

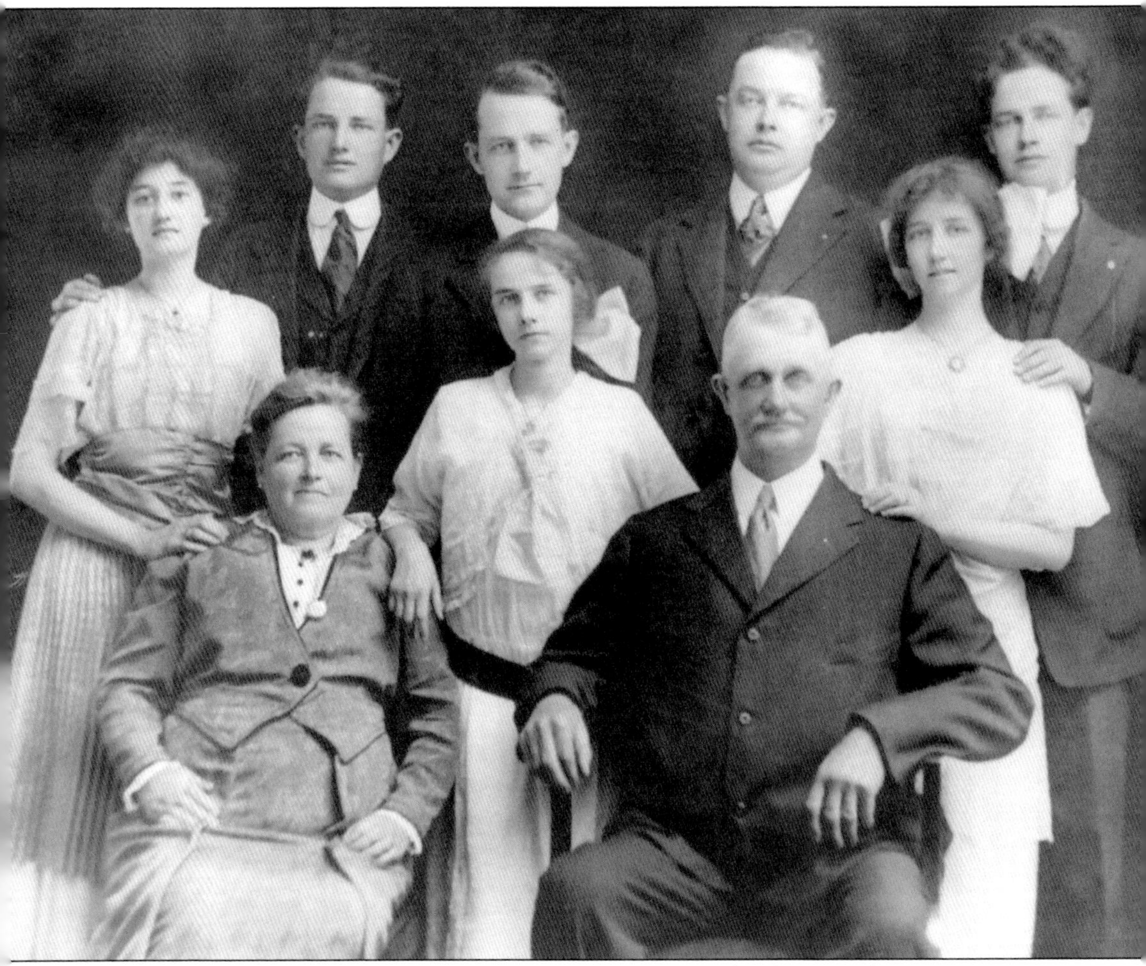

This photograph of the Spain family, a prominent Mahopac family, was taken sometime prior to 1930. Sitting are proud parents Margaret Fenaughty Spain and Darius Spain. The young women in the middle are Johanna B. "Dody" Spain, Elieen R. "Dody" Spain, and Mary E. "Molly" Spain. In the top row are Maurice "Doc" Spain, William H. Spain, Thomas R. Spain, and Darius J. Spain. Darius was born in Killoughnane, Ireland, on February 8, 1861, and died on August 17, 1930. (William D. Spain Jr.)

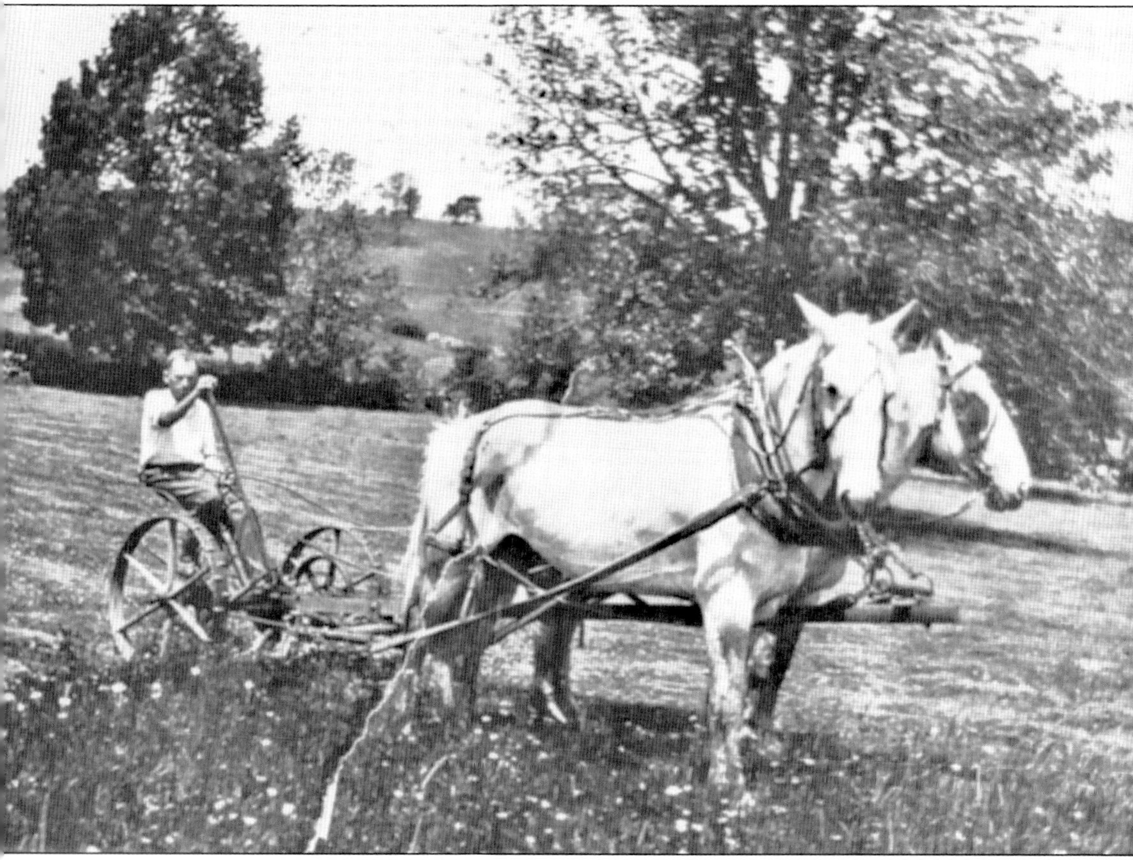

Howard W. Smith is shown in this c. 1920 photograph raking hay to feed his cattle on his Locust Hill Farm, located along Shear Hill Road near what is now Lake Drive. Much of the hay fields seen here, as well as the stonewall visible behind Howard, were inundated by the creation of Lake Casse. (Richard Smith.)

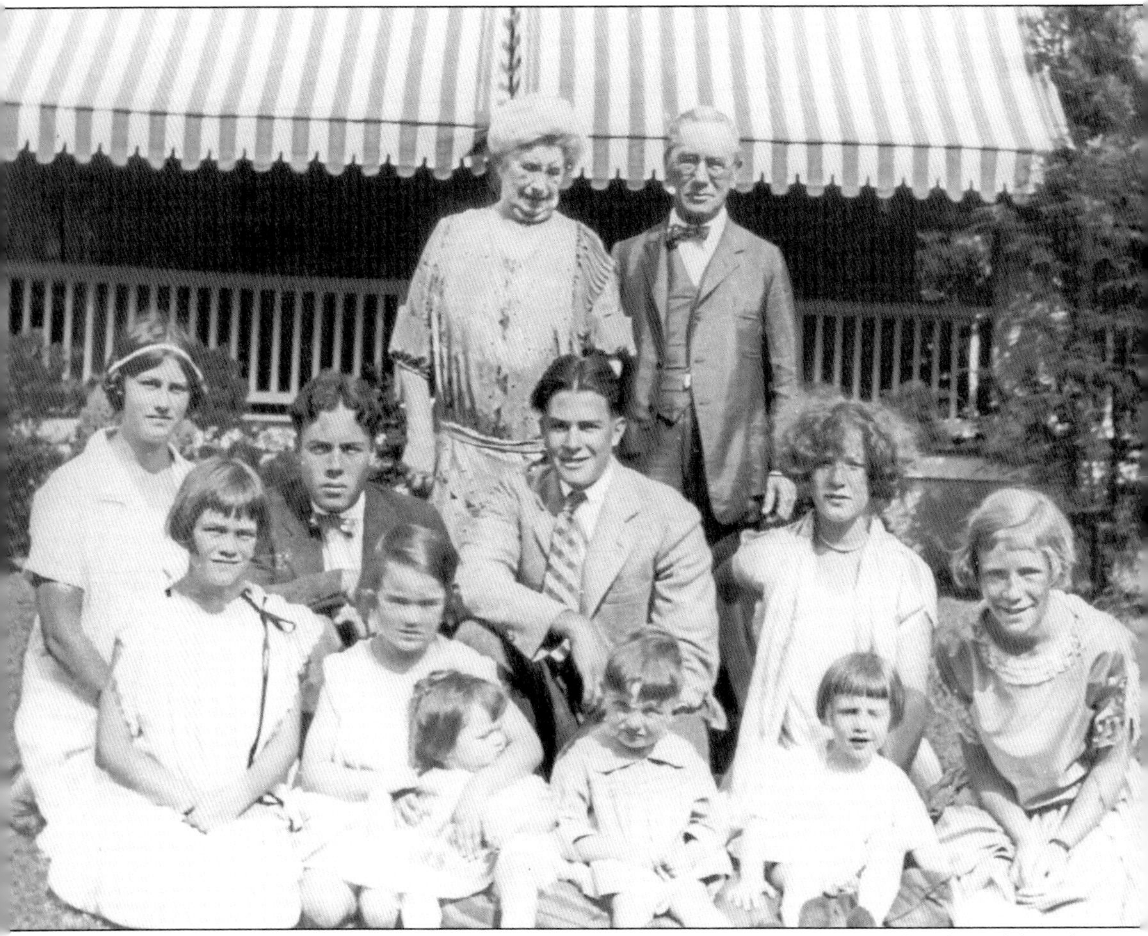

This is a photograph taken in 1923 of Julius DeLong and his wife, Sara, with family and friends. The DeLongs had three girls: Henrietta Ethel, Lydie and Sara. Around 1900, the family began spending summers at Lake Mahopac at the Forest House. Julius later built a home on East Lake Boulevard near St. John the Evangelist Catholic Church. Julius eventually donated the house and property to St. John's Parish. The church demolished the house and built St. John's Chapel on the property. DeLong's residence was the first home on Lake Mahopac to be insulated for year-round use. He died on January 10, 1929. (Susan Brady Mauldin.)

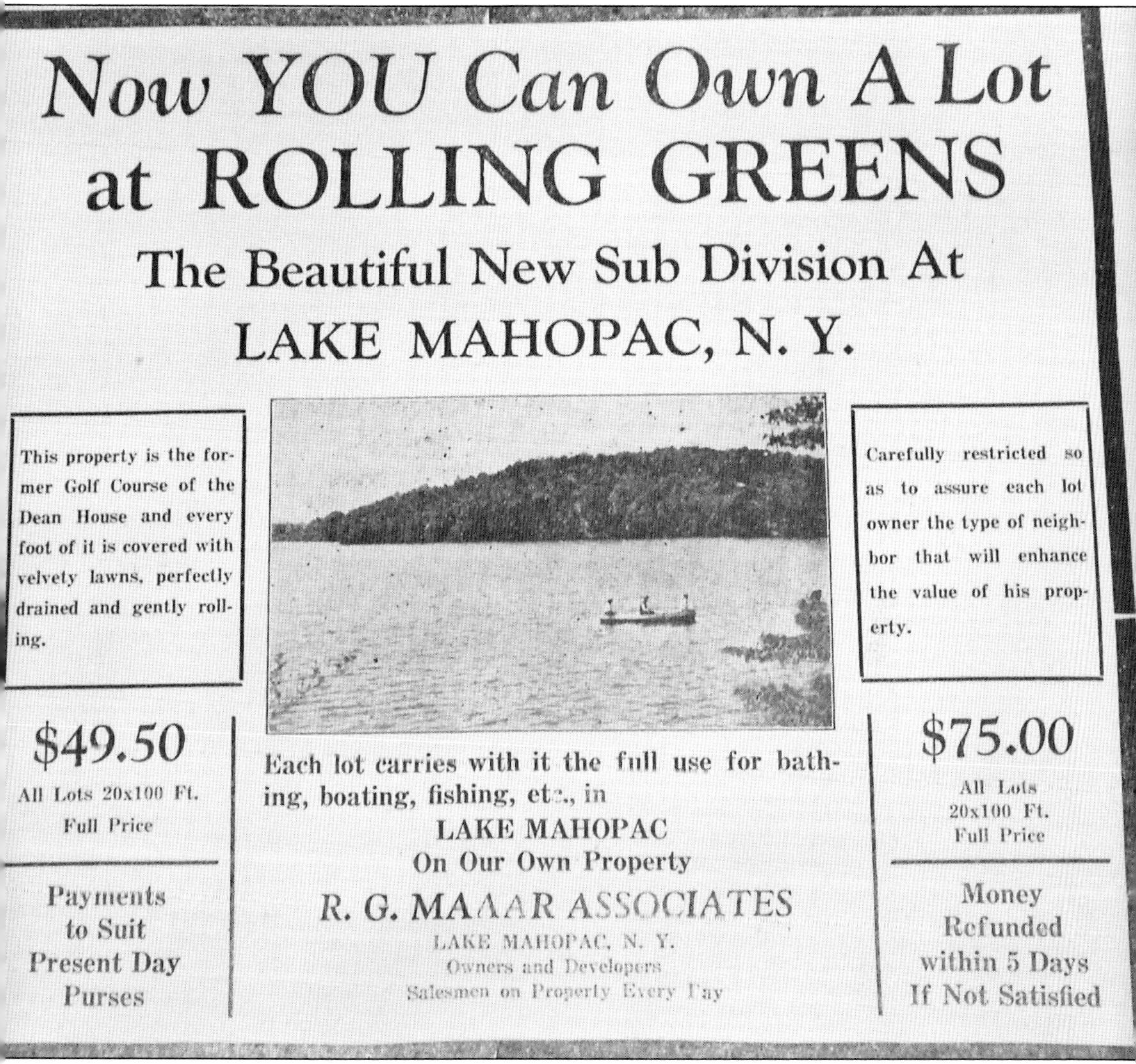

This 1937 advertisement offers lots for sale in the Rolling Greens residential development. The land was the former golf course for the Dean House on Lake Mahopac. Apparently two types of lots, each 20 feet by 100 feet, were offered for sale at prices of $49.50 or $75. Ownership of the lots came with lake rights. Money would be refunded within five days if not satisfied. Anachronistic wordage assuring prospective buyers that sales were restricted to the types of people that would only enhance the values of the properties are evident. The first residence built there was along Gleneida Boulevard across from modern-day Mahopac High School. (The Putnam County Historian's Office.)

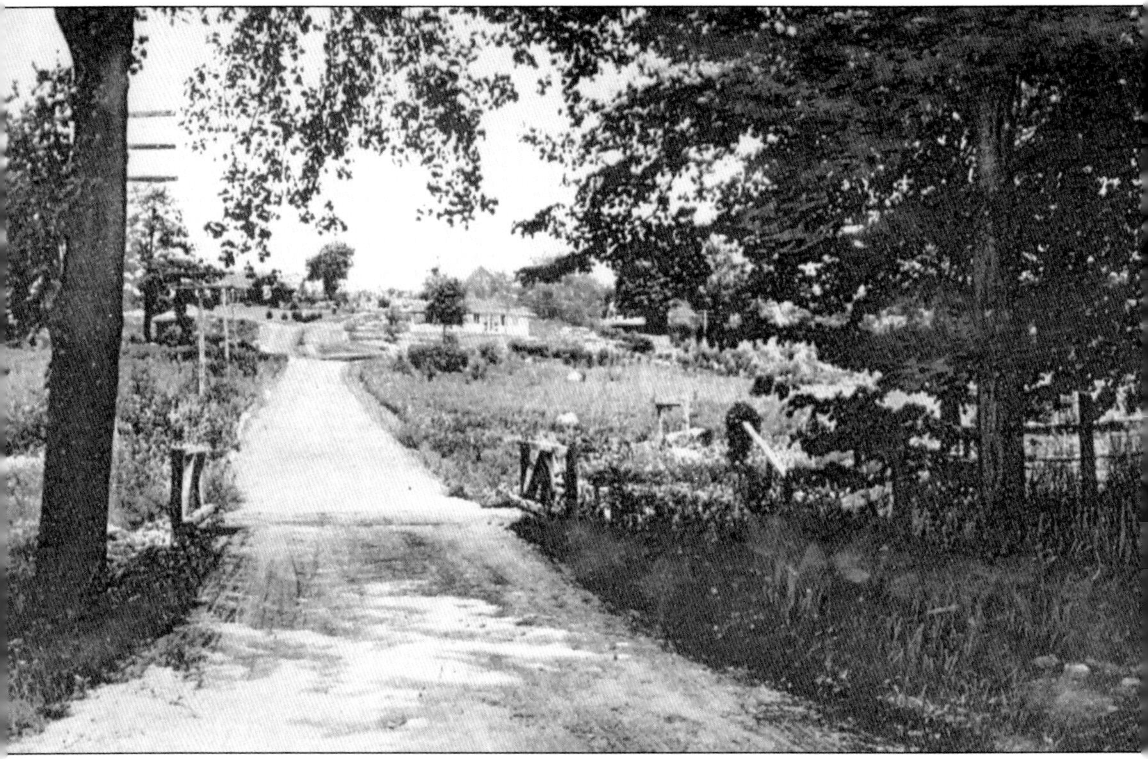

The entrance to the Bungalow Colony on Lake Mahopac was very rural as seen in this c. 1925 image. The houses, however, were electrified at the time as seen by the utility poles leading into the community. The colony was eventually renamed Mahopac Hills to make it more respectable. Leslie P. Dodge, a noted real estate and insurance agent, was one of the first residents of the colony. Dodge was one of the charter members of the Lake Mahopac Rotary and a leader, along with his wife, Helen, in many Mahopac community organizations. Perhaps Leslie Dodge's greatest contribution to local history was his diary, which included daily weather conditions in the Mahopac area from 1944 to 1970 for use in his insurance business. (Loretta Post Billington.)

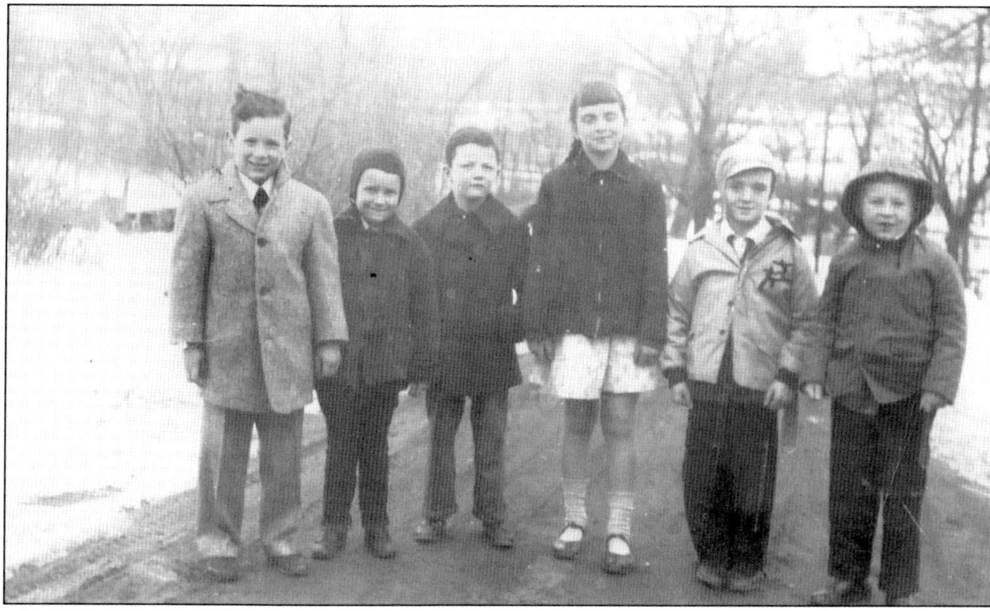

This gathering of children occurred March 1, 1949, a chilly, late winter day, on the occasion of the eighth birthday of Larry Lacina. The photograph was taken in the driveway of the Lacina family's 18th-century home off Myrtle Avenue. The children are, from left to right, Bernard Jacobs, Larry Lacina (birthday boy), Joe Costello, Barbara Lacina (Larry's sister), Johnny Post, and Wesley Clark. (Barbara Lacina Bosch.)

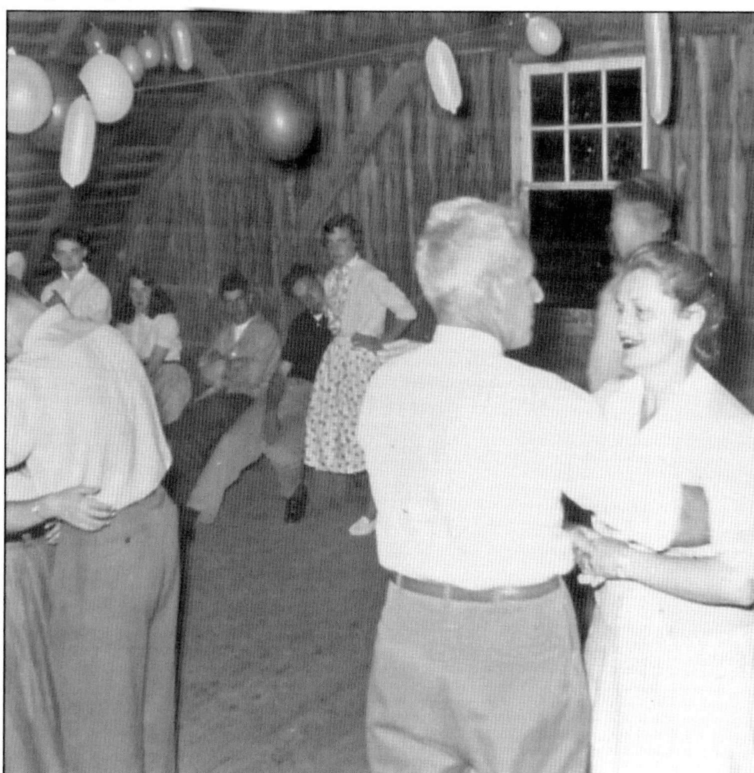

This c. 1960 photograph shows a barn dance taking place at the Agor Farm Dude Ranch off of Hill Street. Barn dances and hayrides for friends, family, and guests were a common occurrence at the farm. Shown dancing in the right foreground of the image are Jessie and Ruth Crane Agor, the owners of the property. (John Agor.)

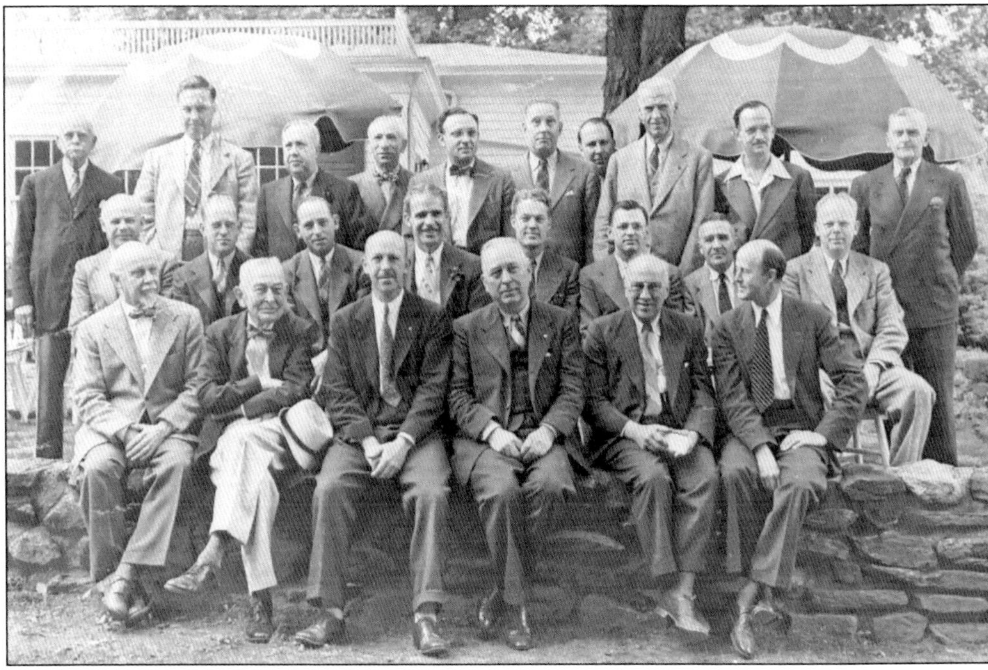

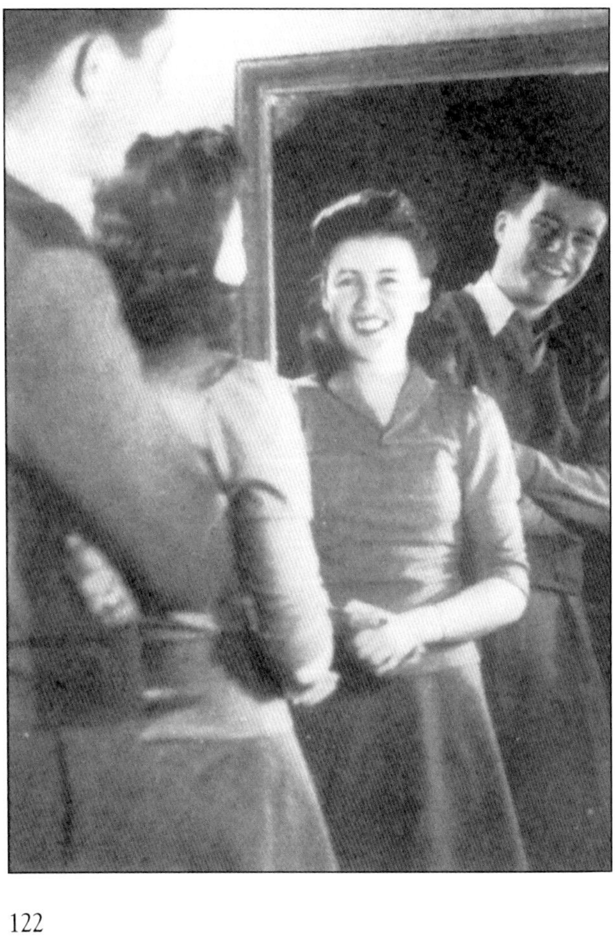

This c. 1955 photograph shows members of the Lake Mahopac-Carmel Rotary club at one of their weekly meetings, which at the time were held at the Lakeshore Club. The Rotary Club was chartered by Rotary International and organized in 1932 as the Lake Mahopac-Carmel Rotary Club with John W. Dain as its first president. In 1967, the club split into the Lake Mahopac Rotary Club and the Carmel Rotary Club. (Lake Mahopac Rotary Club.)

The senior-year students shown in this 1943 Mahopac High School yearbook photograph are Edward "Ted" Dwyer and Kathleen Welch. Both were voted best-looking Mahopac High School seniors that year. Ted was a lifelong resident of Mahopac and proprietor of the Dwyer Real Estate and Insurance Agency. He was a member of the Mahopac Rotary for over 50 years and in 2011 was named Lake Mahopac Rotarian of the year. (Lorretta Post Billington.)

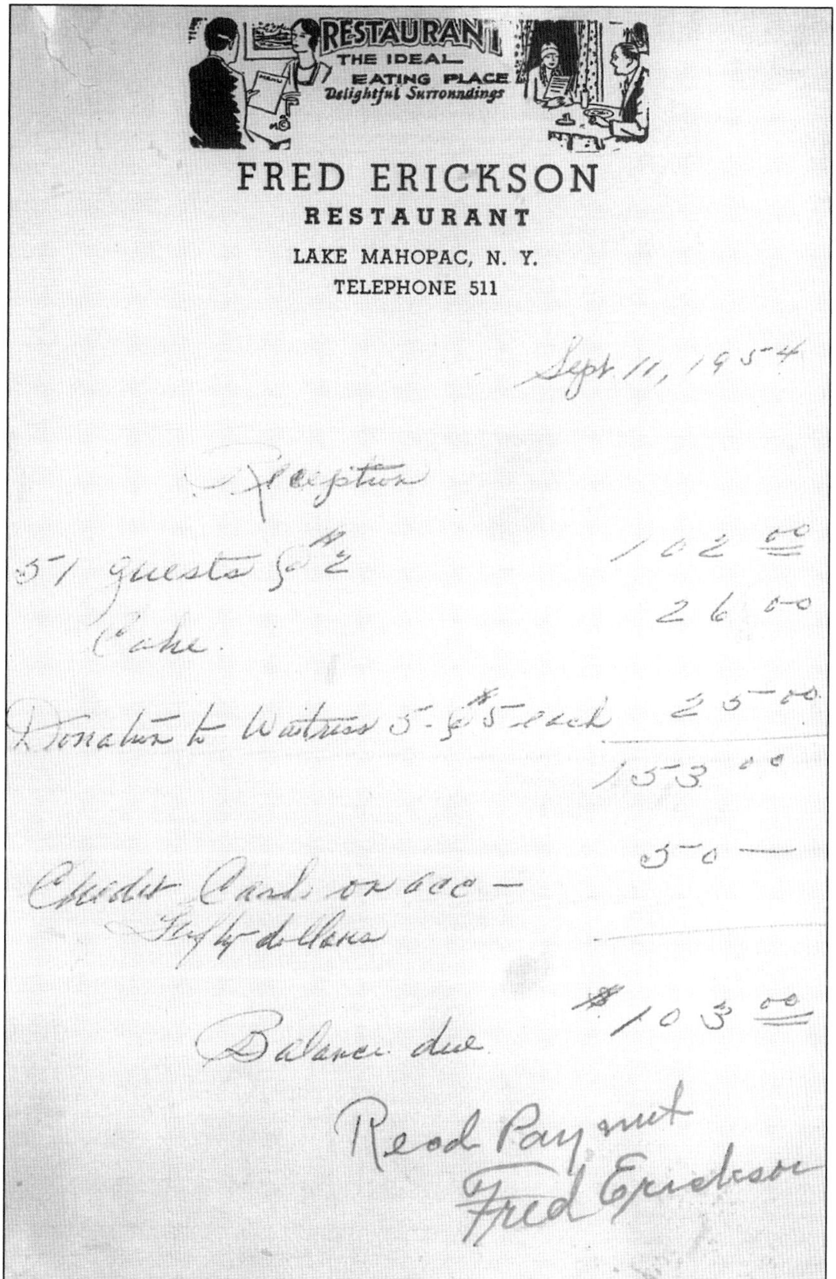

RESTAURANT
THE IDEAL
EATING PLACE
Delightful Surroundings

FRED ERICKSON
RESTAURANT
LAKE MAHOPAC, N. Y.
TELEPHONE 511

Sept 11, 1954

Reception

51 guests @ 2 — 102.00
Cake — 26.00
Donation to Waitress 5 @ $5 each — 25.00
153.00
50 —
Credit Card. on acc — Fifty dollars

Balance due $103.00

Recd Payment
Fred Erickson

The wedding of George and Olive Britton Bennett occurred on September 11, 1954, during Hurricane Edna. The reception was held at Erickson's Restaurant and Ice Cream Parlor. The bridesmaid was Joan Marx Mancuse and the best man was Franklin Glover. John Millicker and Donald Parker served as ushers. George at the time was in the US Navy and stationed at Guantanamo Bay, Cuba. The Bennetts had 51 guests. The total cost for the reception, as seen on Erickson's bill was $153. This included the meal ($102), cake ($26), and a $5 donation to each of the five waitresses working the party ($25). Erickson's Restaurant later became the Mahopac Public Library. (George and Olive Bennett.)

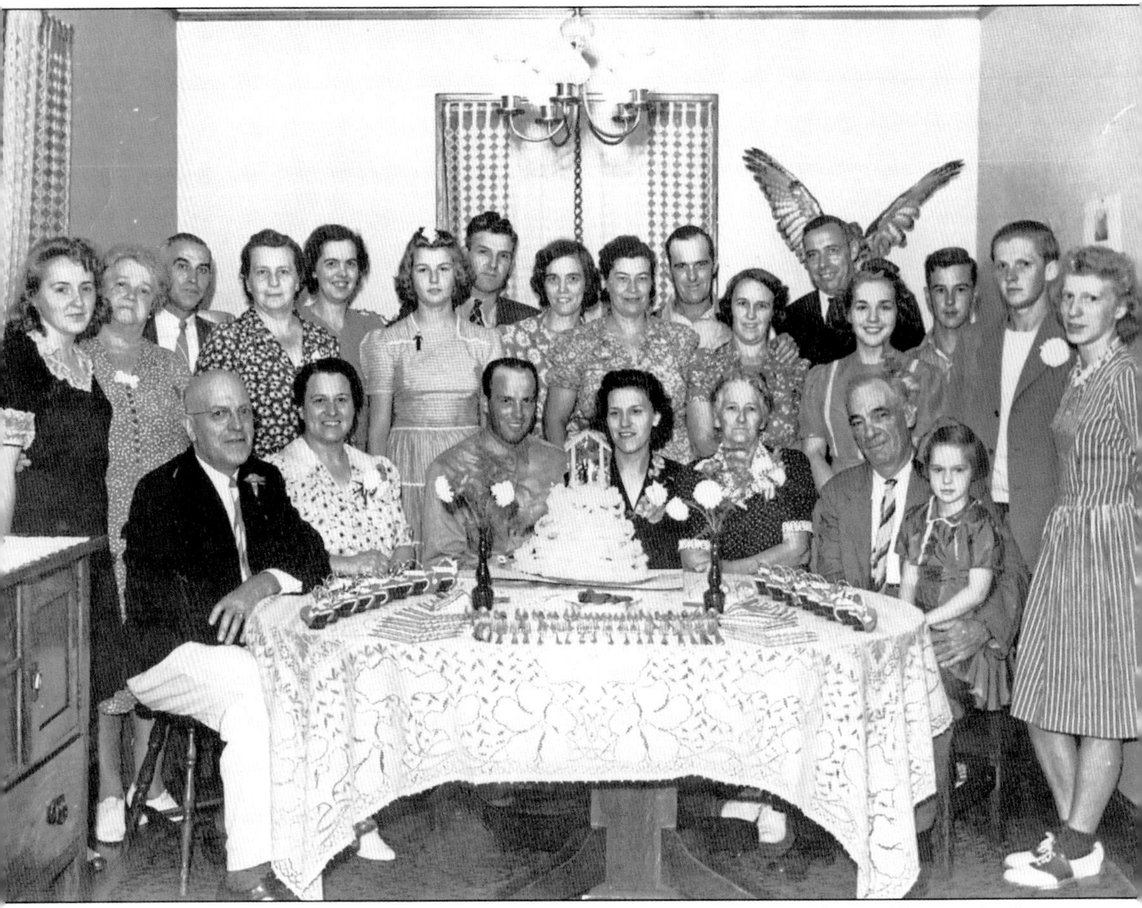

This is a photograph of Walter and Lois Agor's wedding reception. The wedding took place on May 30, 1942, in Louisiana where Walter, a soldier, was stationed. Lois Agor traveled there, and they were married by a justice. The couple later had a reception in Lois's father's apartment on the second floor of the Agor Bros. store in Red Mills. The reception took place in the late summer or autumn of 1942. The guests shown at the reception are, from left to right, (standing) Virginia Agor, Mrs. ? Miller, Hugh and Kathleen MacIntyre, Rachel Miller, Irene Swarm, Oscar Swarm, Mabel Swarm, Anna Miller, Louis Miller, Theresa Miller, Bill Booth, Muriel Agor, Robert Miller, Donald Hill, and Jean Agor; (seated) Kelsie Agor, Neva Agor, Walter Miller, Lois Agor Miller, Mrs. Anna Miller, and Mr. William Miller with Frances Miller on his lap. (Muriel Agor Hill, Darlene Hill Lampe, and Karen Hill Czsyz.)

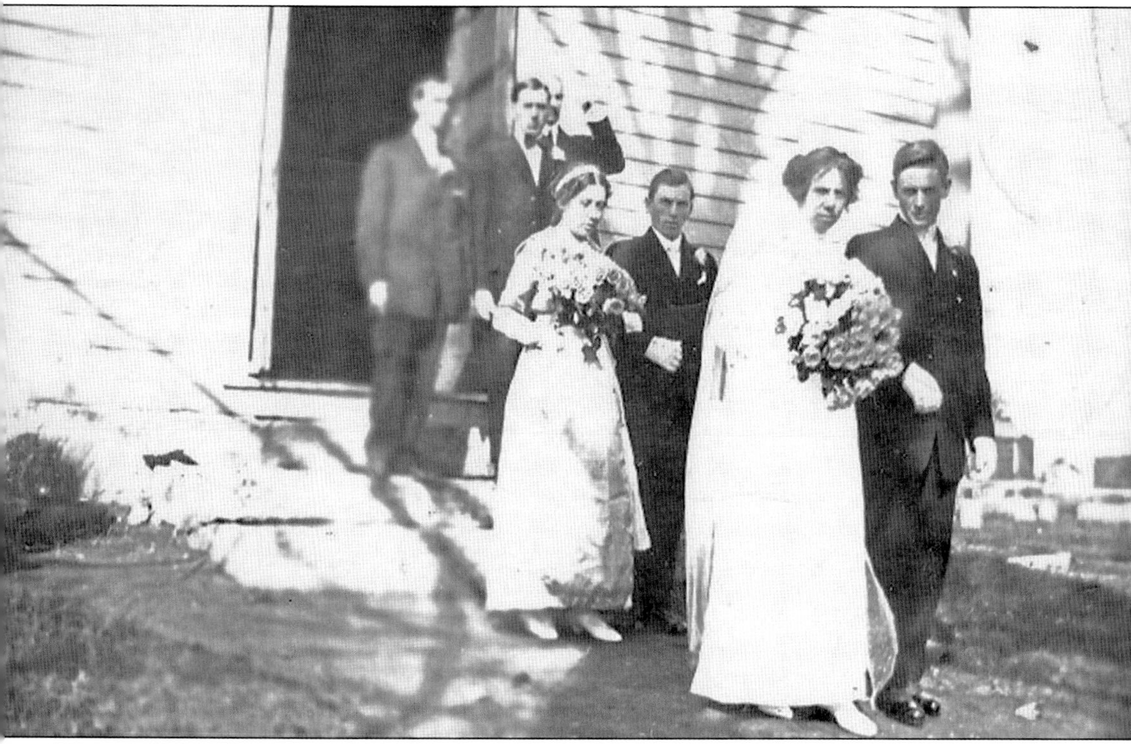

Howard W. Smith and Minnie E. Shear were married at the Union Valley Methodist-Episcopal Chapel on August 24, 1910. Rev. Frederick Withey performed the nuptials. The wedding party follows the newlyweds from the church. Howard was the son of William W. Smith and Mary Samantha Tompkins. Howard and Minnie farmed Locust Hill Farm on the corner of Shear Hill Road and the road that now passes by Lake Casse. The lake was artificially created and inundated part of Locust Hill Farm. (Richard Smith.)

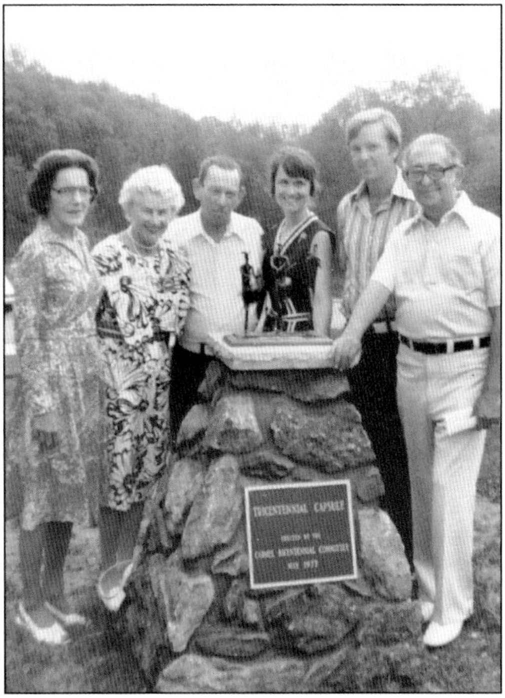

This image records the dedication of the Carmel Tercentenary Time Capsule by the Town of Carmel Historical Society in May 1977, at Carmel Town Hall in Mahopac. It is still there near the Christopher Columbus statue. Photographs, documents, and other artifacts relating to the town are included in the capsule. Memento categories include newspapers, churches and synagogues, religious organizations, libraries, hospitals, government, bicentennial items, banking, and schools and education. (The Town of Carmel Historical Society.)

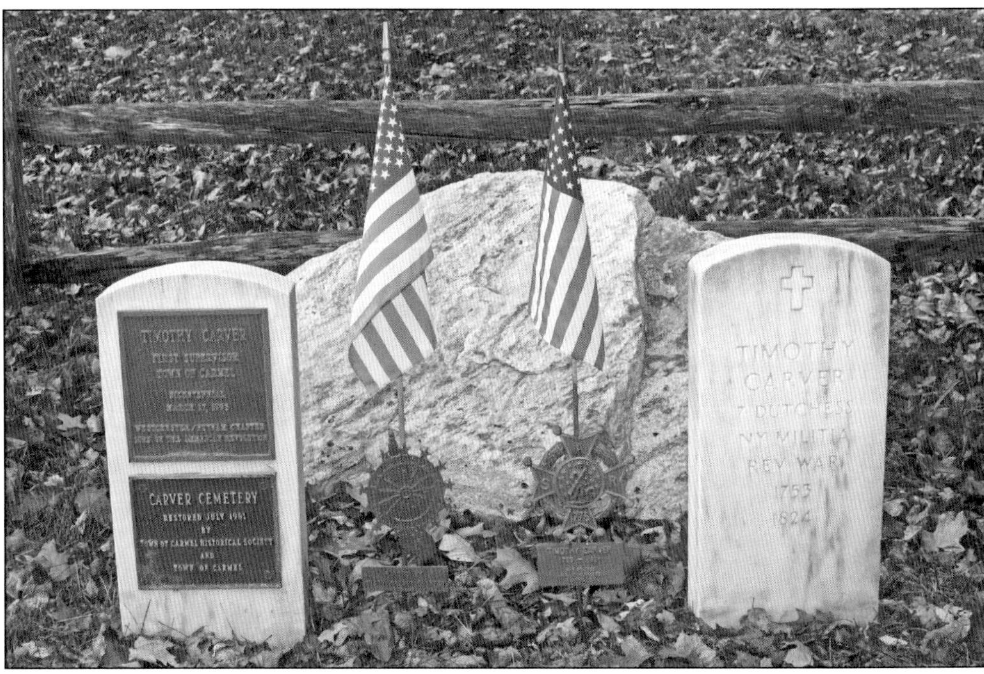

This photograph marks the burial site of Timothy Carver, a veteran of the Revolutionary War and first supervisor of the Town of Carmel. He came from Bridgewater, Massachusetts, with his wife, Rebecca, to homestead in Mahopac in 1757. Rebecca's ancestors came to the New World on the Mayflower. Timothy drowned in 1824 after falling off a bridge spanning the Croton River's West Branch. The bridge became known as Carver's Bridge. Its former location is now inundated beneath the Croton Reservoir. (Brian Vangor.)

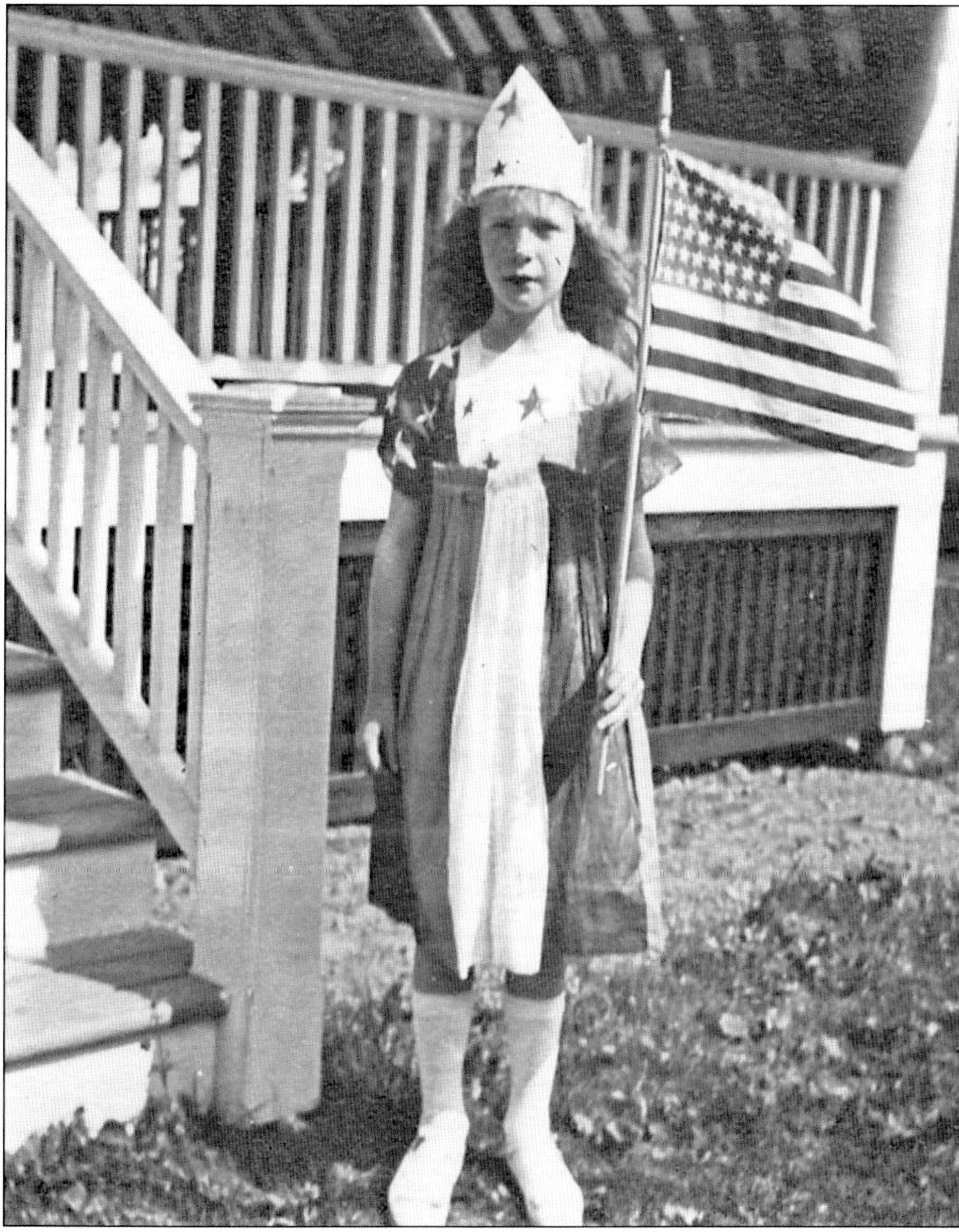

The young lady shown here is Ruth Rowley (later Ruth Grub) on July 4 around 1920. Ruth was born on December 5, 1909. She was the granddaughter of Julius DeLong. Ruth's parents, Paul Rowley and Henrietta Ethel DeLong Rowley, spent many summers in Mahopac on East Lake Boulevard. They eventually rented the house that belonged to the Westcott family near what is now St. John the Evangelist Church. The Westcott home later belonged to Edith Westcott Steacy and her husband, Dr. George Steacy, who was the doctor at Mahopac's Emergency First Aid Station. The photograph was taken in front of the Westcott home. (Susan Brady Mauldin.)

Consistent with our mission to preserve history on a local level, this book was printed in South Carolina on American-made paper and manufactured entirely in the United States. Products carrying the accredited Forest Stewardship Council (FSC) label are printed on 100 percent FSC-certified paper.

MADE IN THE USA